# Lecture Notes in Computer Science     9824

*Commenced Publication in 1973*
Founding and Former Series Editors:
Gerhard Goos, Juris Hartmanis, and Jan van Leeuwen

More information about this series at http://www.springer.com/series/7410

Michael Franz · Panos Papadimitratos (Eds.)

# Trust and
# Trustworthy Computing

9th International Conference, TRUST 2016
Vienna, Austria, August 29–30, 2016
Proceedings

 Springer

*Editors*
Michael Franz
University of California
Irvine, CA
USA

Panos Papadimitratos
KTH Royal Institute of Technology
Stockholm
Sweden

ISSN 0302-9743 ISSN 1611-3349 (electronic)
Lecture Notes in Computer Science
ISBN 978-3-319-45571-6 ISBN 978-3-319-45572-3 (eBook)
DOI 10.1007/978-3-319-45572-3

Library of Congress Control Number: 2016948785

LNCS Sublibrary: SL4 – Security and Cryptology

Printed on acid-free paper

This Springer imprint is published by Springer Nature
The registered company is Springer International Publishing AG Switzerland

# Preface

This volume contains the proceedings of the 9th International Conference on Trust and Trustworthy Computing (TRUST), held in Vienna, Austria, on August 29–30, 2016. TRUST 2016 was hosted and organized by SBA Research.

Continuing the tradition of the previous conferences, held in Villach (2008), Oxford (2009), Berlin (2010), Pittsburgh (2011), Vienna (2012), London (2013), and Heraklion (2014 and 2015), TRUST 2016 provided a unique interdisciplinary forum for researchers, practitioners, and decision makers to explore new ideas and discuss experiences in building, designing, using, and understanding trustworthy computing systems.

The conference program of TRUST 2016 shows that research in trust and trustworthy computing is active, at a high level of competency, and spans a wide range of areas and topics. Topics discussed in this year's research contributions included anonymous and layered attestation, revocation, captchas, runtime integrity, trust networks, key migration, and PUFs.

We received 25 valid submissions in response to the Call for Papers. All submissions were carefully reviewed by at least three Program Committee members or external experts according to the criteria of scientific novelty, importance to the field, and technical quality. After an online discussion of all reviews, 8 papers were selected for presentation and publication in the conference proceedings. This amounts to an acceptance rate of less than one third. Furthermore, the conference program included keynote presentations by Prof. Virgil Gligor (Carnegie Mellon University, USA) and Prof. Stefan Katzenbeisser (Technische Universität Darmstadt, Germany).

We would like to express our gratitude to those people without whom TRUST 2016 would not have been this successful, and whom we mention now in no particular order: the publicity chairs, Drs. Somayeh Salimi and Moritz Wiese, the members of the Steering Committee, the local Organizing Committee (and especially Yvonne Poul), and the keynote speakers. We also want to thank all Program Committee members and their external reviewers; their hard work made sure that the scientific program was of high quality and reflected both the depth and diversity of research in this area. Our special thanks go to all those who submitted papers, and to all those who presented papers at the conference.

July 2016

Michael Franz
Panos Papadimitratos

# Organization

## Steering Committee

| | |
|---|---|
| Alessandro Acquisti | Carnegie Mellon University, USA |
| Boris Balacheff | Hewlett Packard, UK |
| Paul England | Microsoft, USA |
| Andrew Martin | University of Oxford, UK |
| Chris Mitchell | Royal Holloway, University of London, UK |
| Sean Smith | Dartmouth College, USA |
| Ahmad-Reza Sadeghi | TU Darmstadt/Fraunhofer SIT, Germany |
| Claire Vishik | Intel, UK |

## General Chair

| | |
|---|---|
| Edgar Weippl | SBA Research, Austria |

## Technical Program Committee Chairs

| | |
|---|---|
| Michael Franz | University of California, Irvine, USA |
| Panos Papadimitratos | KTH, Stockholm, Sweden |

## Publicity and Publication Chairs

| | |
|---|---|
| Somayeh Salimi | KTH, Stockholm, Sweden |
| Moritz Wiese | KTH, Stockholm, Sweden |

## Technical Program Committee

| | |
|---|---|
| John Baras | University of Maryland, USA |
| Elisa Bertino | Purdue University, USA |
| Matt Bishop | University of California, Davis, USA |
| Mike Burmester | Florida State University, USA |
| Christian Collberg | University of Arizona, USA |
| Mauro Conti | University of Padua, Italy |
| George Cybenko | Dartmouth College, USA |
| Jack Davidson | University of Virginia, USA |
| Bjorn De Sutter | Ghent University, Belgium |
| Sven Dietrich | City University of New York, USA |
| Aurélien Francillon | EURECOM, France |
| Michael Franz | University of California, Irvine, USA |
| Virgil Gligor | Carnegie Mellon University, USA |

| | |
|---|---|
| Kevin Hamlen | The University of Texas at Dallas, USA |
| Andrei Homescu | Immunant Inc., USA |
| Michael Huth | Imperial College, UK |
| Sotiris Ioannidis | FORTH, Greece |
| Stefan Katzenbeisser | TU Darmstadt, Germany |
| Farinaz Koushnafar | University of California, San Diego, USA |
| Rick Kuhn | NIST, USA |
| Michael Locasto | University of Calgary, Canada |
| Stephen Magill | Galois, USA |
| Andrew Martin | Oxford University, UK |
| Jonathan McCune | Google, USA |
| Tyler Moore | University of Tulsa, USA |
| Peter G. Neumann | SRI International, USA |
| Hamed Okhravi | MIT Lincoln Laboratory, USA |
| Panos Papadimitratos | KTH, Sweden |
| Mathias Payer | Purdue University, USA |
| Christian Probst | DTU, Denmark |
| David Pym | University College London, UK |
| Pierangela Samarati | Università degli Studi di Milano, Italy |
| Matthias Schunter | Intel, Germany |
| Jean-Pierre Seifert | TU Berlin, Germany |
| R. Sekar | Stony Brook University, USA |
| Sean Smith | Dartmouth College, USA |
| Alfonso Valdes | University of Illinois at Urbana-Champaign, USA |
| Ingrid Verbauwhede | KU Leuven, Belgium |
| Stijn Volckaert | University of California, Irvine, USA |
| Moti Yung | Google, USA |

## Additional Reviewers

| | |
|---|---|
| Moreno Ambrosin | University of Padua, Italy |
| Robert Buhren | TU Berlin, Germany |
| Ruan de Clercq | KU Leuven, Belgium |
| Riccardo Lazzeretti | University of Padua, Italy |
| Pieter Maene | KU Leuven, Belgium |
| Marta Piekarska | TU Berlin, Germany |
| Shahin Tajik | TU Berlin, Germany |

# Contents

# Anonymous Attestation Using the Strong Diffie Hellman Assumption Revisited

Jan Camenisch[1], Manu Drijvers[1,2(✉)], and Anja Lehmann[1]

[1] IBM Research – Zurich, Säumerstrasse 4, 8803 Rüschlikon, Switzerland
{jca,mdr,anj}@zurich.ibm.com
[2] Department of Computer Science, ETH Zurich, 8092 Zürich, Switzerland

**Abstract.** Direct Anonymous Attestation (DAA) is a cryptographic protocol for privacy-protecting authentication. It is standardized in the TPM standard and implemented in millions of chips. A variant of DAA is also used in Intel's SGX. Recently, Camenisch et al. (PKC 2016) demonstrated that existing security models for DAA do not correctly capture all security requirements, and showed a number of flaws in existing schemes based on the LRSW assumption. In this work, we identify flaws in security proofs of a number of qSDH-based DAA schemes and point out that none of the proposed schemes can be proven secure in the recent model by Camenisch et al. (PKC 2016). We therefore present a new, provably secure DAA scheme that is based on the qSDH assumption. The new scheme is as efficient as the most efficient existing DAA scheme, with support for DAA extensions to signature-based revocation and attributes. We rigorously prove the scheme secure in the model of Camenisch et al., which we modify to support the extensions. As a side-result of independent interest, we prove that the BBS+ signature scheme is secure in the type-3 pairing setting, allowing for our scheme to be used with the most efficient pairing-friendly curves.

## 1 Introduction

Direct anonymous attestation (DAA) is a cryptographic authentication protocol that lets a platform, consisting of a secure element and a host, create anonymous attestations. These attestations are signatures on messages and convince a verifier that the message was signed by a authorized secure element, while preserving the privacy of the platform. DAA was designed for the Trusted Platform Module (TPM) by Brickell, Camenisch, and Chen [9] and was standardized in the TPM 1.2 specification in 2004 [34]. Their paper inspired a large body of work on DAA schemes [4,10,11,13,15,22–24,26], including more efficient scheme using bilinear pairings as well as different security definitions and proofs. One result of these works is the recent TPM 2.0 specification [31,35] that includes support for multiple pairing-based DAA schemes, two of which are standardized by ISO [30].

---

This work has been supported by the ERC under Grant PERCY #321310.

M. Franz and P. Papadimitratos (Eds.): TRUST 2016, LNCS 9824, pp. 1–20, 2016.
DOI: 10.1007/978-3-319-45572-3_1

DAA is widely used in the area of trusted computing. Over 500 million TPMs have been sold[1], making DAA probably the most complex cryptographic scheme that is widely implemented. Additionally, an extension of DAA is used in the Intel Software Guard Extensions (SGX) [27], the most recent development in the area of trusted computing.

A number of functional extensions to DAA have been proposed. Brickell and Li [12,14] introduced Enhanced Privacy ID (EPID), which extends DAA with signature-based revocation. This extension allows one to revoke a platform based on a previous signature from that platform. This is an improvement over the private key revocation used in DAA schemes, where a TPM cannot be revoked without knowing its secret key.

Chen and Urian [25] introduced DAA with attributes (DAA-A), in which the membership credential can also contain attributes. These attributes might include more information about the platform, such as the vendor or model, or other information, such as an expiration date of the credential. When signing, the platform can selectively disclose attributes, e.g., reveal that the signature was created by a TPM of a certain manufacturer, or create more advanced proofs, such as proving that the expiration date of the credential lies in the future.

Unfortunately, in spite of being used in practice, many of the existing schemes are not provably secure. Recently, Camenisch et al. [15] showed that previous security definitions of DAA are not satisfactory, meaning that security proofs using these security models do not guarantee security. They further point out that many of the DAA schemes based on the LRSW assumption [32] are flawed. They finally provide a comprehensive security model and provide a LRSW-based scheme that is provably secure in their model. However, there is to date no scheme based on the qSDH assumption [6] that is secure in their model.

Indeed, in this work we show that also many of the DAA schemes based on the qSDH assumption are flawed. The most efficient qSDH-based schemes [13, 22,25] use a credential which is not provably secure against adaptive chosen message attacks, leaving room for an attacker to forge credentials. Moreover, these schemes use a flawed proof-of-knowledge of credentials, which in fact does not prove possession of such a credential. Finally, the security of all existing qSDH-based schemes has only been analyzed in the type-2 pairing setting [29]. However, these schemes are often used in the more efficient type-3 setting, where there is no efficient isomorphism from $\mathbb{G}_2$ to $\mathbb{G}_1$, As the security proofs rely on such an isomorphism, they do not apply to a type-3 setting, meaning there is no evidence of security.

Apart from pointing out flaws in the existing qSDH-based DAA schemes, this paper provides two more main contributions. Second, we fix the issues and present a qSDH-based DAA scheme with support for attributes and signature-based revocation. Like previous work, we use the BBS+ signature [1] for credentials, but unlike previous work we move to the more efficient and flexible type-3 pairing setting. Third, we extend the security model by Camenisch et al. [15] to

---

[1] http://www.trustedcomputinggroup.org/solutions/authentication.

capture signature-based revocation and support attributes, and rigorously prove our scheme secure in this model.

## 2 Flaws in Existing qSDH-based Schemes

The first DAA scheme by Brickell et al. [9] is based on the strong RSA assumption. Due to the large keys required for RSA, this protocol was inefficient and hard to implement. A lot of research has gone into designing more efficient DAA schemes using bilinear pairings and improving the security model of DAA. The work on efficient DAA schemes can be split in two chains of work, one based on the LRSW assumption [32], and one on the qSDH assumption [6]. The schemes based on the LRSW assumption have recently been studied by Camenisch et al. [15]. In this section we now discuss the existing qSDH-based schemes and their proofs of security. We start by giving an overview of existing security models for DAA and DAA with extensions, and then show that none of the existing qSDH-based are efficient and provably secure.

### 2.1 Security Models for DAA

One of the most challenging tasks in cryptography is to formally define a security model that allows for rigorous security proofs. Before we discuss security models, we give some intuition on the required security properties of DAA. First, signatures must be *unforgeable*, meaning only platforms that the issuer allowed to join can create signatures. Second, signatures must be *anonymous*. A basename is used to control anonymity, and an adversary given two signatures valid with respect to two distinct basenames must not be able to decide whether the signatures were created by the same platform. Third, we require *non-frameability*. When a platform signs with respect to the same basename multiple times, a verifier can link these signatures, meaning it realizes both signatures stem from the same platform. No adversary should be able to frame a platform, meaning it cannot create a signature on a message $m$ that links to some platform's signatures, while that platform never signed $m$.

There are multiple ways to define a security model. Property-based definitions are a set of security games, where every game defines a security property, and a scheme is secure when every property holds. Simulation-based definitions consist of a trusted third party. In a so-called ideal world, every protocol participant hands their inputs to the trusted third party rather than executing the protocol, and outputs are generated by the trusted third party. As the trusted third party performs the task in a way secure by design, the ideal world performs the desired task securely. A protocol is considered secure if the real world, in which protocol participants execute the protocol, is as secure as the ideal world.

The first security model for DAA as introduced by Brickell et al. [9] follows the simulation-based paradigm. Therein, signature generation and verification is modeled as an interactive process, meaning a signature must always be verified immediately and cannot be used further. Camenisch et al. [15] define a simulation-based security model for DAA that outputs signatures and allows them to be used in any way.

In an attempt to simplify the security model of DAA, Brickell et al. [11] introduce a property-based definition for DAA. Unfortunately, this definition does not cover non-frameability, and the notion for unforgeability allows forgeable schemes to be proven secure: A scheme in which one value is a signature on every message can fulfill the security model, while clearly being insecure. Chen [22] extends this definition with a property for non-frameability, but the other issues remain. Brickell and Li create a property-based security model for enhanced privacy ID (EPID) [14] very similar to the model of Brickell et al. [11], and containing the same flaws.

Camenisch et al. [15] give a more detailed overview of the security models for DAA.

## 2.2  qSDH-Based DAA Schemes and Proofs

Chen and Feng [26] introduce the first DAA scheme based on the qSDH assumption. The scheme requires the TPM to work in the target group $\mathbb{G}_T$, which is inefficient and makes implementation more involved. Chen [22] improves the efficiency of the previous schemes by removing one element of the membership credential. Brickell and Li [13] further improve the efficiency by changing the distribution of work between the host and TPM such that the TPM only performs computations in $\mathbb{G}_1$. Being the most efficient scheme, it is supported by the TPM 2.0 standard and ISO standardized [30].

All three schemes come with proofs of security using the security models by Brickell et al. [11] and Brickell and Li [14]. However, as these models allow one to prove insecure schemes secure, proofs in these models are not actual evidence of security. Furthermore, the proofs of the two most efficient schemes [13,22] are invalid, as the membership credential is not proven to be existentially unforgeable against adaptive chosen message attacks. The proof aims to reduce a credential forgery to breaking the qSDH assumption, meaning that the issuer private key is an unknown value defined by the qSDH instance. They start by using the Boneh-Boyen trick [6] to create $q - 1$ weak BB signatures under the issuer key, on previously chosen $e_i$ values. From every weak BB signature, one membership credential on a (potentially adversarial) platform key can be created. For one randomly selected honest platform joining, it returns a credential on a key chosen during the parameter selection of the scheme. It can create this credential without consuming a BB04 signature due to the special selection of parameters. Since the key is chosen like an honest platform would, this simulation is valid for honest platforms. Finally, the authors claim that when a credential forgery occurs that reuses part of an issued credential, with probability $\frac{1}{q}$, it is reusing part of the specially crafted credential. This is not true, as there may not even be honest platforms joining, or the adversary may disregard credentials issued to honest platforms. To fix the proof, one must be able to issue the special credential also to corrupt platforms, i.e., on a key chosen by the adversary, but this does not seem possible.

Related to this issue, the proofs of knowledge proving knowledge of a credential in these schemes do not prove the correct statement. The prover proves knowledge of TPM secret $gsk$ and of values $a, b$. The proof only proves knowledge of a valid credential when $b = a \cdot gsk$, but this structure of $b$ is not proven. This means that from a signature that passes verification, one cannot always extract a valid signature, which prevents proving unforgeability. This could be fixed by also proving $b = a \cdot gsk$ in zero knowledge.

Finally, the security proofs of all the pairing-based schemes mentioned here make use of an isomorphism from $\mathbb{G}_2$ to $\mathbb{G}_1$ in the security proof. This prevents the schemes from being used with the more efficient type-3 curves [29]. However, the TPM 2.0 standard [31,35], designed to support the DAA scheme by Brickell and Li [13], uses such type-3 curves. As there is no efficient isomorphism in this setting, any security proof requiring an isomorphism is not applicable, leaving the security of the scheme unproven.

*DAA with Extensions.* Two extensions of DAA have been proposed. Brickell and Li [14] present EPID based on the qSDH assumption. This extends DAA with signature-based revocation, allowing revocation of platforms based on a signature from that platform. Unfortunately, they do not show how the work of the platform can be split between a TPM and host. Chen and Urian [25] introduce DAA with attributes (DAA-A), where the membership credential does not only contain the TPM key, but also attribute values. This allows for many new use cases, such as showing that a signature was created by a platform of a certain vendor, or adding expiration dates to credentials. The authors present two instantiations, one based on the LRSW assumption and one based on the qSDH assumption. Unfortunately, the schemes do not come with security proofs. The qSDH scheme suffers from the same flaws as the most recent qSDH DAA schemes discussed above, i.e., the credential is not proven to be unforgeable. Worse, the LRSW scheme is forgeable using the trivial credential $A = B = C = D = E_1 = \ldots = E_L = 1_{\mathbb{G}_1}$ that signs all attributes and keys, so anyone can sign with respect to any desired set of attributes.

# 3   A New Security Model for DAA with Extensions

In this section we present our security model for DAA with attributes and signature-based revocation, which is defined as an ideal functionality $\mathcal{F}_{\mathsf{daa+}}^l$ in the UC framework [21]. In UC, an environment $\mathcal{E}$ passes inputs and outputs to the protocol parties. The network is controlled by an adversary $\mathcal{A}$ that may communicate freely with $\mathcal{E}$. In the ideal world, the parties forward their inputs to the ideal functionality $\mathcal{F}$, which then (internally) performs the defined task and creates outputs that the parties forward to $\mathcal{E}$. Roughly, a real-world protocol $\Pi$ is said to securely realize a functionality $\mathcal{F}$, if the real world is indistinguishable from the ideal world, meaning for every adversary performing an attack in the real world, there is an ideal world adversary (often called simulator) $\mathcal{S}$ that performs the same attack in the ideal world.

**Setup**
1. **Issuer Setup.** On input (SETUP, $sid$) from issuer $\mathcal{I}$
   - Verify that $sid = (\mathcal{I}, sid')$ and output (SETUP, $sid$) to $\mathcal{S}$.
2. **Set Algorithms.** On input (ALG, $sid$, sig, ver, link, identify, ukgen) from $\mathcal{S}$
   - Check that ver, link and identify are deterministic **(i)**.
   - Store $(sid, \text{sig}, \text{ver}, \text{link}, \text{identify}, \text{ukgen})$ and output (SETUPDONE, $sid$) to $\mathcal{I}$.

**Join**
3. **Join Request.** On input (JOIN, $sid$, $jsid$, $\mathcal{M}_i$) from host $\mathcal{H}_j$.
   - Create a join session record $\langle jsid, \mathcal{M}_i, \mathcal{H}_j, \perp, status \rangle$ with $status \leftarrow request$.
   - Output (JOINSTART, $sid$, $jsid$, $\mathcal{M}_i$, $\mathcal{H}_j$) to $\mathcal{S}$.
4. **Join Request Delivery.** On input (JOINSTART, $sid$, $jsid$) from $\mathcal{S}$
   - Update the session record $\langle jsid, \mathcal{M}_i, \mathcal{H}_j, \perp, status \rangle$ to $status \leftarrow delivered$.
   - Abort if $\mathcal{I}$ or $\mathcal{M}_i$ is honest and a record $\langle \mathcal{M}_i, *, *, * \rangle \in$ Members already exists **(ii)**.
   - Output (JOINPROCEED, $sid$, $jsid$, $\mathcal{M}_i$) to $\mathcal{I}$.
5. **Join Proceed.** On input (JOINPROCEED, $sid$, $jsid$, $attrs$) from $\mathcal{I}$, with $attrs \in \mathbb{A}_1 \times \ldots \times \mathbb{A}_L$
   - Update the session record $\langle jsid, \mathcal{M}_i, \mathcal{H}_j, attrs, status \rangle$ to $status \leftarrow complete$.
   - Output (JOINCOMPLETE, $sid$, $jsid$, $attrs'$) to $\mathcal{S}$, where $attrs' \leftarrow \perp$ if $\mathcal{M}_i$ and $\mathcal{H}_j$ are honest and $attrs' \leftarrow attrs$ otherwise.
6. **Platform Key Generation.** On input (JOINCOMPLETE, $sid$, $jsid$, $gsk$) from $\mathcal{S}$.
   - Look up record $\langle jsid, \mathcal{M}_i, \mathcal{H}_j, attrs, status \rangle$ with $status = complete$.
   - If $\mathcal{M}_i$ and $\mathcal{H}_j$ are honest, set $gsk \leftarrow \perp$.
   - Else, verify that the provided $gsk$ is eligible by checking
     - CheckGskHonest$(gsk) = 1$ **(iii)** if $\mathcal{H}_j$ is corrupt and $\mathcal{M}_i$ is honest, or
     - CheckGskCorrupt$(gsk) = 1$ **(iv)** if $\mathcal{M}_i$ is corrupt.
   - Insert $\langle \mathcal{M}_i, \mathcal{H}_j, gsk, attrs \rangle$ into Members and output (JOINED, $sid$, $jsid$) to $\mathcal{H}_j$.

**Fig. 1.** The Setup and Join related interfaces of $\mathcal{F}_{\mathsf{daa}+}^l$. *(The roman numbers are labels for the different checks made within the functionality and will be used as references in the analysis of the functionality and the proof.)*

## 3.1   Ideal Functionality $\mathcal{F}_{\mathsf{daa}+}^l$

We now formally define our ideal functionality $\mathcal{F}_{\mathsf{daa}+}^l$, which is a modification of $\mathcal{F}_{\mathsf{daa}}^l$ as defined by Camenisch et al. [15]. The modifications extend the functionality to support signature-based revocation and attributes.

The UC framework allows us to focus our analysis on a single protocol instance with a globally unique session identifier sid. Here we use session identifiers of the form $sid = (\mathcal{I}, sid')$ for some issuer $\mathcal{I}$ and a unique string $sid'$. To allow several sub-sessions for the join and sign related interfaces we use unique sub-session identifiers $jsid$ and $ssid$. Our ideal functionality $\mathcal{F}_{\mathsf{daa}+}^l$ is parametrized by a leakage function $l : \{0,1\}^* \rightarrow \{0,1\}^*$, that we need to model the information leakage that occurs in the communication between a host $\mathcal{H}_i$ and TPM $\mathcal{M}_j$. As our functionality supports attributes, we have parameters $L$ and $\{\mathbb{A}_i\}_{0<i\leq L}$, where $L$ is the amount of attributes every credential contains and $\mathbb{A}_i$ the set from which the $i$-th attribute is taken. A parameter $\mathbb{P}$ is used to describe which proofs over the attributes platforms can make. This generic approach lets the functionality capture both simple protocols that only support selective

**Sign**

7. **Sign Request.** On input $(\mathsf{SIGN}, sid, ssid, \mathcal{M}_i, m, \mathsf{bsn}, p, \mathsf{SRL})$ from $\mathcal{H}_j$ with $p \in \mathbb{P}$
   - If $\mathcal{H}_j$ is honest and no entry $\langle \mathcal{M}_i, \mathcal{H}_j, *, attrs \rangle$ with $p(attrs) = 1$ exists in Members, abort.
   - Create a sign session record $\langle ssid, \mathcal{M}_i, \mathcal{H}_j, m, \mathsf{bsn}, p, \mathsf{SRL}, status \rangle$ with $status \leftarrow request$.
   - Output $(\mathsf{SIGNSTART}, sid, ssid, l(m, \mathsf{bsn}, p, \mathsf{SRL}), \mathcal{M}_i, \mathcal{H}_j)$ to $\mathcal{S}$.

8. **Sign Request Delivery.** On input $(\mathsf{SIGNSTART}, sid, ssid)$ from $\mathcal{S}$.
   - Update the session record $\langle ssid, \mathcal{M}_i, \mathcal{H}_j, m, \mathsf{bsn}, p, \mathsf{SRL}, status \rangle$ to $status \leftarrow delivered$.
   - Output $(\mathsf{SIGNPROCEED}, sid, ssid, m, \mathsf{bsn}, p, \mathsf{SRL})$ to $\mathcal{M}_i$.

9. **Sign Proceed.** On input $(\mathsf{SIGNPROCEED}, sid, ssid)$ from $\mathcal{M}_i$.
   - Look up record $\langle ssid, \mathcal{M}_i, \mathcal{H}_j, m, \mathsf{bsn}, p, \mathsf{SRL}, status \rangle$ with $status = delivered$.
   - Output $(\mathsf{SIGNCOMPLETE}, sid, ssid)$ to $\mathcal{S}$.

10. **Signature Generation.** On input $(\mathsf{SIGNCOMPLETE}, sid, ssid, \sigma)$ from $\mathcal{S}$.
    - If $\mathcal{I}$ is honest, check that $\langle \mathcal{M}_i, \mathcal{H}_j, *, attrs \rangle$ with $p(attrs) = 1$ exists in Members.
    - For every $(\sigma', m', \mathsf{bsn}') \in \mathsf{SRL}$, find all $(gsk_i, \mathcal{M}_i)$ from $\langle \mathcal{M}_i, *, gsk_i \rangle \in$ Members and $\langle \mathcal{M}_i, *, gsk_i \rangle \in$ DomainKeys where $\mathsf{identify}(\sigma', m', \mathsf{bsn}', gsk_i) = 1$.
      - Check that there are no two distinct $gsk$ values matching $\sigma'$ **(v)**.
      - Check that no pair $(gsk_i, \mathcal{M}_i)$ was found **(vi)**.
    - If $\mathcal{M}_i$ and $\mathcal{H}_j$ are honest, ignore the adversary's signature and internally generate the signature for a fresh or established $gsk$:
      - Find $gsk$ from $\langle \mathcal{M}_i, \mathsf{bsn}, gsk \rangle \in$ DomainKeys. If no such $gsk$ exists, set $gsk \leftarrow \mathsf{ukgen}()$, check $\mathsf{CheckGskHonest}(gsk) = 1$ **(vii)**, and store $\langle \mathcal{M}_i, \mathsf{bsn}, gsk \rangle$ in DomainKeys.
      - Compute signature $\sigma \leftarrow \mathsf{sig}(gsk, m, \mathsf{bsn}, p, \mathsf{SRL})$, check $\mathsf{ver}(\sigma, m, \mathsf{bsn}, p, \mathsf{SRL}) = 1$ **(viii)**.
      - Check $\mathsf{identify}(\sigma, m, \mathsf{bsn}, gsk) = 1$ **(ix)** and that there is no $\mathcal{M}_i' \neq \mathcal{M}_i$ with key $gsk'$ registered in Members or DomainKeys with $\mathsf{identify}(\sigma, m, \mathsf{bsn}, gsk') = 1$ **(x)**.
    - If $\mathcal{M}_i$ is honest, store $\langle \sigma, m, \mathsf{bsn}, \mathcal{M}_i, p, \mathsf{SRL} \rangle$ in Signed.
    - Output $(\mathsf{SIGNATURE}, sid, ssid, \sigma)$ to $\mathcal{H}_j$.

**Verify**

11. **Verify.** On input $(\mathsf{VERIFY}, sid, m, \mathsf{bsn}, \sigma, p, \mathsf{RL}, \mathsf{SRL})$ from some party $\mathcal{V}$.
    - Retrieve all pairs $(gsk_i, \mathcal{M}_i)$ from $\langle \mathcal{M}_i, *, gsk_i \rangle \in$ Members and $\langle \mathcal{M}_i, *, gsk_i \rangle \in$ DomainKeys where $\mathsf{identify}(\sigma, m, \mathsf{bsn}, gsk_i) = 1$. Set $f \leftarrow 0$ if at least one of the following conditions hold:
      - More than one key $gsk_i$ was found **(xi)**.
      - $\mathcal{I}$ is honest and no pair $(gsk_i, \mathcal{M}_i)$ was found for which an entry $\langle \mathcal{M}_i, *, *, attrs \rangle \in$ Members exists with $p(attrs) = 1$ **(xii)**.
      - There is an honest $\mathcal{M}_i$ but no entry $\langle *, m, \mathsf{bsn}, \mathcal{M}_i, p, \mathsf{SRL} \rangle \in$ Signed exists **(xiii)**.
      - There is a $gsk' \in \mathsf{RL}$ where $\mathsf{identify}(\sigma, m, \mathsf{bsn}, gsk') = 1$ and no pair $(gsk_i, \mathcal{M}_i)$ for an honest $\mathcal{M}_i$ was found **(xiv)**.
      - For some matching $gsk_i$ and $(\sigma', m', \mathsf{bsn}') \in \mathsf{SRL}$, $\mathsf{identify}(\sigma', m', \mathsf{bsn}', gsk_i) = 1$ **(xv)**.
    - If $f \neq 0$, set $f \leftarrow \mathsf{ver}(\sigma, m, \mathsf{bsn}, p, \mathsf{SRL})$ **(xvi)**.
    - Add $\langle \sigma, m, \mathsf{bsn}, \mathsf{RL}, f \rangle$ to VerResults and output $(\mathsf{VERIFIED}, sid, f)$ to $\mathcal{V}$.

**Link**

12. **Link.** On input $(\mathsf{LINK}, sid, \sigma, m, p, \mathsf{SRL}, \sigma', m', p', \mathsf{SRL}', \mathsf{bsn})$ from a party $\mathcal{V}$.
    - Output $\bot$ to $\mathcal{V}$ if at least one signature $(\sigma, m, \mathsf{bsn}, p, \mathsf{SRL})$ or $(\sigma', m', \mathsf{bsn}, p', \mathsf{SRL}')$ is not valid (verified via the verify interface with $\mathsf{RL} = \emptyset$) **(xvii)**.
    - For each $gsk_i$ in Members and DomainKeys compute $b_i \leftarrow \mathsf{identify}(\sigma, m, \mathsf{bsn}, gsk_i)$ and $b_i' \leftarrow \mathsf{identify}(\sigma', m', \mathsf{bsn}, gsk_i)$ and do the following:
      - Set $f \leftarrow 0$ if $b_i \neq b_i'$ for some $i$ **(xviii)**.
      - Set $f \leftarrow 1$ if $b_i = b_i' = 1$ for some $i$ **(xix)**.
    - If $f$ is not defined yet, set $f \leftarrow \mathsf{link}(\sigma, m, \sigma', m', \mathsf{bsn})$.
    - Output $(\mathsf{LINK}, sid, f)$ to $\mathcal{V}$.

**Fig. 2.** The Sign, Verify, and Link related interfaces of $\mathcal{F}_{\mathsf{daa}+}^l$

disclosure and more advanced protocols that support arbitrary predicates. Every element $p \in \mathbb{P}$ is a predicate over the attributes: $\mathbb{A}_1 \times \ldots \times \mathbb{A}_L \to \{0, 1\}$.

The full definition of $\mathcal{F}^l_{\mathsf{daa}+}$ is presented in Figs. 1 and 2. Two macros are used to simplify the presentation of the functionality:

CheckGskHonest($gsk$) =
$$\forall \langle \sigma, m, \mathsf{bsn}, \mathcal{M} \rangle \in \mathtt{Signed} : \mathsf{identify}(\sigma, m, \mathsf{bsn}, gsk) = 0 \quad \wedge$$
$$\forall \langle \sigma, m, \mathsf{bsn}, *, 1 \rangle \in \mathtt{VerResults} : \mathsf{identify}(\sigma, m, \mathsf{bsn}, gsk) = 0$$

CheckGskCorrupt($gsk$) = $\nexists \sigma, m, \mathsf{bsn}$ :
$$\left( \Big( \langle \sigma, m, \mathsf{bsn}, * \rangle \in \mathtt{Signed} \vee \langle \sigma, m, \mathsf{bsn}, *, 1 \rangle \in \mathtt{VerResults} \Big) \wedge \right.$$
$$\exists gsk' : \Big( gsk \neq gsk' \wedge \big( \langle *, *, gsk' \rangle \in \mathtt{Members} \vee \langle *, *, gsk' \rangle \in \mathtt{DomainKeys} \big) $$
$$\left. \wedge\ \mathsf{identify}(\sigma, m, \mathsf{bsn}, gsk) = \mathsf{identify}(\sigma, m, \mathsf{bsn}, gsk') = 1 \Big) \right)$$

Camenisch et al. [15] give an extensive argumentation of why their functionality guarantees the desired properties. We now argue that our changes indeed allow for attributes and signature-based revocation and that they do not have a negative impact on the other properties guaranteed by the functionality.

*Attributes.* The issuer is in charge of the attributes, and must explicitly allow a platform to be issued certain attributes with the JOINPROCEED output and input. The verification interface now checks whether the signer has the correct attributes, fulfilling the attribute predicate (Check **(xii)**). This guarantees that no platform can create valid signatures with respect to attribute predicates that do not hold for the attributes of this platform.

*Signature-based Revocation.* The sign interface now takes a signature-based revocation list SRL as input. The functionality does not sign for platforms that are revoked by SRL, which it enforces via Check **(vi)**. Further, the verification interface will reject signatures from platforms revoked in SRL by checking whether any of those signatures is based on the key $gsk$ from the signature being verified.

Our functionality enforces that every signature matches to only one $gsk$ value. To ensure this also for the signatures specified in SRL, Check **(v)** has been added and the CheckGsk macros have been extended to also take the SRL values into consideration.

## 4   Building Blocks

In this section we introduce the building blocks used by our construction. In addition to the standard building blocks such as bilinear pairings and the qSDH assumption, we introduce the BBS+ signature without requiring an isomorphism between the bilinear groups. Up to now, this signature has only been proven secure using such an isomorphism, limiting the settings in which the signature can be used.

### 4.1 Bilinear Maps

Let $\mathbb{G}_1$, $\mathbb{G}_2$, and $\mathbb{G}_T$ be groups of prime order $p$. A map $e : \mathbb{G}_1 \times \mathbb{G}_2 \to \mathbb{G}_T$ must satisfy bilinearity, i.e., $e(g_1^x, g_2^y) = e(g_1, g_2)^{xy}$; non-degeneracy, i.e., for all generators $g_1 \in \mathbb{G}_1$ and $g_2 \in \mathbb{G}_2$, $e(g_1, g_2)$ generates $\mathbb{G}_T$; and efficiency, i.e., there exists an efficient algorithm $\mathcal{G}(1^\tau)$ that outputs the bilinear group $(p, \mathbb{G}_1, \mathbb{G}_2, \mathbb{G}_T, e, g_1, g_2)$ and an efficient algorithm to compute $e(a, b)$ for any $a \in \mathbb{G}_1$, $b \in \mathbb{G}_2$.

Galbraith et al. [29] distinguish three types of pairings: type-1, in which $\mathbb{G}_1 = \mathbb{G}_2$; type-2, in which $\mathbb{G}_1 \neq \mathbb{G}_2$ and there exists an efficient isomorphism $\psi : \mathbb{G}_2 \to \mathbb{G}_1$; and type-3, in which $\mathbb{G}_1 \neq \mathbb{G}_2$ and no such isomorphism exists.

Type-3 pairings currently allow for the most efficient operations in $\mathbb{G}_1$ given a security level using BN curves with a high embedding degree [2]. Therefore it is desirable to describe a cryptographic scheme in a type-3 setting, i.e., without assuming $\mathbb{G}_1 = \mathbb{G}_2$ or the existence of an efficient isomorphism from $\mathbb{G}_2$ to $\mathbb{G}_1$.

### 4.2 q-Strong Diffie-Hellman Assumption

The $q$-Strong Diffie-Hellman (qSDH) problem has two versions. The first version by Boneh and Boyen is defined in a type-1 and type-2 pairing setting [6]. This version, to which we refer as the Eurocrypt version, is informally stated as follows:

Given a $q+2$-tuple $(g_1, g_2, g_2^x, g_2^{(x^2)}, \ldots, g_2^{(x^q)}) \in \mathbb{G}_1 \times \mathbb{G}_2^{q+1}$ with $g_1 = \psi(g_2)$, output a pair $(c, g_1^{1/(x+c)}) \in \mathbb{Z}_p^* \times \mathbb{G}_1$.

Boneh and Boyen created a new version of the qSDH problem to support type-3 settings [7]. The so-called JOC version is informally stated as follows:

Given a $q+3$-tuple $(g_1, g_1^x, g_1^{(x^2)}, \ldots, g_1^{(x^q)}, g_2, g_2^x) \in \mathbb{G}_1^{q+1} \times \mathbb{G}_2^2$, output a pair $(c, g_1^{1/(x+c)}) \in \mathbb{Z}_p \setminus \{-x\} \times \mathbb{G}_1$.

### 4.3 BBS+ Signatures

We recall the BBS+ signature, as described by Au et al. [1], which is inspired by the group signature scheme by Boneh et al. [8].

**Key Generation.** Take $(h_0, \ldots, h_L) \xleftarrow{\$} \mathbb{Z}_p^{L+1}$, $x \xleftarrow{\$} \mathbb{Z}_p^*$, $w \leftarrow g_2^x$, and set $sk = x$ and $pk = (w, h_0, \ldots, h_L)$.

**Signature.** On input message $(m_1, \ldots, m_L) \in \mathbb{Z}_p^L$ and secret key $x$, pick $e, s \xleftarrow{\$} \mathbb{Z}_p$ and compute $A \leftarrow (g_1 h_0^s \prod_{i=1}^L h_i^{m_i})^{\frac{1}{e+x}}$. Output signature $\sigma \leftarrow (A, e, s)$.

**Verification.** On input a public key $(w, h_0, \ldots, h_L) \in \mathbb{G}_2 \times \mathbb{G}_1^{L+1}$, message $(m_1, \ldots, m_L) \in \mathbb{Z}_p^L$, and purported signature $(A, e, s) \in \mathbb{G}_1 \times \mathbb{Z}_p^2$, check $e(A, wg_2^e) = e(g_1 h_0^s \prod_{i=1}^L h_i^{m_i}, g_2)$.

Au et al. prove the BBS+ signature secure under the Eurocrypt version of the qSDH assumption, making use of the isomorphism between the groups in the security proof. As in type-3 pairings no such isomorphism exists, this means the proof is not valid when this isomorphism does not exist and we do not know whether the signature is secure in this setting. We modify the proof by Au et al. to use the JOC version of the qSDH assumption and no longer rely on an isomorphism in the proof, allowing us to use BBS+ signatures with type-3 pairings.

**Theorem 1.** *The BBS+ signature scheme is existentially unforgeable against adaptive chosen message attacks under the JOC version of the qSDH assumption and the DL assumption, in particular in pairing groups where no efficient isomorphism between $\mathbb{G}_2$ and $\mathbb{G}_1$ exists.*

Due to space contraints, the proof is presented in the full version of the paper [16].

### 4.4  Proof Protocols

When referring to the zero-knowledge proofs of knowledge of discrete logarithms and statements about them, we will follow the notation introduced by Camenisch and Stadler [19] and formally defined by Camenisch, Kiayias, and Yung [17].

For instance, $PK\{(a, b, c) : y = g^a h^b \wedge \tilde{y} = \tilde{g}^a \tilde{h}^c\}$ denotes a *"zero-knowledge proof of knowledge of integers a, b and c such that $y = g^a h^b$ and $\tilde{y} = \tilde{g}^a \tilde{h}^c$ holds,"* where $y, g, h, \tilde{y}, \tilde{g}$ and $\tilde{h}$ are elements of some groups $\mathbb{G} = \langle g \rangle = \langle h \rangle$ and $\tilde{\mathbb{G}} = \langle \tilde{g} \rangle = \langle \tilde{h} \rangle$. Given a protocol in this notation, it is straightforward to derive an actual protocol implementing the proof [17]. Indeed, the computational complexities of the proof protocol can be easily derived from this notation: for each term $y = g^a h^b$, the prover and the verifier have to perform an equivalent computation, and to transmit one group element and one response value for each exponent.

*SPK* denotes a signature proof of knowledge, that is a non-interactive transformation of a proof with the Fiat-Shamir heuristic [28] in the random oracle model [3]. From these non-interactive proofs, the witness can be extracted by rewinding the prover and programming the random oracle. Alternatively, these proofs can be extended to be online-extractable, by verifiably encrypting the witness to a public key defined in the common reference string (CRS). A practical instantiation is given by Camenisch and Shoup [18] using Paillier encryption, secure under the DCR assumption [33].

## 5  Construction

In this section, we present our DAA protocol with attributes and signature-based revocation called $\Pi_{\text{daa+}}$. On a high level, it is similar to previous work on qSDH-based DAA. A platform, consisting of a TPM and a host, must once run the join protocol before it can create signatures. In the join protocol, the TPM authenticates to the issuer. The issuer can decide whether the TPM is allowed to join, and if so, it creates a credential for the platform. The credential is BBS+ signature on a commitment to the TPM chosen secret key $gsk$, and on attribute values as determined by the issuer. Note that the issuer can choose the attribute values, as we expect the issuer to issue only credentials containing attributes where it knows the 'correct' attribute values, such as the model or vendor of the TPM (which it knows as the TPM authenticated), or an expiration date of the credential. After receiving a credential, the platform can sign a message $m$ by creating a signature proof-of-knowledge proving that it has a credential. A basename bsn controls linkability. Choosing a fresh bsn yields a signature that cannot be linked to any signature that the platform previously generated, meaning the platform can be fully anonymous. Only when it chooses to reuse a basename, the signatures based on the same basename can be linked, i.e., a verifier can notice that they stem from the same platform. The platform also chooses which attributes it will disclose to a verifier.

Our protocol is parametrized by $L$, the amount of attributes a credential contains, attribute sets $\mathbb{A}_1, \ldots, \mathbb{A}_L$, and $l$, the leakage of the secure channels used. For simplicity of the presentation, we describe our construction supporting only selective disclosure as attribute predicates, although it is simple to see how the construction can be extended to allow for more advanced predicates using standard proof techniques. We describe the predicates using a set $D \subseteq \{1, \ldots, L\}$ indicating which attributes are disclosed, and a tuple $I = (a_1, \ldots, a_L)$ setting the desired attribute values. For example, the predicate $D \leftarrow \{2\}$, $I = (\bot, 123, \bot)$ is only true for platforms with credentials in which the second attribute value equals 123. Let $\bar{D} = \{1, \ldots, L\} \setminus D$ be the set of undisclosed attributes.

We assume that a common reference string functionality $\mathcal{F}_{\mathsf{crs}}$ and a certificate authority functionality $\mathcal{F}_{\mathsf{ca}}$ are available to all parties. $\mathcal{F}_{\mathsf{crs}}$ will be used to provide the protocol participants with the system parameters consisting of a security parameter $\tau$, a bilinear group $\mathbb{G}_1, \mathbb{G}_2, \mathbb{G}_T$ of prime order $p$ with generators $g_1, h_0, \ldots, h_L$ of $\mathbb{G}_1$ and $g_2$ of $\mathbb{G}_2$ and bilinear map $e$, generated via $\mathcal{G}(1^\tau)$. $\mathcal{F}_{\mathsf{ca}}$ allows the issuer to register his public key. We further use random oracles $H_1 : \{0,1\}^* \rightarrow \mathbb{G}_1$ that is used for the computation of pseudonyms and $H : \{0,1\}^* \rightarrow \{0,1\}^\tau$ which is used for the Fiat-Shamir heuristic in the zero-knowledge proofs.

The TPM and issuer must have an authenticated communication channel in the join protocol. This can be achieved in multiple ways, we abstract away from this by using an ideal functionality for this authenticated channel. As the host forwards messages, it can block the communication, so the standard $\mathcal{F}_{\mathsf{auth}}$ does not capture the desired security. Instead we use $\mathcal{F}_{\mathsf{auth}*}$ which was introduced by Camenisch et al. [15] specifically for this type of authenticated channel. The communication between a TPM and host is modeled using secure message transmission functionality $\mathcal{F}_{\mathsf{smt}}^l$. For definitions of the standard functionalities $\mathcal{F}_{\mathsf{crs}}, \mathcal{F}_{\mathsf{ca}}$ and $\mathcal{F}_{\mathsf{smt}}^l$ we refer to [20,21].

For the sake of readability, we will not explicitly call $\mathcal{F}^l_{\mathsf{smt}}$ for communication between a TPM and host, nor write down that parties query $\mathcal{F}_{\mathsf{crs}}$ and $\mathcal{F}_{\mathsf{ca}}$ to retrieve the system parameters and the issuer public key. When a party receives an input or message it does not expect, e.g., protocol messages received out of order, or any of the protocol checks fails, the protocol outputs with failure message $\perp$. For efficiency, a host should precompute values $e(g_1, g_2)$ and $e(h_0, w)$ after joining and a verifier should in addition precompute $e(h_i, g_2)$ for $i = 0, \ldots, L$ to minimize the number of pairing computations, but for readability we write the full pairing function.

## 5.1    Our DAA Protocol with Extensions $\Pi_{\mathsf{daa}+}$

**Issuer Setup.** In the setup phase, the issuer $\mathcal{I}$ creates a key pair of the BBS+-signature scheme and registers the public key with $\mathcal{F}_{\mathsf{ca}}$.

1. $\mathcal{I}$ upon input (SETUP, $sid$) generates his key pair:
   - Check that $sid = (\mathcal{I}, sid')$ for some $sid'$.
   - Choose $x \xleftarrow{\$} \mathbb{Z}_p$ and set $w \leftarrow g_2^x$. Prove knowledge of the private key by creating $\pi \xleftarrow{\$} SPK\{x : w = g_2^x\}$. Initiate $\mathcal{L}_{\mathsf{JOINED}} \leftarrow \emptyset$.
   - Register the public key $w, \pi$ at $\mathcal{F}_{\mathsf{ca}}$, and store the secret key $x$.
   - Output (SETUPDONE, $sid$).

**Join Request.** The join protocol runs between the issuer $\mathcal{I}$ and a platform, consisting of a TPM $\mathcal{M}_i$ and a host $\mathcal{H}_j$. The platform authenticates to the issuer and, if the issuer allows the platform to join with certain attributes, obtains a credential that subsequently enables the platform to create signatures. A unique sub-session identifier $jsid$ distinguishes several join sessions that might run in parallel.

1. $\mathcal{H}_j$ upon input (JOIN, $sid, jsid, \mathcal{M}_i$) parses $sid = (\mathcal{I}, sid')$ and sends the message (JOIN, $sid, jsid$) over $\mathcal{I}$.
2. $\mathcal{I}$ upon receiving (JOIN, $sid, jsid$) from a party $\mathcal{H}_j$ chooses a fresh nonce $n \xleftarrow{\$} \{0, 1\}^\tau$ and sends $(sid, jsid, n)$ back to $\mathcal{H}_j$.
3. $\mathcal{H}_j$ upon receiving $(sid, jsid, n)$ from $\mathcal{I}$, sends $(sid, jsid, n)$ to $\mathcal{M}_i$.
4. $\mathcal{M}_i$ upon receiving $(sid, jsid, n)$ from $\mathcal{H}_j$, generates its secret key:
   - Check that no key record exists.
   - Choose $gsk \xleftarrow{\$} \mathbb{Z}_p$ and store the key as $(sid, \mathcal{H}_j, gsk, \perp)$.
   - Set $Q \leftarrow h_1^{gsk}$ and compute $\pi_1 \xleftarrow{\$} SPK\{(gsk) : Q = h_1^{gsk}\}(n)$.
   - Store key record $(sid, \mathcal{H}_j, gsk)$.
   - Send $(Q, \pi_1)$ via the host to $\mathcal{I}$ using $\mathcal{F}_{\mathsf{auth}*}$.
5. $\mathcal{H}_j$ notices $\mathcal{M}_i$ sending $(Q, \pi_1)$ over $\mathcal{F}_{\mathsf{auth}*}$ to the issuer, it appends its own identity in the unauthenticated part of the message and forwards the full message to the issuer. It also keeps state as $(jsid, Q)$.
6. $\mathcal{I}$ upon receiving $(Q, \pi_1)$ authenticated by $\mathcal{M}_i$ and identity $\mathcal{H}_j$ unauthenticated over $\mathcal{F}_{\mathsf{auth}*}$, it verifies $\pi_1$ and checks that $\mathcal{M}_i \notin \mathcal{L}_{\mathsf{JOINED}}$. It stores $(jsid, Q, \mathcal{M}_i, \mathcal{H}_j)$ and outputs (JOINPROCEED, $sid, jsid, \mathcal{M}_i$).

**Join Proceed.** The join session is completed when the issuer receives an explicit input telling him to proceed with join session *jsid* and issue attributes *attrs* = $(a_1, \ldots, a_L)$.

1. $\mathcal{I}$ upon input (JOINPROCEED, *sid*, *jsid*, *attrs*) generates the BBS+ credential:
   - Retrieve the record $(jsid, Q, \mathcal{M}_i, \mathcal{H}_j)$ and add $\mathcal{M}_i$ to $\mathcal{L}_{\text{JOINED}}$.
   - Choose random $e, f \in \mathbb{Z}_p$.
   - $A \leftarrow (g_1 \cdot h_0^f \cdot Q \cdot \prod_{i=1}^{L} h_{i+1}^{a_i})^{1/(e+x)}$
   - Send the credential to the host by sending $(sid, jsid, A, e, f, attrs)$ to $\mathcal{H}_j$ over $\mathcal{F}_{\text{smt}}$.
2. $\mathcal{H}_j$ upon receiving $(sid, jsid, A, e, f, attrs)$ from $\mathcal{I}$ verifies and stores the credential.
   - Check that $e(A, wg_2^e) = e(g_1 \cdot h_0^f \cdot Q \cdot \prod_{i=1}^{L} h_{i+1}^{a_i}, g_2)$.
   - Store $(sid, \mathcal{M}_i, (A, e, f), attrs)$ and output (JOINED, *sid*, *jsid*).

**Sign Request.** The sign protocol runs between a TPM $\mathcal{M}_i$ and a host $\mathcal{H}_j$. After joining, together they can sign a message $m$ with respect to a basename **bsn**, attribute predicate $(D, I)$, and signature-based revocation list **SRL**. Again, we use a unique sub-session identifier *ssid* to allow for multiple sign sessions.

1. $\mathcal{H}_j$ upon input (SIGN, *sid*, *ssid*, $\mathcal{M}_i$, $m$, **bsn**, $(D, I)$, **SRL**) checks whether his attributes fulfill the predicate and randomizes the BBS+ credential:
   - Retrieve the join record $(sid, \mathcal{M}_i, (A, e, f), attrs)$.
   - Check that the attributes fulfill the predicate: Parse $I$ as $(a'_1, \ldots, a'_L)$ and *attrs* as $(a_1, \ldots, a_L)$ and check that $a_i = a'_i$ for every $i \in D$.
   - Choose $a \xleftarrow{\$} \mathbb{Z}_p$ and set $A' \leftarrow A \cdot h_0^a$.
   - Send $(sid, ssid, m, \text{bsn}, (D, I), \text{SRL})$ to $\mathcal{M}_i$ and store $(sid, ssid, a)$
2. $\mathcal{M}_i$ upon receiving $(sid, ssid, m, \text{bsn}, (D, I), \text{SRL})$ from $\mathcal{H}_j$ asks for permission to proceed.
   - Check that a join record $(sid, \mathcal{H}_j, gsk)$ exists.
   - Store $(sid, ssid, m, \text{bsn}, (D, I), \text{SRL})$ and output (SIGNPROCEED, *sid*, *ssid*, $m$, **bsn**, $(D, I)$, **SRL**).

**Sign Proceed.** The signature is completed when $\mathcal{M}_i$ gets permission to proceed for *ssid*.

1. $\mathcal{M}_i$ upon input (SIGNPROCEED, *sid*, *ssid*) computes the pseudonym **nym** and starts the computation of the following zero knowledge proof.

$$SPK\{(gsk, \{a_i\}_{i \in \bar{D}}, e, a, b) :$$

$$\frac{e(A', w)}{e(g_1, g_2) \prod_{i \in D} e(h_{i+1}, g_2)^{a_i}} = e(A', g_2)^{-e} e(h_0, g_2)^b e(h_1, g_2)^{gsk} e(h_0, w)^a$$

$$\cdot \prod_{i \in \bar{D}} e(h_{i+1}, g_2)^{a_i} \;\wedge\; \mathbf{nym} = H_1(\mathbf{bsn})^{gsk}\}(m)$$

– Retrieve join record $(sid, \mathcal{H}_j, gsk)$ and sign record $(sid, ssid, m, \mathbf{bsn}, (D, I), \mathbf{SRL})$.
– Set $\mathbf{nym} \leftarrow H_1(\mathbf{bsn})^{gsk}$.
– Take $r_{gsk} \xleftarrow{\$} \mathbb{Z}_p$ and compute $E \leftarrow h_1^{r_{gsk}}$ and $L \leftarrow H_1(\mathbf{bsn})^{r_{gsk}}$.
– Send $(sid, ssid, E, L, \mathbf{nym})$ to $\mathcal{H}_j$.

2. $\mathcal{H}_j$ upon receiving $(sid, ssid, E, L, \mathbf{nym})$ from $\mathcal{M}_i$, completes the commitment phase of the zero-knowledge proof.

– Take $r_{a_i} \xleftarrow{\$} \mathbb{Z}_p$ for $i \in \bar{D}$, and $r_e, r_a, r_b \xleftarrow{\$} \mathbb{Z}_p$.
– Compute $t$-value

$$t \leftarrow e(A', g_2)^{r_e} e(h_0, g_2)^{r_b} e(E, g_2) e(h_0, w)^{r_a} \prod_{i \in \bar{D}} e(h_{i+1}, g_2)^{r_{a_i}}$$

$$= e(A'^{r_e} \cdot h_0^{r_b} \cdot E \cdot \prod_{i \in \bar{D}} h_{i+1}^{r_{a_i}}, g_2) e(h_0, w)^{r_a}$$

– Compute $c' \leftarrow H(A', \mathbf{nym}, t, L, g_1, h_0, \ldots, h_L, w)$.
– Send $(sid, ssid, c')$ to $\mathcal{M}_i$.

3. $\mathcal{M}_i$ upon receiving $(sid, ssid, c')$ from $\mathcal{H}_j$.

– Take a nonce $n \xleftarrow{\$} \{0,1\}^\tau$.
– Compute $c \leftarrow H(n, c', m, \mathbf{bsn}, (D, I), \mathbf{SRL})$.
– Set $s_{gsk} \leftarrow r_{gsk} + c \cdot gsk$.
– Send $(sid, ssid, s_{gsk})$ to $\mathcal{H}_j$.

4. $\mathcal{H}_j$ upon receiving $(sid, ssid, s_{gsk})$ from $\mathcal{M}_i$, completes the zero-knowledge proof.

– Set $b \leftarrow f + a \cdot e$, $s_{a_i} \leftarrow r_{a_i} + c a_i$ for $i \in \bar{D}$, $s_e \leftarrow r_e - ce$, $s_a \leftarrow r_a + ca$, $s_b \leftarrow r_b + cae$.
– Set $\pi \leftarrow (c, s_{gsk}, \{s_{a_i}\}_{i \in \bar{D}}, s_e, s_a, s_b, n)$.

5. As signature-based revocation is used, a revocation list $\mathbf{SRL}$ containing tuples $(\mathbf{bsn}_i, \mathbf{nym}_i)$ is given, and the platform must prove that $H_1(\mathbf{bsn}_i)^{gsk} \neq \mathbf{nym}_i$. It does so using the Camenisch-Shoup proof of inequality of discrete logarithms [18]: take a random $\gamma$, compute $C \leftarrow (H_1(\mathbf{bsn}_i)^{gsk}/\mathbf{nym}_i)^\gamma$, and prove $SPK\{(\alpha, \beta) : C = H_1(\mathbf{bsn}_i)^\alpha (\frac{1}{\mathbf{nym}_i})^\beta \wedge 1 = H_1(\mathbf{bsn})^\alpha (\frac{1}{\mathbf{nym}})^\beta\}$. For every $(\mathbf{bsn}_i, \mathbf{nym}_i) \in \mathbf{SRL}$, the platform takes the following steps.

(a) Host $\mathcal{H}_j$ sends $(sid, ssid, \mathbf{bsn}_i)$ to $\mathcal{M}_i$.

(b) Upon receiving $(sid, ssid, \mathbf{bsn}_i)$, the TPM $\mathcal{M}_i$ starts the commitment phase of this proof of non-revocation.

– Take $r_{i,\alpha} \xleftarrow{\$} \mathbb{Z}_p$ and compute $t'_{i,1} \leftarrow H_1(\mathbf{bsn}_i)^{r_{i,\alpha}}$, $t'_{i,2} \leftarrow H_1(\mathbf{bsn})^{r_{i,\alpha}}$, $K \leftarrow H_1(\mathbf{bsn}_i)^{gsk}$.
– Send $(sid, ssid, t'_{i,1}), t'_{i,2}, K)$ to $\mathcal{H}_j$.

(c) Upon receiving $(sid, ssid, t'_{i,1}), t'_{i,2}, K)$, $\mathcal{H}_j$ completes the commitment phase of the non-revocation proof.

– Take $\gamma_i \xleftarrow{\$} \mathbb{Z}_p$ and set $C_i \leftarrow (K/\mathbf{nym}_i)^{\gamma_i}$.
– Check $C_i \neq 1_{\mathbb{G}_1}$.
– Take $r_{i,\beta} \xleftarrow{\$} \mathbb{Z}_p$ and set $t_{i,1} \leftarrow t'^{r_{i,\beta}}_{i,1} \cdot (\frac{1}{\mathbf{nym}_i})^{r_{i,\beta}}$ and $t_{i,2} \leftarrow t'^{\gamma_i}_{i,2} \cdot (\frac{1}{\mathbf{nym}})^{r_{i,\beta}}$.
– Compute $c' \leftarrow H(C, \mathbf{bsn}_i, \mathbf{bsn}, \mathbf{nym}_i, \mathbf{nym}, n, t_{i,1}, t_{i,2})$

- Send $(sid, ssid, c')$ to $\mathcal{M}_i$.
(d) $\mathcal{M}_i$ upon receiving $(sid, ssid, c')$ from $\mathcal{H}_j$
    - Take nonce $n_i \stackrel{\$}{\leftarrow} \{0,1\}^\tau$ and compute $c \leftarrow H(n_i, c)$.
    - Set $s'_{i,\alpha} \leftarrow r_{i,\alpha} + c \cdot gsk$ and send $(sid, ssid, s'_{i,\alpha}, n_i)$ to $\mathcal{H}_j$.
(e) Upon receiving $(sid, ssid, s'_{i,\alpha}, n_i)$ from $\mathcal{M}_i$, host $\mathcal{H}_j$ finishes the non-revocation proof.
    - Compute $c \leftarrow H(n_i, c')$.
    - Set $s_{i,\alpha} \leftarrow \gamma \cdot s'_{i,gsk}$ and $s_{i,\beta} \leftarrow r_{i,\beta} + c \cdot \gamma$.
    - Set $\pi_i \leftarrow (c, n_i, C_i, s_{i,\alpha}, s_{i,\beta})$.
6. The host outputs $(\mathsf{SIGNATURE}, sid, ssid, (A', \mathbf{nym}, \pi, \{\pi_i\}))$.


**Verify.** The verify algorithm allows one to check whether a signature $\sigma$ on message $m$ with respect to basename $\mathbf{bsn}$, attribute disclosure $(D, I)$, private key revocation list $\mathsf{RL}$, and signature revocation list $\mathsf{SRL}$ is valid.

1. $\mathcal{V}$ upon input $(\mathsf{VERIFY}, sid, m, \mathbf{bsn}, \sigma, (D, I), \mathsf{RL}, \mathsf{SRL})$ verifies the signature:
    - Parse $\sigma$ as $(A', \mathbf{nym}, \pi, \{\pi_i\})$.
    - Verify $\pi$ with respect to $A'$ and $\mathbf{nym}$:
        - Parse $\pi$ as $(c, s_{gsk}, \{s_{a_i}\}_{i \in \bar{D}}, s_e, s_a, s_b, n)$.
        - Set $\hat{L} \leftarrow h_1^{s_{gsk}} \cdot \mathbf{nym}^{-c}$ and

$$\hat{t} \leftarrow e(A', g_2^{s_e} \cdot w^{-c})e(h_0, g_2)^{s_b}e(h_1, g_2)^{s_{gsk}}e(h_0, w)^{s_a} \prod_{i \in \bar{D}} e(h_{i+1}, g_2)^{s_{a_i}}$$
$$\cdot e(g_1, g_2)^c \prod_{i \in D} e(h_{i+1}, g_2)^{a_i \cdot c}$$

- Check
  $$c = H(n, H(A', \mathbf{nym}, t, L, g_1, h_0, \ldots, h_L, w), m, \mathbf{bsn}, (D, I), \mathsf{SRL}).$$
- For every $(\mathbf{bsn}_i, \pi_i) \in \mathsf{SRL}$:
    - Parse $\pi_i$ as $(c, n_i, C_i, s_{i,\alpha}, s_{i,\beta})$.
    - Check $C \neq 1_{\mathbb{G}_1}$.
    - Set $\hat{t}_{i,1} \leftarrow H(\mathbf{bsn})^{s_{i,\alpha}} \frac{1}{\mathbf{nym}_i}^{s_{i,\beta}}$ and $\hat{t}_{i,2} \leftarrow H(\mathbf{bsn})^{s_{i,\alpha}} \frac{1}{\mathbf{nym}}^{s_{i,\beta}}$.
    - Check $c = H(n_i, H(C, \mathbf{bsn}_i, \mathbf{bsn}, \mathbf{nym}_i, \mathbf{nym}, n, \hat{t}_{i,1}, \hat{t}_{i,2}))$.
- If all tests pass, set $f \leftarrow 1$, otherwise $f \leftarrow 0$.
- Output $(\mathsf{VERIFIED}, sid, f)$.


**Link.** The verify algorithm allows one to check whether two signatures $\sigma, \sigma'$, on messages $m, m'$ respectively, that were generated for the same basename $\mathbf{bsn}$ were created by the same TPM.

1. $\mathcal{V}$ upon input $(\mathsf{LINK}, sid, \sigma, m, p, \mathsf{SRL}, \sigma', m', p', \mathsf{SRL}', \mathbf{bsn})$ verifies the signatures and compares the pseudonyms contained in $\sigma, \sigma'$:
    - Check that both signatures $\sigma, \sigma'$ are valid with respect to $m, \mathbf{bsn}, p, \mathsf{SRL}$ and $m', \mathbf{bsn}, p', \mathsf{SRL}'$ respectively. Output $\perp$ if they are not both valid.
    - Parse the signatures as $(A', \mathbf{nym}, \pi, \{\pi_i\}) \leftarrow \sigma$, $(A'', \mathbf{nym}', \pi', \{\pi_i'\}) \leftarrow \sigma'$.
    - If $\mathbf{nym} = \mathbf{nym}'$, set $f \leftarrow 1$, otherwise $f \leftarrow 0$.
    - Output $(\mathsf{LINK}, sid, f)$.

## 5.2   Comparison with Previous DAA Schemes

Our protocol is very similar to the most recent qSDH-based DAA schemes [13, 22, 25]. However, a few key changes were needed to achieve provable security and address the problems mentioned in Sect. 2. First, we use a BBS+ signature for the membership credential, instead of the simplified credential where the $s$-value is ommited as used in the recent schemes [13, 22, 25]. The BBS+ is proven to be unforgeable, and with this extra element, the proof of knowledge which is part of DAA signatures allows one to extract valid credentials, whereas in the most recent schemes one could not.

Compared to the most recent EPID scheme by Brickell and Li [14], we introduce a way to split the workload between a TPM and host, and add basenames steering linkability. The usage of basenames is required to prevent the TPM from serving as a static Diffie-Hellman oracle towards the host. For non-revocation proofs, the platform must prove that its pseudonym $\mathtt{nym} = B^{gsk}$ is based on a different key than a pseudonym in a revoked signature $\mathtt{nym}' = B'^{gsk'}$. A host proving the inequality of the keys with the help of a TPM using the method by Camenisch and Shoup will learn $B'^{gsk}$, for any $B'$ of its choosing. By requiring basenames, i.e., $B = H_1(\mathtt{bsn})$, learning $B'^{gsk} = H_1(\mathtt{bsn})^{gsk}$ does not give a corrupt host any information, as in the random oracle model this can be simulated without knowing $gsk$.

For the reason mentioned above, the fully anonymous option $\mathtt{bsn} = \perp$ from previous DAA schemes is not supported by our scheme, but we argue that this does not affect privacy: A platform can choose a fresh basename it only uses once to be fully anonymous. Any verifier that accepts fully anonymous signatures can simply accept signatures with respect to any basename.

Compared to the existing DAA-A scheme [25], we store all attributes except the secret key on the host for efficiency. This still guarantees unforgeability with an honest TPM and corrupt host. Anonymity is not affected either, as in either case, the host must be trusted for anonymity.

In Table 1 we compare the computational efficiency of our scheme with the other qSDH-based DAA schemes. In particular, we show the computational cost for the TPM in the sign algorithm, for the host in the sign algorithm, and for the verifier in the verify algorithm, as these are the algorithms that will be used frequently. We denote $k$ exponentiations in group $\mathbb{G}_i$ by $k\mathbb{G}_i$, $k\mathbb{G}_i^j$ denotes $k$ $j$-multi-exponentiations, and $kP$ denotes $k$ pairing operations. Table 2 we compare the size of credentials and signatures with other DAA schemes. Here, $k\mathbb{G}$ denotes the bits required to represent $k$ elements of $\mathbb{G}$, and $H$ denotes the bit length of the hash output. CU15-1 denotes the LRSW-based DAA-A scheme by Chen and Urian [25], and CU15-2 the qSDH-based instantiation. We analyzed both schemes for signatures with only the secret key on the TPM, which is used to create a pseudonym, and all other attributes held by the host. We let $L$ denote the amount of attributes, with $D$ the amount of disclosed attributes and $U$ the amount of undisclosed attributes. Revocation lists and revocation checks are omitted for these efficiency numbers. To compare this scheme with previous DAA schemes, we consider the efficiency without attributes, i.e., $L = D = U = 0$. In computation, our scheme is as efficient as the scheme by Brickell and Li [13], which is currently the most efficient DAA scheme. Our credentials contain one extra element of $\mathbb{Z}_p$ to achieve provable security. Signatures in our scheme are one element of $\mathbb{G}_1$ smaller than signatures in the Brickell and Li scheme, which follows from the fact that we always use a basename, so we do not need to transmit the base for the computation of the pseudonym.

We stress that many of the listed schemes are not provably secure, whereas we rigorously prove our scheme secure.

**Table 1.** A comparison of the efficiency of DAA schemes.

| | $\mathcal{M}$ Sign | $\mathcal{H}$ Sign | Verify |
|---|---|---|---|
| CF08 [26] | $2\mathbb{G}_1, 1\mathbb{G}_T$ | $1\mathbb{G}_1, 2\mathbb{G}_1^2, 1\mathbb{G}_T, 1P$ | $1\mathbb{G}_1^2, 2\mathbb{G}_1^3, 1\mathbb{G}_T^5, 3P$ |
| Che10 [22] | $2\mathbb{G}_1, 1\mathbb{G}_T$ | $1\mathbb{G}_1, \mathbb{G}_T^3$ | $1\mathbb{G}_1^2, 1\mathbb{G}_2^2, 1\mathbb{G}_T^4, 1P$ |
| BL10 [13] | $3\mathbb{G}_1$ | $1\mathbb{G}_1, 1\mathbb{G}_1^2, 1\mathbb{G}_T, 1P$ | $1\mathbb{G}_1^2, 1\mathbb{G}_2^2, 1\mathbb{G}_T^4, 1P$ |
| CPS10 [24] | $3\mathbb{G}_1$ | $4\mathbb{G}_1$ | $2\mathbb{G}_1^2, 2P$ |
| CU15-1 [25] | $3\mathbb{G}_1$ | $(4+L+U)\mathbb{G}_1$ | $2\mathbb{G}_1, 2\mathbb{G}_1^L, 2\mathbb{G}_1^D, 2\mathbb{G}_1^U, 6P$ |
| CU15-2 [25] | $3\mathbb{G}_1$ | $2\mathbb{G}_1, 1\mathbb{G}_1^{U+2}, 2P$ | $1\mathbb{G}_1^2, 1\mathbb{G}_1^{4+L}, 2P$ |
| CDL16 [15] | $5\mathbb{G}_1$ | $4\mathbb{G}_1$ | $2\mathbb{G}_1^2, 4P$ |
| This work | $3\mathbb{G}_1$ | $1\mathbb{G}_1, 1\mathbb{G}_1^{2+U}, 1\mathbb{G}_T, 1P$ | $1\mathbb{G}_1^2, 1\mathbb{G}_2^2, 1\mathbb{G}_T^{4+L}, 1P$ |

**Table 2.** A comparison of the credential and signature size of DAA schemes.

| | Cred. size | | Signature size | | | |
|---|---|---|---|---|---|---|
| CF08 [26] | $2\mathbb{Z}_p$ | $1\mathbb{G}_1$ | $6\mathbb{Z}_p$ | $2\mathbb{G}_1$ | $2\mathbb{G}_T$ | $1H$ |
| Che10 [22] | $1\mathbb{Z}_p$ | $1\mathbb{G}_1$ | $4\mathbb{Z}_p$ | $3\mathbb{G}_1$ | | $1H$ |
| BL10 [13] | $1\mathbb{Z}_p$ | $1\mathbb{G}_1$ | $4\mathbb{Z}_p$ | $3\mathbb{G}_1$ | | $1H$ |
| CPS10 [24] | | $4\mathbb{G}_1$ | $1\mathbb{Z}_p$ | $4\mathbb{G}_1$ | | $1H$ |
| CU15-1 [25] | | $(5+L)\mathbb{G}_1$ | $(2+U)\mathbb{Z}_p$ | $(7+L)\mathbb{G}_1$ | | $1H$ |
| CU15-2 [25] | $1\mathbb{Z}_p$ | $1\mathbb{G}_1$ | $(5+U)\mathbb{Z}_p$ | $3\mathbb{G}_1$ | | $1H$ |
| CDL16 [15] | | $4\mathbb{G}_1$ | $1\mathbb{Z}_p$ | $4\mathbb{G}_1$ | | $1H$ |
| This work | $2\mathbb{Z}_p$ | $1\mathbb{G}_1$ | $(5+U)\mathbb{Z}_p$ | $2\mathbb{G}_1$ | | $1H$ |

## 6  Security Analysis

**Theorem 2.** *The protocol $\Pi_{\mathsf{daa+}}$ presented in Sect. 5 securely realizes $\mathcal{F}_{\mathsf{daa+}}^l$ in the $(\mathcal{F}_{\mathsf{auth}*}, \mathcal{F}_{\mathsf{ca}}, \mathcal{F}_{\mathsf{smt}}^l, \mathcal{F}_{\mathsf{crs}}^D)$-hybrid model using random oracles and static corruptions, if the DL, DDH and JOC version of the qSDH assumptions hold, and the proofs-of-knowledge are online extractable.*

Due to space constraints, the proof is given in the full version of the paper [16].

## 7   Conclusion

DAA is one of the most complex cryptographic protocols deployed in practice. It is implemented in multiple platforms for trusted computing, including the Trusted Computing Group's TPM and Intel's SGX. A number of functional extensions to DAA have been proposed, including signature-based revocation and embedding of attributes. However, as we have shown in this paper, the security models and security proofs of the proposed DAA schemes based on the qSDH assumptions are not satisfactory. This includes the extended DAA schemes and the standardized DAA schemes. Bleichenbacher's attack [5] on PKCS#1 demonstrates the importance of rigorous security proofs, in particular for cryptographic standards. It remains as future work, to revisit the concerned standards to eliminate the schemes' flaws and ensure that they are provably secure.

As a first step towards this, we have in this paper proposed a new DAA scheme with support for attributes and signature-based revocation. Our scheme is as efficient as the most efficient existing DAA scheme. While the existing schemes do not have valid security proofs, our scheme is proven secure in the model by Camenisch et al. [15], extended to support attributes and signature-based revocation. As a side result, we have proven the BBS+ signature scheme to be secure in type-3 pairing settings, meaning our scheme can be used with the most efficient pairing-friendly elliptic curve groups.

## References

1. Au, M.H., Susilo, W., Mu, Y.: Constant-size dynamic $k$-TAA. In: Prisco, R., Yung, M. (eds.) SCN 2006. LNCS, vol. 4116, pp. 111–125. Springer, Heidelberg (2006)
2. Barreto, P.S.L.M., Naehrig, M.: Pairing-friendly elliptic curves of prime order. In: Preneel, B., Tavares, S. (eds.) SAC 2005. LNCS, vol. 3897, pp. 319–331. Springer, Heidelberg (2006)
3. Bellare, M., Rogaway, P.: Random oracles are practical: a paradigm for designing efficient protocols. In: CCS 1993 (1993)
4. Bernhard, D., Fuchsbauer, G., Ghadafi, E., Smart, N.P., Warinschi, B.: Anonymous attestation with user-controlled linkability. Int. J. Inf. Secur. **12**(3), 219–249 (2013)
5. Bleichenbacher, D.: Chosen ciphertext attacks against protocols based on the RSA encryption standard PKCS #1. In: Krawczyk, H. (ed.) CRYPTO 1998. LNCS, vol. 1462, pp. 1–12. Springer, Heidelberg (1998)
6. Boneh, D., Boyen, X.: Short signatures without random oracles. In: Cachin, C., Camenisch, J.L. (eds.) EUROCRYPT 2004. LNCS, vol. 3027, pp. 56–73. Springer, Heidelberg (2004)
7. Boneh, D., Boyen, X.: Short signatures without random oracles and the SDH assumption in bilinear groups. J. Cryptology **21**(2), 149–177 (2007)
8. Boneh, D., Boyen, X., Shacham, H.: Short group signatures. In: Franklin, M. (ed.) CRYPTO 2004. LNCS, vol. 3152, pp. 41–55. Springer, Heidelberg (2004)
9. Brickell, E., Camenisch, J., Chen, L.: Direct anonymous attestation. In: CCS 2004 (2004)
10. Brickell, E., Chen, L., Li, J.: A new direct anonymous attestation scheme from bilinear maps. In: Lipp, P., Sadeghi, A.-R., Koch, K.-M. (eds.) Trust 2008. LNCS, vol. 4968, pp. 166–178. Springer, Heidelberg (2008)

11. Brickell, E., Chen, L., Li, J.: Simplified security notions of direct anonymous attestation and a concrete scheme from pairings. Int. J. Inf. Secur. **8**(5), 315–330 (2009)
12. Brickell, E., Li, J.: Enhanced privacy ID: a direct anonymous attestation scheme with enhanced revocation capabilities. In: WPES 2007 (2007)
13. Brickell, E., Li, J.: A pairing-based DAA scheme further reducing TPM resources. Cryptology ePrint Archive, Report 2010/067 (2010)
14. Brickell, E., Li, J.: Enhanced privacy ID from bilinear pairing for hardware authentication and attestation. Int. J. Inf. Priv. Secur. Integrity **1**(1), 3–33 (2011)
15. Camenisch, J., Drijvers, M., Lehmann, A.: Universally composable direct anonymous attestation. In: Cheng, C.-M., Chung, K.-M., Persiano, G., Yang, B.-Y. (eds.) PKC 2016. LNCS, vol. 9615, pp. 234–264. Springer, Heidelberg (2016). doi:10.1007/978-3-662-49387-8_10
16. Camenisch, J., Drijvers, M., Lehmann, A.: Anonymous Attestation Using the Strong Diffie Hellman Assumption Revisited. Cryptology ePrint Archive, Report 2016/663 (2016)
17. Camenisch, J., Kiayias, A., Yung, M.: On the portability of generalized schnorr proofs. In: Joux, A. (ed.) EUROCRYPT 2009. LNCS, vol. 5479, pp. 425–442. Springer, Heidelberg (2009)
18. Camenisch, J.L., Shoup, V.: Practical verifiable encryption and decryption of discrete logarithms. In: Boneh, D. (ed.) CRYPTO 2003. LNCS, vol. 2729, pp. 126–144. Springer, Heidelberg (2003)
19. Camenisch, J.L., Stadler, M.A.: Efficient group signature schemes for large groups. In: Kaliski Jr., B.S. (ed.) CRYPTO 1997. LNCS, vol. 1294, pp. 410–424. Springer, Heidelberg (1997)
20. Canetti, R.: Universally composable signature, certification, and authentication. In: Computer Security Foundations Workshop (2004)
21. Canetti, R.: Universally composable security: a new paradigm for cryptographic protocols. Cryptology ePrint Archive, Report 2000/067 (2000)
22. Chen, L.: A DAA scheme requiring less TPM resources. In: Bao, F., Yung, M., Lin, D., Jing, J. (eds.) Inscrypt 2009. LNCS, vol. 6151, pp. 350–365. Springer, Heidelberg (2010)
23. Chen, L., Morrissey, P., Smart, N.P.: Pairings in trusted computing. In: Galbraith, S.D., Paterson, K.G. (eds.) Pairing 2008. LNCS, vol. 5209, pp. 1–17. Springer, Heidelberg (2008)
24. Chen, L., Page, D., Smart, N.P.: On the design and implementation of an efficient DAA scheme. In: Gollmann, D., Lanet, J.-L., Iguchi-Cartigny, J. (eds.) CARDIS 2010. LNCS, vol. 6035, pp. 223–237. Springer, Heidelberg (2010)
25. Chen, L., Urian, R.: DAA-A: direct anonymous attestation with attributes. In: Conti, M., Schunter, M., Askoxylakis, I. (eds.) TRUST 2015. LNCS, vol. 9229, pp. 228–245. Springer, Heidelberg (2015)
26. Chen, X., Feng, D.: Direct anonymous attestation for next generation TPM. J. Comput. **3**(12), 43–50 (2008)
27. Costan, V., Devadas, S.: Intel SGX explained. Cryptology ePrint Archive, Report 2016/086 (2016)
28. Fiat, A., Shamir, A.: How to prove yourself: practical solutions to identification and signature problems. In: Odlyzko, A.M. (ed.) CRYPTO 1986. LNCS, vol. 263, pp. 186–194. Springer, Heidelberg (1987)
29. Galbraith, S.D., Paterson, K.G., Smart, N.P.: Pairings for cryptographers. Discrete Appl. Math. **156**(16), 3113–3121 (2008)
30. International Organization for Standardization. ISO/IEC 20008: Information technology - Security techniques - Anonymous digital signatures (2013)

31. International Organization for Standardization. ISO/IEC 11889: Information technology - Trusted platform module library (2015)
32. Lysyanskaya, A., Rivest, R.L., Sahai, A., Wolf, S.: Pseudonym systems (Extended Abstract). In: Heys, H.M., Adams, C.M. (eds.) SAC 1999. LNCS, vol. 1758, pp. 184–199. Springer, Heidelberg (2000)
33. Paillier, P.: Public-key cryptosystems based on composite degree residuosity classes. In: Stern, J. (ed.) EUROCRYPT 1999. LNCS, vol. 1592, pp. 223–238. Springer, Heidelberg (1999)
34. Trusted Computing Group: TPM main specification version 1.2 (2004)
35. Trusted Computing Group. TPM library specification, family "2.0" (2014)

# Practical Signing-Right Revocation

Michael Till Beck[1], Stephan Krenn[2],
Franz-Stefan Preiss[3], and Kai Samelin[3,4(✉)]

[1] Ludwig-Maximilians-Universität München, Munich, Germany
michael.beck@ifi.lmu.de
[2] AIT Austrian Institute of Technology GmbH, Vienna, Austria
stephan.krenn@ait.ac.at
[3] IBM Research – Zurich, Rüschlikon, Switzerland
{frp,ksa}@zurich.ibm.com
[4] Technische Universität Darmstadt, Darmstadt, Germany

**Abstract.** One of the key features that must be supported by every modern PKI is an efficient way to determine (at verification) whether the signing key had been revoked. In most solutions, the verifier periodically contacts the certificate authority (CA) to obtain a list of blacklisted, or whitelisted, certificates. In the worst case this has to be done for every signature verification. Besides the computational costs of verification, after revocation *all* signatures under the revoked key become invalid. In the solution by Boneh et al. at USENIX '01, the CA holds a share of the private signing key and contributes to the signature generation. After revocation, the CA simply denies its participation in the interactive signing protocol. Thus, the revoked user can no longer generate valid signatures. We extend this solution to also cover privacy, non-trusted setups, and time-stamps. We give a formal definitional framework, and provide elegantly simple, yet provably secure, instantiations from efficient standard building blocks such as digital signatures, commitments, and partially blind signatures. Finally, we propose extensions to our scheme.

## 1 Introduction

Digital signatures [24] provide meaningful security as long as the signing key stays secret. However, in the real-world, signing keys can be compromised very easily, e.g., through hacker attacks, lost hardware tokens, or simply by accident. Furthermore, it is often required to revoke signing rights, e.g., when an employee leaves a company. Consequently, deployed solutions such as X.509, and related standards, always allow for revocation of certificates [12,19]. Here, two main approaches (and potentially combinations thereof) are deployed. First, in a *white-list* approach, the certificate authority (CA) vouches for the fact that a given certificate is not revoked. Alternatively, the CA can publish a *black-list*

This work was partially funded by the European Commission through grant agreement numbers 321310 (PERCY), 644962 (PRISMACLOUD), and 653454 (CREDENTIAL).

© Springer International Publishing Switzerland 2016
M. Franz and P. Papadimitratos (Eds.): TRUST 2016, LNCS 9824, pp. 21–39, 2016.
DOI: 10.1007/978-3-319-45572-3_2

containing all revoked certificates. Now, a verifier directly rejects a signature if the used key has been black-listed. Thus, if one requires up-to-date information, this means that the lists must be retrieved *for every signature verification*, causing a high — and sometimes too high — computational and communicational overhead. Thus, in either case, the verifiers contact the CA to determine whether a given certificate is still valid. Thus, every verifier must periodically update the published lists in both approaches to have meaningful security guarantees.

Moreover, as noted by Boneh et al. [9], these *total* revocation mechanisms have several drawbacks. For example, as mentioned previously, to check the revocation status of a given certificate, the verifier must have access to an up-to-date certificate revocation list (CRL), or the CA has to be queried for each signature verification. The latter may not be possible, however, as the verifier may not have a network connection, or communication is too costly. Furthermore, if a certificate is revoked, all signatures corresponding to the contained public key pk, including the ones that were generated honestly, become invalid after revocation. However, it is desirable that all signatures under a secret key sk that were generated prior to the corruption of sk (or prior to the revocation of the corresponding certificate) remain valid, while the generation of new signatures under sk is not possible. For example, consider Spider-Man sending the message $m$="I admit that you, Iron Man, are more powerful than me."[1] Clearly, if $m$ is signed with Spider-Man's secret key sk, Iron Man can publish the signature to prove to the public that he is more powerful than Spider-Man. However, if Spider-Man revokes his certificate, the signature becomes invalid, and there is no way for Iron Man to prove that the statement is valid. This is because if the secret key sk is corrupted, it cannot be proven that Iron Man is not the adversarial party generating *new* bogus signatures on behalf of Spider-Man. The problem is that signatures are not associated with their generation time, i.e., a new signature is as good as an old one, if no further means such as time-stamping services are involved. Thus, all signatures have to be revoked in this setting. Refer to Gutmann for additional problems of PKIs in their current form [25].

**Our Contribution.** We address the aforementioned unsatisfactory situation by introducing the notion of CA-assisted signature generation with time-stamping, message privacy, and non-trusted setup. In a nutshell, our scheme requires that a *partially* trusted CA blindly signs the message $m$ in question plus potentially a time-stamp (and some other technical values such as keys, etc.), while a trusted setup is not required. In particular, the CA checks whether the corresponding user's pk is revoked, and signs $m$ only if pk not revoked. The signature generated by the CA is then additionally signed with a standard digital signature scheme by the user. Both signatures are subsequently sent to, and verified, by the verifier. Signatures can be generated as long as the corresponding public key is not revoked. Therefore, all generated signatures remain valid after revocation as the CA simply stops assisting the signer after the key gets revoked.

---

[1] For all Spider-Man fans: please reverse the roles of Spider-Man and Iron Man.

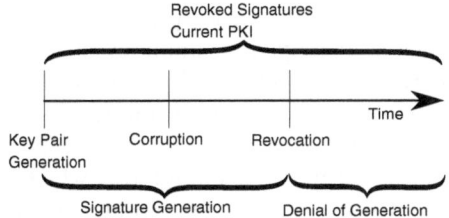

**Fig. 1.** Revocation of certificates.

While technically being relatively simple, our construction solves most of the mentioned problems, and, interestingly enough, is even more efficient than most deployed solutions, as the CAs are no longer queried for each verification. Moreover, we want that our solution can be added "on-top" of the existing PKI, i.e., the users do not require new keys, while the existing method can co-exist. If a time-stamping authority and traditional revocation lists are naïvely used to solve the problem, the signing process needs to be interactive similar to our construction (because the time-stamp needs to be bound to the signed message). However, our solution does not require *any* interactivity upon verification, which is needed in the naïve solution in order to update revocation information. Moreover, our construction paradigm is elegantly simple, yet versatile. We show how it can easily be extended to cover additional application scenarios. Interestingly, when one tries to close the remaining gap between corruption and revocation (cf. Fig. 1), the resulting construction becomes very similar to the naïve solution again (cf. Sect. 4.1). However, in this case it is easy to see that interactivity is needed for signing (because of the time-stamp) as well as for verification (to check whether a signature key has been revoked "into the past").

Even though the CA is only partially trusted, we do not lose anything, as some kind of trust anchor is always required for a PKI anyway. Our approach actually requires less trust: for white-lists, the CA learns if signatures for a specific public key are verified, while in a black-list approach everyone sees which certificates are revoked. In our solution, the CA only learns when a signature is generated, which happens less frequently. Moreover, we have a fall-back mode, which allows to revert to standard signatures.

**State-of-the-Art.** The idea to let a (semi-)trusted entity such as a CA also contribute to signature generation has been introduced by Boneh et al. [9] and Rivest [34], but neither present a formalization. The approach by Boneh et al. is based on standard 2-out-of-2 threshold signatures [8,21]. In particular, the secret key sk is split between the CA and the signer. The server denies its contribution to signature generation, if the presented certificate is marked as revoked. However, their approach requires trusted setup (the suggested mitigation strategy of using a distributed key generation algorithm here is too inefficient in practice), new keys for each participant, and cannot add time-stamps to generated signatures. Moreover, an adversarial server may also learn the message to be signed, i.e., in contrast to our solution no privacy guarantees are given to the user. A similar approach is deployed in anonymous credentials such as Identity Mixer [12,16], where the credential holder proves that it is not revoked at presentation of the credential, e.g., using accumulators [6,13,20,33]. Here, the prover has to prove knowledge of a witness (in zero-knowledge) such that its revocation handle is contained in the accumulator, which resembles a white-list approach. Clearly, the witnesses have to be updated for each revocation, while credentials are, compared to digital signatures, only valid once at presentation.

Blind signatures have been introduced by Chaum [17]. In a nutshell, blind signatures allow an external entity to receive a signature $\sigma$ on a message $m$ (of its own choice) such that the signer learns nothing about the message $m$, and cannot link a signing transcript to the final signature. Chaum's work was later formalized and proven secure [4,27]. Later, constructions in the standard model [14], based on different assumptions other than RSA [8], additional security guarantees [22], but also some impossibility results were published [23]. The initial idea was also extended to cover some form of partial blindness, where the signature is issued on the blinded message $m$, but also some public information info known to both parties [1,18]. These partially blind signatures are mostly used to prevent misuse of blind signatures. We use this possibility to bind a signature to a public key, and add time-stamps.

There is also the notion of certificate-less cryptography [2,26]. In our case we only require a certificate, there are no *ephemeral* keys, and no identity management. However, the ideas are very similar, and can thus be seen as related. Likewise, the concept of *virtual smart cards* [15] is related. However, in contrast to our approach, the additional server is not trusted by outsiders and the signer has to provide an additional password. Moreover, for an outsider (i.e., verifier), a signature generated with their scheme is indistinguishable from a traditional signature. This is not what we want, i.e., a verifier must be able to decide whether a signature was generated using out method.

There are also other primitives which may be used in our context, e.g., threshold signatures [21], proxy signatures [29], server-assisted signatures [7], multi signatures [5], aggregate signatures [10], or sanitizable signatures [3,11,28]. However, all these approaches do not offer privacy (i.e., they reveal the message to the server) without further modifications. We therefore chose to use primitives which directly give us the required guarantees.

## 2   Preliminaries and Building Blocks

**Notation.** $\lambda \in \mathbb{N}$ denotes our security parameter. All algorithms implicitly take $1^\lambda$ as an additional input. We write $a \leftarrow A(x)$ if $a$ is assigned the output of algorithm $A$ with input $x$. An algorithm is efficient if it runs in probabilistic polynomial time (ppt) in the length of its input. The algorithms may return a special error symbol $\bot \notin \{0,1\}^*$, denoting an exception. For the remainder of this paper, all algorithms are ppt if not explicitly mentioned otherwise. If we have a list, we require that we have an injective, and efficiently reversible encoding mapping the list to $\{0,1\}^*$. If we have a set $S$, we assume a lexicographical ordering on the elements. A message space $\mathcal{M}$, and the randomness space $\mathcal{R}$, may implicitly depend on a corresponding public key. If not otherwise stated, we assume that $\mathcal{M} = \{0,1\}^*$ to reduce unhelpful boilerplate notation. A function $\nu : \mathbb{N} \rightarrow [0,1]$ is *negligible*, if it vanishes faster than every inverse polynomial, i.e., $\forall k \in \mathbb{N}, \exists n_0 \in \mathbb{N}$ such that $\nu(n) \leq n^{-k}, \forall n > n_0$.

**Non-interactive Commitments.** Non-interactive commitment schemes allow one party to commit itself to a value without revealing it. Later, the committing party can give some opening information to the receiver, which can then "open" the commitment.

**Definition 1 (Non-Interactive Commitments).** *A non-interactive commitment scheme* COM *consists of three ppt algorithms* {ParGen, Commit, Open}, *such that:*

ParGen. *This algorithm takes as input a security parameter $\lambda$ and outputs the public parameters* pp, *i.e.,* pp $\leftarrow$ ParGen$(1^\lambda)$.
Commit. *This algorithm takes as input a message $m$ and outputs a commitment $C$ together with corresponding opening information $O$, i.e., $(C,O) \leftarrow$* Commit(pp, $m$).
Open. *This deterministic algorithm takes as input a commitment $C$ with corresponding opening information $O$ and outputs message $m \in \mathcal{M}$, i.e., $m \leftarrow$* Open(pp, $C, O$).

**Definition 2 (Binding).** *A non-interactive commitment scheme is* binding, *if for all ppt adversaries $\mathcal{A}$ there is a negligible function $\nu(\cdot)$ such that*

$$\Pr \left[ \begin{array}{l} \mathsf{pp} \leftarrow \mathsf{ParGen}(1^\lambda), (C^*, O^*, O'^*) \leftarrow \mathcal{A}(\mathsf{pp}), m \leftarrow \mathsf{Open}(\mathsf{pp}, C^*, O^*), \\ m' \leftarrow \mathsf{Open}(\mathsf{pp}, C^*, O'^*) : m \neq m' \ \wedge \ m \neq \perp \ \wedge \ m' \neq \perp \end{array} \right] \leq \nu(\lambda).$$

**Definition 3 (Perfectly Hiding).** *A non-interactive commitment scheme is* perfectly hiding, *if for all unbounded adversaries $\mathcal{A}$ we have*

$$\Pr \left[ \begin{array}{c} (\mathsf{pp}, m_0, m_1, \mathsf{state}) \leftarrow \mathcal{A}(1^\lambda), b \leftarrow \{0,1\}, \\ (C,O) \leftarrow \mathsf{Commit}(\mathsf{pp}, m_b), b^* \leftarrow \mathcal{A}(C, \mathsf{state}) : \\ b = b^* \end{array} \right] - \frac{1}{2} = 0.$$

We say that a commitment scheme COM is correct, if for all $\lambda \in \mathbb{N}$, all pp $\leftarrow$ ParGen$(1^\lambda)$, for all messages $m$, for all $(C,O) \leftarrow$ Commit(pp, $m$), we have Open(pp, $C, O$) = $m$.

A non-interactive commitment scheme COM is secure, if it is correct, binding, and perfectly hiding. An example for such a commitment-scheme are Pedersen-Commitments [32]. We stress that the message space of the Pedersen-Commitments can be extended using collision-resistant hash-functions.

**Digital Signatures.** Digital signatures allow the holder of a secret key sk to sign a message $m$, while with knowledge of the corresponding public key pk everyone can verify whether a given signature was actually endorsed by the signer.

**Definition 4 (Digital Signatures).** *A standard digital signature scheme* DSIG *consists of three algorithms* {KGen, Sign, Verify} *such that:*

KGen. *The algorithm* KGen *outputs the public and private key of the signer, where $\lambda$ is the security parameter:* (pk, sk) $\leftarrow$ KGen($1^\lambda$).
Sign. *The algorithm* Sign *gets as input the secret key* sk, *and the message* $m \in \mathcal{M}$ *to sign. It outputs a signature* $\sigma \leftarrow$ Sign(sk, $m$).
Verify. *The algorithm* Verify *outputs a decision bit* $d \in \{false, true\}$, *indicating if the signature* $\sigma$ *is valid, w.r.t.* pk, *and* $m$: $d \leftarrow$ Verify(pk, $m$, $\sigma$).

For each DSIG we require the correctness properties to hold. In particular, we require that for all $\lambda \in \mathbb{N}$, for all (pk, sk) $\leftarrow$ KGen($1^\lambda$), for all $m \in \mathcal{M}$ we have Verify(pk, $m$, Sign(sk, $m$)) = true. This definition captures perfect correctness.

*Unforgeability.* Now, we define unforgeability of digital signature schemes, as given in [24]. In a nutshell, we require that an adversary $\mathcal{A}$ cannot (except with negligible probability) come up with a signature $\sigma^*$ for a *new* message $m^*$. The adversary $\mathcal{A}$ can adaptively query for signatures on messages of its own choice.

**Experiment eUNF** $-$ **CMA**$_{\mathcal{A}}^{\mathsf{DSIG}}(\lambda)$
  (sk, pk) $\leftarrow$ KGen($1^\lambda$)
  $\mathcal{Q} \leftarrow \emptyset$
  $(m^*, \sigma^*) \leftarrow \mathcal{A}^{\mathsf{Sign}'(\mathsf{sk},\cdot)}(\mathsf{pk})$
      where oracle Sign' on input $m$:
        set $\mathcal{Q} \leftarrow \mathcal{Q} \cup \{m\}$
        return $\sigma \leftarrow$ Sign(sk, $m$)
  return 1, if Verify(pk, $m^*$, $\sigma^*$) = true $\wedge$ $m^* \notin \mathcal{Q}$
  return 0

**Fig. 2.** Unforgeability

**Definition 5 (Unforgeability).** *A signature scheme* DSIG *is unforgeable, if for any ppt adversary $\mathcal{A}$ there exists a negligible function $\nu$ such that* $\Pr[\mathsf{eUNF} - \mathsf{CMA}_{\mathcal{A}}^{\mathsf{DSIG}}(1^\lambda) = 1] \leq \nu(\lambda)$. *The corresponding experiment is depicted in Fig. 2.*

We call a digital signature scheme DSIG secure, if it is correct, and unforgeable.

**Partially Blind Signatures.** Blind Signatures [17,27] allow the holder of a secret key to sign a message $m$ for a second entity. The signer does not learn what message it signs, and also cannot link a signature generation transcript against the final signature. Partially Blind Signatures [1] also allow to add some piece of "public" information, known to both parties, to the final signature. Note, for the following definition, we omit the case where some "public parameters" are generated, as it depends on the underlying scheme whether this algorithm is required. An extension is straightforward.

**Definition 6 (Partially Blind Signatures).** *A partially blind signature scheme* BSIG *consists of two algorithms* (KGen, Verify), *and an interactive protocol* ⟨B, U⟩ *such that:*

KGen. *The algorithm* KGen *outputs the public and private key of the signer, where* λ *is the security parameter:* (pk, sk) ← KGen(1^λ).

⟨B, U⟩. *The algorithm* ⟨B, U⟩ *is interactive. The user* U *receives input* m, *public information* info, *and* pk. *The signer* B *inputs the secret key* sk, *and some string* info, *while the user* U *inputs a public key* pk, *a message* m, *and the string* info. *At the end of the protocol, only the user* U *receives a signature* σ, *while* B *receives nothing. We denote this as* (⊥, σ) ← ⟨B(sk, info), U(pk, m, info)⟩. *We write* ⟨·, U(·, ·, ·)⟩^∞ *if the adversary plays the role of the signer* B, *can start a new signing session with* U *as often as it wants to, and can arbitrarily schedule the interactions. Likewise, if we write* ⟨B(·, ·), ·⟩^1, *the adversary acts as the user, and can interact with the signer only once. We also require that every entity is able to decide to what step of which "session" a given protocol message corresponds, and also when a given "signing session" is finished, and was successful. In particular, we say a signing session is finished once* B *sends its last message to* U, *and* U *can actually extract a valid signature.*

Verify. *The algorithm* Verify *outputs a decision bit* d ∈ {false, true}, *indicating the validness of the signature* σ, *w.r.t.* pk, info, *and* m: d ← Verify(pk, m, info, σ).

For each BSIG we require the correctness properties to hold. In particular, we require that for all λ ∈ ℕ, for all (pk, sk) ← KGen(1^λ), for all m ∈ M, for all info ← {0, 1}* we have Verify(pk, m, info, σ) = true, where σ is taken from (⊥, σ) ← ⟨B(sk, info), U(pk, m, info)⟩. This captures perfect correctness.

We now introduce the security requirements needed for our construction.

*Unforgeability.* Now, we define unforgeability of partially blind signature schemes, as given in [1, 31], but adjusted for our notation. In a nutshell, we require that an adversary A cannot (except with negligible probability) come up with more signatures for different message/information pair (m, info) than successful, i.e., completed, signing queries. Note, the adversary can interleave signing queries.

**Definition 7 (Unforgeability).** *A signature scheme* BSIG *is unforgeable, if for any ppt adversary* A *there exists a negligible function* ν *such that* Pr[omUNF − CMA_A^BSIG(1^λ) = 1] ≤ ν(λ). *The corresponding experiment is depicted in Fig. 3.*

Note, we define "weak" unforgeability, i.e., once a signature for a given message/information pair (m, info) becomes known, the adversary may be able to derive new signatures.

**Experiment** $\mathsf{omUNF-CMA}_{\mathcal{A}}^{\mathsf{BSIG}}(\lambda)$

$(\mathsf{sk},\mathsf{pk}) \leftarrow \mathsf{KGen}(1^\lambda)$

$((m_1,\sigma_1,\mathsf{info}_1),\ldots,(m_\ell,\sigma_\ell,\mathsf{info}_\ell)) \leftarrow \mathcal{A}^{\langle\mathcal{B}(\mathsf{sk},\cdot,\cdot),\cdot\rangle^\infty}(\mathsf{pk})$

return 1, if $\forall i \in \{1,2,\ldots,\ell\}$ : $\mathsf{Verify}(\mathsf{pk},m_i,\mathsf{info}_i,\sigma_i) = \mathsf{true}$

and oracle $\langle\mathcal{B}(\mathsf{sk},\cdot),\cdot\rangle$ finished less than $\ell$ times, and

all $(m_i,\mathsf{info}_i)$ are pairwise distinct

return 0

**Fig. 3.** Unforgeability

*Blindness.* Now, we define blindness of partially blind signature schemes, derived from [31]. In a nutshell, we require that an adversary $\mathcal{A}$ cannot (except with negligible probability) decide what message is signed, and cannot link a signing transscript against the final signature. This must even be true, if it can generate the public key, chose the messages to be signed, and also the public string info.

**Experiment** $\mathsf{Blindness}_{\mathcal{A}}^{\mathsf{BSIG}}(\lambda)$

$(\mathsf{pk}^*,\{m_0,m_1\},\mathsf{info},\mathsf{state}_1) \leftarrow \mathcal{A}(1^\lambda)$

$b \leftarrow \{0,1\}$

$\mathsf{state}_2 \leftarrow \mathcal{A}^{\langle\cdot,\mathcal{U}_0(\mathsf{pk}^*,m_b,\mathsf{info})\rangle^1,\langle\cdot,\mathcal{U}_1(\mathsf{pk}^*,m_{1-b},\mathsf{info})\rangle^1}(\mathsf{state}_1)$

let $\sigma_0$, and $\sigma_1$ denote the output of $\mathcal{U}_0$, and $\mathcal{U}_1$

If $\sigma_0 = \bot \vee \sigma_1 = \bot$, let $\sigma \leftarrow \bot$

Else, set $\sigma \leftarrow (\sigma_b,\sigma_{1-b})$

$a \leftarrow \mathcal{A}(\mathsf{state}_2,\sigma)$

return 1, if $a = b$

return 0

**Fig. 4.** Blindness

**Definition 8 (Blindness).** *A partially blind signature scheme* $\mathsf{BSIG}$ *is blind, if for any ppt adversary* $\mathcal{A}$ *there exists a negligible function* $\nu$ *such that* $\Pr[\mathsf{Blindness}_{\mathcal{A}}^{\mathsf{BSIG}}(1^\lambda) = 1] \leq \nu(\lambda)$. *The corresponding experiment is depicted in Fig. 4.*

We call a partially blind signature scheme $\mathsf{BSIG}$ secure, if it is correct, unforgeable, and blind. Jumping ahead, we use the public information to embed the current time-stamp, and the signer's public key into the signature.

## 3    CA-Assisted Signatures

We now introduce CA-Assisted Signatures. As already discussed in the introduction, the main idea is that a CA helps generating a signature.

## 3.1  Syntax

In the following we now give a formal specification of the algorithms and their interfaces in such schemes. We require that each party has access to a common clock which is synchronized across all parties. In practice, this can be realized, e.g., by using the Network Time Protocol [30], and checking that the time-stamp is in an acceptable range, say, e.g., 30 s.

**Definition 9 (CA-Assisted Signatures).** *A CA-assisted digital signature scheme* CASIG *consists of four algorithms* {KGen$_u$, KGen$_c$, Revoke, Verify} *and one interactive protocol* $\langle \mathcal{CA}, \mathcal{U} \rangle$ *such that:*

KGen$_u$. *The algorithm* KGen$_u$ *outputs the public and private key of each user, where* $\lambda$ *is the security parameter:* $(\mathsf{pk}_u, \mathsf{sk}_u) \leftarrow \mathsf{KGen}(1^\lambda)$.

KGen$_c$. *The algorithm* KGen$_c$ *outputs the public and private key of a* $\mathcal{CA}$, *where* $\lambda$ *is the security parameter:* $(\mathsf{pk}_c, \mathsf{sk}_c) \leftarrow \mathsf{KGen}(1^\lambda)$.

$\langle \mathcal{CA}, \mathcal{U} \rangle$. *The protocol* $\langle \mathcal{CA}, \mathcal{U} \rangle$ *is interactive. The user* $\mathcal{U}$ *receives input* $m$, $\mathsf{pk}_s$, *time, and* $\mathsf{sk}_u$. *The* $\mathcal{CA}$ *inputs the secret key* $\mathsf{sk}_c$, *time, and* $\mathsf{pk}_u$. *At the end of the protocol, only the user* $\mathcal{U}$ *receives a signature* $\sigma$ *(which may be* $\bot$ *for a revoked user), while* $\mathcal{CA}$ *receives nothing:* $(\bot, \sigma) \leftarrow \langle \mathcal{CA}(\mathsf{sk}_s, \mathsf{pk}_u, \mathit{time})), \mathcal{U}(\mathsf{sk}_u, \mathsf{pk}_u, m, \mathit{time}) \rangle$. *As for partially blind signatures, we assume that each party knows to which signing session, and which protocol step a received message belongs to, and is successful.*

Revoke. *The algorithm* Revoke *allows to revoke a given public key* $\mathsf{pk}_u$. *In a nutshell, the CA no longer agrees to start a signing protocol for revoked* $\mathsf{pk}_u$. *Thus, revocation of a* $\mathsf{pk}_u$ *does not affect already ongoing signing sessions for this* $\mathsf{pk}_u$. *This algorithm outputs nothing.*

Verify. *The algorithm* Verify *outputs a decision bit* $d \in \{\mathit{false}, \mathit{true}\}$, *indicating the validness of the signature* $\sigma$, *with respect to* $\mathsf{pk}_c$, $\mathsf{pk}_s$, *time, and* $m$: $d \leftarrow$ Verify$(\mathsf{pk}_c, \mathsf{pk}_u, m, \mathit{time}, \sigma)$.

## 3.2  Definitional Framework for CA-Assisted Signatures

We now define the formal requirements for CA-assisted signatures. In a nutshell, those are correctness, unforgeability against malicious users and CAs, and blindness/privacy against CAs and outsiders.

*Correctness.* As usual, we require correctness of any CASIG. In particular, we require that with overwhelming probability in the security parameter it holds that Verify$(\mathsf{pk}_c, \mathsf{pk}_u, m, \mathit{time}, \sigma) = \mathsf{true}$, where $(\mathsf{pk}_u, \mathsf{sk}_u) \leftarrow$ KGen$_u(1^\lambda)$, $(\mathsf{pk}_c, \mathsf{sk}_c) \leftarrow$ KGen$_c(1^\lambda)$, $m \in \mathcal{M}$, time $\in \mathbb{N}$, $(\bot, \sigma) \leftarrow \langle \mathcal{CA}(\mathsf{sk}_c, \mathsf{pk}_s, \mathit{time}), \mathcal{U}(\mathsf{sk}_s, \mathsf{pk}_u, m, \mathit{time}) \rangle$, and $\mathsf{pk}_u$ was not revoked *before the signature generation request.* The probability space is here given by all random coins in all involved algorithms. The scheme is said to be *perfectly correct*, if $\sigma$ verifies correctly with probability 1.

*Unforgeability.* Unforgeability of CA-assisted signatures covers two aspects. On the one hand, a malicious user must not be able to fake signatures of the CA. On the other hand, a malicious CA must not be able to impersonate a user. Together, those two definitions clearly also imply that an outsider is not able to forge any valid signatures.

For signer unforgeability, we allow an adversary to obtain arbitrarily many signatures on arbitrary messages, and public keys, of its choice. Furthermore, for every signature, the adversary may define the current time (except that it may not turn back the time). Also, he can generate and revoke user keys at convenience. Similarly to Definition 7, the adversary now wins if it can output more message/signature pairs than he queried from the oracle; furthermore, each of those pairs must only verify for a public key and time that have been used in a signing query. Finally, signatures may only verify if the corresponding user public key has not been revoked before starting the respective signing session. For simplicity, we define that if a signing oracle is tagged as "non-called", if the corresponding public key was revoked before the current time. In the case that revocation and signing were done at the very same point in time, we do not consider the signature a forgery even if the revocation request was submitted first in the experiment; one the one hand, this is a purely academic issue anyways, and on the other hand "before" and "after" do not have any semantics within a fixed point in time.

**Definition 10 (Signer Unforgeability).** *A CA-assisted signature scheme* CASIG *is signer unforgeable, if for any ppt adversary $\mathcal{A}$ there exists a negligible function $\nu$ such that $\Pr[\text{seUNF} - \text{CMA}_{\mathcal{A}}^{\text{CASIG}}(1^\lambda) = 1] \leq \nu(\lambda)$. The corresponding experiment is depicted in Fig. 5.*

---

**Experiment** $\text{seUNF} - \text{CMA}_{\mathcal{A}}^{\text{CASIG}}(\lambda)$

  $(\text{sk}_c, \text{pk}_c) \leftarrow \text{KGen}_c(1^\lambda)$
  $\text{time} \leftarrow 0$
  $((m_1, \sigma_\ell, \text{time}_1, \text{pk}_1), \ldots, (m_\ell, \sigma_\ell, \text{time}_\ell, \text{pk}_\ell)) \leftarrow \mathcal{A}^{\langle \mathcal{CA}(\text{sk}_c, \cdot, \text{time}), \cdot \rangle^\infty, \text{Timestamp}(\cdot), \text{Revoke}(\cdot)}(\text{pk}_c)$
  where oracle Timestamp on input time′:
    if time′ ≤ time, ignore
    let time ← time′
  return 1, if $\forall i \in \{1, 2, \ldots, \ell\}$ : $\text{Verify}(\text{pk}_c, \text{pk}_i, m_i, \text{time}_i, \sigma_i) = \textbf{true}$
    and oracle $\langle \mathcal{CA}(\text{sk}, \cdot, \cdot), \cdot \rangle$ finished less than $\ell$ times, and
    all $(m_i, \text{time}_i, \text{pk}_i)$ are pairwise distinct
  return 1, if $\text{Verify}(\text{pk}_c, \text{pk}_1, m_1, \text{time}_1, \sigma_1) = \textbf{true}$,
    and $\text{pk}_1$ was revoked before $\text{time}_1$
  return 0

**Fig. 5.** Signer unforgeability

---

Complementary to signer unforgeability, we also require that the CA cannot generate valid signatures for a specific user without its contribution. We therefore let the adversary (controlling the CA) obtain arbitrarily many signatures for a user public key $pk_u$, where again $\mathcal{A}$ has full control over time. The adversary now wins if he can output a signature on a message that was not asked for that specific define point in time. This definition is similar to the standard definition of unforgeability, cf. Definition 5.

Note that as before, the adversary is allowed to interleave signing queries. Further note that the given definition is only presented in its weak formulation, i.e., the adversary is allowed to output fresh signatures for message/time pairs for which it obtained honest signatures. Extending the definition to strong unforgeability is straightforward.

**Definition 11 (CA Unforgeability).** *A CA-assisted signature scheme* CASIG *is CA unforgeable, if for any ppt adversary $\mathcal{A}$ there exists a negligible function $\nu$ such that* $\Pr[\mathsf{ceUNF} - \mathsf{CMA}_{\mathcal{A}}^{\mathsf{CASIG}}(1^\lambda) = 1] \leq \nu(\lambda)$. *The corresponding experiment is depicted in Fig. 6.*

**Experiment** $\mathsf{ceUNF} - \mathsf{CMA}_{\mathcal{A}}^{\mathsf{CASIG}}(\lambda)$
  $(sk_u, pk_u) \leftarrow \mathsf{KGen}_u(1^\lambda)$
  $\mathsf{time} \leftarrow 0$
  $(m^*, \sigma^*, \mathsf{time}^*, pk^*) \leftarrow \mathcal{A}^{\langle \cdot, \mathcal{U}(sk_u, \cdot, \cdot, \mathsf{time}) \rangle^\infty, \mathsf{Timestamp}(\cdot)}(pk_u)$
  where oracle $\mathsf{Timestamp}$ on input $\mathsf{time}'$:
    if $\mathsf{time}' \leq \mathsf{time}$, ignore
    let $\mathsf{time} \leftarrow \mathsf{time}'$
  return 1, if $\mathsf{Verify}(pk^*, pk_u, m^*, \mathsf{time}^*, \sigma^*) = \mathsf{true}$,
    and oracle $\langle \cdot, \mathcal{U}(sk_u, \cdot, \cdot, \cdot) \rangle$ was never queried for $(pk^*, m^*, \mathsf{time}^*)$.
  return 0

**Fig. 6.** CA unforgeability

*Blindness.* Blindness is concerned with the privacy of the user towards the CA. While a secure CA-assisted signature scheme must satisfy both aspects of unforgeability, blindness comes in two flavors giving different privacy guarantees.

The first flavor, called *CA blindness*, is similar in spirit to Definition 8. There, the CA (controlled by the adversary) may trigger signing protocols on two messages of its choice in a random order, gets the resulting signatures, and then needs to link the transcripts to the messages.

In the second flavor, called *CA weak-blindness*, we only require that the adversary does not learn which message it signed. In particular, the adversary does not gain access to the signatures, and may only trigger a single signing query. It is easy to see that CA blindness implies CA weak-blindness, but not vice versa. The decision which level of blindness/privacy is required must be made on a case-to-case basis, depending on the concrete use case.

Similar to Definition 8, the adversary is restricted to a single interaction with each oracle in our blindness definitions. However, blindness against multiple protocol runs directly follows from a simple hybrid argument.

**Definition 12 (CA Blindness).** *A CA-assisted signature scheme* CASIG *is CA blind, if for any ppt adversary $\mathcal{A}$ there exists a negligible function $\nu$ such*

**Experiment** $\mathsf{CA} - \mathsf{Blindness}_{\mathcal{A}}^{\mathsf{CASIG}}(\lambda)$
  $(\mathsf{sk}_u, \mathsf{pk}_u) \leftarrow \mathsf{KGen}_u(1^\lambda)$
  $(\mathsf{pk}^*, \{m_0, m_1\}, \mathsf{time}, \mathsf{state}_1) \leftarrow \mathcal{A}(\mathsf{pk}_u)$
  $b \leftarrow \{0, 1\}$
  $\mathsf{state}_2 \leftarrow \mathcal{A}^{\langle \cdot, \mathcal{U}_0(\mathsf{sk}_u, \mathsf{pk}^*, m_b, \mathsf{time})\rangle^1, \langle \cdot, \mathcal{U}_1(\mathsf{sk}_u, \mathsf{pk}^*, m_{1-b}, \mathsf{time})\rangle^1, \mathsf{Revoke}(\cdot)}(\mathsf{state}_1)$
  let $\sigma_0$, and $\sigma_1$ denote the output of $\mathcal{U}_0$, and $\mathcal{U}_1$.
  If $\sigma_0 = \bot \vee \sigma_1 = \bot$, let $\sigma \leftarrow \bot$.
  Else, set $\sigma \leftarrow (\sigma_b, \sigma_{b-1})$
  $a \leftarrow \mathcal{A}(\mathsf{state}_2, \sigma)$
  return 1, if $a = b$
  return 0

**Fig. 7.** CA blindness

that $\Pr[\mathsf{CA} - \mathsf{Blindness}_{\mathcal{A}}^{\mathsf{CASIG}}(1^\lambda) = 1] \leq \nu(\lambda)$. *The corresponding experiment is depicted in Fig. 7.*

**Definition 13 (CA Weak-Blindness).** *A CA-assisted signature scheme* CASIG *is* weakly CA-blind, *if for any ppt adversary $\mathcal{A}$ there exists a negligible function $\nu$ such that* $\Pr[\mathsf{CA} - \mathsf{WBlindness}_{\mathcal{A}}^{\mathsf{CASIG}}(1^\lambda) = 1] \leq \nu(\lambda)$. *The corresponding experiment is depicted in Fig. 8.*

**Experiment** $\mathsf{CA} - \mathsf{WBlindness}_{\mathcal{A}}^{\mathsf{CASIG}}(\lambda)$
  $(\mathsf{sk}_u, \mathsf{pk}_u) \leftarrow \mathsf{KGen}_u(1^\lambda)$
  $(\mathsf{pk}^*, \{m_0, m_1\}, \mathsf{time}, \mathsf{state}) \leftarrow \mathcal{A}(\mathsf{pk}_u)$
  $b \leftarrow \{0, 1\}$
  $a \leftarrow \mathcal{A}^{\langle \cdot, \mathcal{U}(\mathsf{sk}_u, \mathsf{pk}^*, m_b, \mathsf{time})\rangle^1, \mathsf{Revoke}(\cdot)}(\mathsf{state})$
  return 1, if $a = b$
  return 0

**Fig. 8.** Weak CA blindness

We call a CA-assisted signature scheme CASIG *secure and (weakly) blind*, if it is correct, signer unforgeable, CA unforgeable, and CA (weakly) blind.

## 4   Constructions

We now show how to come up with constructions achieving what we want. First, we present a generic construction, which, depending on the used building blocks, achieves weaker, or stronger resp., privacy notions. We stress that our reductions are tight, i.e., we have no reduction losses, and thus omit a probability analysis in the proofs.

**Generic Construction Idea.** Let us introduce the generic idea of our construction first. We then give two different derivations of the generic constructions, but instantiated with different building blocks. Both constructions offer the same unforgeability guarantees, but offer a different level of privacy.

In a nutshell, we let a CA contribute to signature generation, but only if the public key of the requester is not revoked at the time time of the signature request. The CA can then also add some additional information to the final signature such as certificates, and the like. However, from a privacy point of view, it is also required that the CA does not learn which messages are signed, which reflects blindness.

On the one hand, we let the signer commit to a message, and the let the CA sign this commitment, and the signer's public key, if, and only if, the given public key is not revoked. The user, on the other hand, creates an additional signature around the received signature from the CA to protect against bogus CAs. Clearly, there is no joint setup, and thus key generation can be done offline, which is not possible in current schemes. We stress that revoking a public key is simply sending the CA a message "My pk has been revoked", possibly containing a proof of knowledge, which is not necessarily zero-knowledge.

Note, the parties do not need to communicate using a secure channel.

**Construction 1 (Weakly-Blind Construction).** *Let* $\mathsf{CASIG} := (\mathsf{KGen}_u,$ $\mathsf{KGen}_c, \langle \mathcal{CA}, \mathcal{U} \rangle, \mathsf{Revoke}, \mathsf{Verify})$ *such that:*

$\mathsf{KGen}_u$. *Generate a key-pair of a standard digital signature scheme, i.e., return* $(\mathsf{pk}_u, \mathsf{sk}_u) \leftarrow \mathsf{DSIG.KGen}(1^\lambda)$.

$\mathsf{KGen}_c$. *Generate a key-pair of a standard digital signature scheme* $(\mathsf{pk}_c, \mathsf{sk}_c) \leftarrow$ $\mathsf{DSIG.KGen}(1^\lambda)$, *and the public parameters* $\mathsf{pp} \leftarrow \mathsf{COM.ParGen}(1^\lambda)$ *of a commitment scheme. Return* $((\mathsf{pk}_c, \mathsf{pp}), \mathsf{sk}_c)$.

$\langle \mathcal{CA}, \mathcal{U} \rangle$. *See Fig. 9.*

$\mathsf{Verf}$. *To verify a signature* $\sigma = (\sigma', \sigma_c, C, O, \mathsf{time})$ *w.r.t.* $m$, $\mathsf{pk}_c$, *and* $\mathsf{pk}_u$, *check that* $m = \mathsf{COM.Open}(\mathsf{pp}, C, O)$, *and* $\mathsf{DSIG.Verify}(\mathsf{pk}_c, (C, \mathsf{time}, \mathsf{pk}_u), \sigma_c) =$ *true*, $\mathsf{DSIG.Verify}(\mathsf{pk}_u, (\sigma_c, \mathsf{time}, m, C, O, \mathsf{pk}_c, \mathsf{pk}_u), \sigma') =$ *true*. *If all checks pass, output* *true*, *and* *false* *otherwise*.

**Theorem 1.** *If* $\mathsf{DSIG}$ *and* $\mathsf{COM}$ *are secure, then our construction is secure and weakly blind.*

*Proof.* Correctness follows from inspection. Thus, we only consider signer unforgeability, CA unforgeability, weak blindness. We prove each property on its own.

*Signer Unforgeability.* Let $\mathcal{A}$ be an adversary which can break the signer unforgeability of our construction. We can then construct an adversary $\mathcal{B}$ which either breaks the binding property of $\mathsf{COM}$, or the unforgeability of the signature scheme $\mathsf{DSIG}$ used by the CA. Assume that there is a signature $\sigma$ on the message $(\sigma_c, \mathsf{time}, m, C, O, \mathsf{pk}_c, \mathsf{pk}^*)$, where $\sigma_c$ is a signature on the message $(C, \mathsf{time})$, but also a signature $\sigma'$ for $(\sigma_c, \mathsf{time}', m', C, O, \mathsf{pk}_c, \mathsf{pk}'^*)$, where

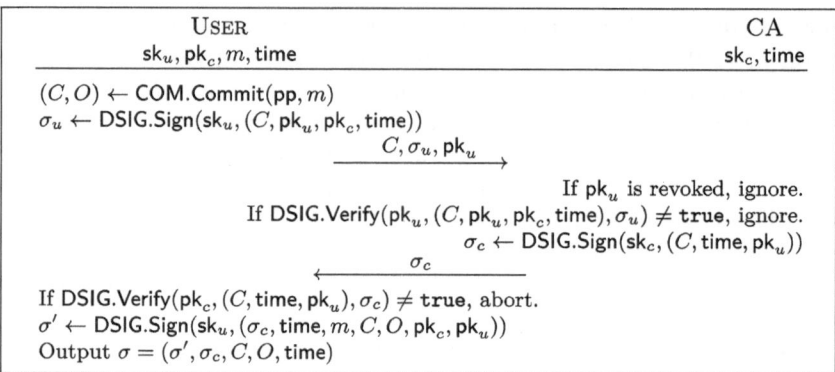

**Fig. 9.** CA-Assisted signing with weak blindness

$(m, \text{time}, \text{pk}^*) \neq (m', \text{time}', \text{pk}'^*)$. Hence, we have two different messages which "are in" the same commitment. Clearly, this breaks the binding property of the commitment scheme used. In the second case, i.e., there is a new commitment $C'$ for $(m, \text{time}) \neq (m', \text{time}')$ never signed by the CA, the adversary must have been able to forge a signature $\sigma_c'$. This also accounts for a revoked public key. In both cases a reduction for $\mathcal{B}$ is trivial, and therefore omitted.

*CA Unforgeability.* This case is trivial as well. If the adversary $\mathcal{A}$ can come up with a signature on a message $(\sigma_c, \text{time}, m, C, O, \text{pk}^*, \text{pk}_u)$, where $(m, \text{time}, \text{pk}^*)$ was never signed, then it can break the unforgeability of the used signature scheme. Again, a reduction is straightforward.

*CA Weak-Blindness.* Trivial, as COM is perfectly hiding, and therefore $\sigma_u$ is independent of $m$, which is the only information sent to the CA, i.e., $\mathcal{A}$.    □

**Construction 2 (Blind Construction).** *Let* $\mathsf{CASIG}' := (\mathsf{KGen}_u, \mathsf{KGen}_c, \langle \mathcal{CA}, \mathcal{U} \rangle, \mathsf{Revoke}, \mathsf{Verify})$ *such that:*

$\mathsf{KGen}_u$. *Generate a key-pair of a standard digital signature scheme, i.e., return* $(\mathsf{pk}_u, \mathsf{sk}_u) \leftarrow \mathsf{DSIG.KGen}(1^\lambda)$.
$\mathsf{KGen}_c$. *Generate a key-pair of a partially blind signature scheme, i.e., return* $(\mathsf{pk}_c, \mathsf{sk}_c) \leftarrow \mathsf{BSIG.KGen}(1^\lambda)$.
$\langle \mathcal{CA}, \mathcal{U} \rangle$. *See Fig. 10.*
Verf. *To verify a signature* $\sigma = (\sigma', \sigma_c, \text{time})$ *w.r.t.* $m$, $\mathsf{pk}_c$, *and* $\mathsf{pk}_u$, *check that* $\mathsf{DSIG.Verify}(\mathsf{pk}_c, (\sigma_c, \text{time}, m, \mathsf{pk}_c, \mathsf{pk}_u), \sigma') = \text{true}$, *and* $\mathsf{BSIG.Verify}(\mathsf{pk}_c, m, (\mathsf{pk}_u, \text{time}), \sigma_c) = \text{true}$. *If all checks pass, output* **true**, *and* **false** *otherwise.*

**Theorem 2.** *If* DSIG *and* BSIG *are secure, then our construction is secure and blind.*

*Proof.* Again, correctness follows by inspection. It remains to prove CA unforgeability, signer unforgeability, and blindness.

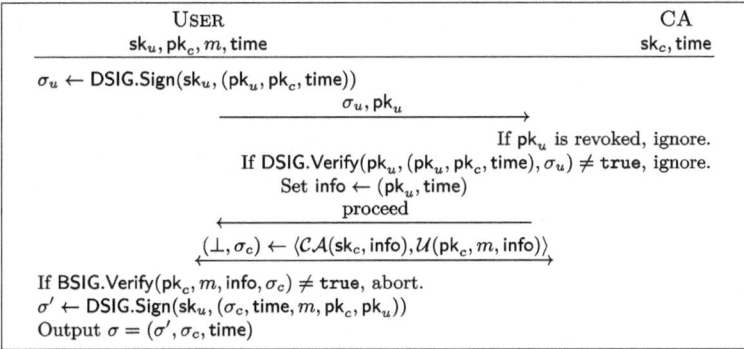

**Fig. 10.** CA-Assisted signing with blindness

*Signer Unforgeability.* Let $\mathcal{A}$ be an adversary which can break the signer unforgeability of our construction. We can then construct an adversary $\mathcal{B}$ which breaks the unforgeability of the partially blind signature scheme. $\mathcal{B}$ receives pk from the BSIG to forge, and embeds the received pk into the public key $\mathsf{pk}_c$. It simply follows the protocol, and uses its own oracle to get signatures. If a given $\mathsf{pk}_i$ is revoked, $\mathcal{B}$ no longer accepts new signing sessions. Eventually, $\mathcal{A}$ outputs $((m_1, \sigma_1, \mathsf{info}_1, \mathsf{pk}_1), \ldots, (m_\ell, \sigma_\ell, \mathsf{time}_\ell, \mathsf{pk}_\ell))$. Clearly, if $\mathsf{pk}_1$ was revoked, $\mathcal{B}$ never asked its own oracle to generate a signature for $(m_1, (\mathsf{pk}_1, \mathsf{time}_1))$, and can thus return all successful runs, and $(m_1, \sigma_1, \mathsf{time}_1, \mathsf{pk}_1)$, as for $(m_1, \mathsf{time}_1)$ is fresh by assumption, as $\mathcal{B}$ never queries its own oracle any longer for fresher time.

*CA Unforgeability.* Essentially the same reduction as for the weakly blind scheme.

*CA Blindness.* Let $\mathcal{A}$ be an adversary which breaks the CA blindness of our scheme. We can then construct an adversary which breaks the blindness of the used BSIG. $\mathcal{B}$ proceeds as follows. It generates $\mathsf{pk}_u$ honestly, which it also gives to $\mathcal{A}$, receiving $(\mathsf{pk}^*, \{m_0, m_1\}, \mathsf{time}, \mathsf{state}_1)$. It then gives $\mathsf{state}_1$ to $\mathcal{A}$, and interacts with its own oracles like $\mathcal{A}$ does with his using $m_0$ and $m_1$, but uses $(\mathsf{pk}_u, \mathsf{time})$ as info. If $\mathcal{A}$ is finished it returns $\mathsf{state}_2$, and $\mathcal{B}$ subsequently receives $(\sigma_1, \sigma_2)$ from its own challenger. Then, $\mathcal{B}$ gives $\mathcal{A}$ $\mathsf{state}_2$, and $(\sigma_1, \sigma_2)$ to $\mathcal{A}$. Whatever $\mathcal{A}$ then outputs, is also output by $\mathcal{B}$.                                              □

**Efficiency.** We want to stress that in the first protocol message the user essentially proves knowledge of the secret key. If the signature on time is not valid, the protocol can directly be aborted. This prohibits that outsiders use the CA to check whether a given certificate is revoked. If this is not wanted for performance reasons, leaving this step out is also possible.

Clearly, both constructions require that a verifier needs to verify two signatures, while the CA has to generate a signature. However, considering that the CA has to vouch that a given certificate was not revoked, it has to generate a signature anyway, if the revocation information needs to be up-to-date, which clearly needs to be verified as well. In other words, our construction is already more efficient after the first signature verification. Moreover, compared to the approach by Boneh et al. [9], an outsider can trivially derive whether our protocol was used to generate the signature, which in turn increases trust in the signature itself, as the verifier can also decide whether it accepts a given $pk_c$ as trustworthy.

## 4.1  Extensions

We now discuss informally how our basic constructions can be extended to account for additional use-cases. We omit full details and proofs due to space limitations, however the intuition should still become clear.

*Signer-Anonymity.* While both our constructions give message-privacy guarantees to the user, they reveal the identity of the signing party to the CA. If this poses a potential privacy problem, it can be mitigated as follows, for instance for the weakly-blind construction, cf. Fig. 9. The commitment is extended to also commit to $pk_u$. Then, instead of signing the tuple in Fig. 9 in the first step, one computes a signature proof of knowledge proving in zero-knowledge that one knows the secret key corresponding to the public key in the commitment, and that this public key is not on the blacklist. This can be done using similar techniques as Idemix [16].

*Revocation into the Past.* Our constructions are well-suited for situations where signing keys should simply be deactivated, e.g., when an employee leaves a company. However, in certain situations, it is also necessary to revoke "into the past" in order to also invalidate signatures issued between key leakage and revocation, cf. Fig. 1. In this case, the CA has to publish a list of revoked keys together with time-stamps of their revocation moment; upon verification, only signatures issued before this point in time would be accepted. From a complexity point of view this solution is similar to the combination of black-list based PKIs and time-stamping authorities, i.e., interaction is needed upon signing and verification.

*Message Policies.* One could also require that the signer proves (in zero-knowledge) that the message to be signed follows certain restrictions, e.g., that a company policy is followed. Only if the proof is valid, and the public key is not revoked, the server contributes to signature-generation. For example, a policy may be that a normal employee can only sign contracts below $1,000. This can even be done on a per-public-key basis. The size of signatures does not grow by this extension, and also the verification costs do not increase. Furthermore, the policy trivially remains hidden from the verifier.

Further extending the scheme efficiently such that also the CA does not learn any information about the policy remains a challenging open problem.

*Robustness.* Even though our security model is fixed for one signer and one CA, one can of course switch to a different CA on-the-fly. This protects against offline CAs, as one can simply use another one. In particular, a user can use a single signing key with different CAs, who act as revocation authorities for different domains (e.g., across different companies). Revocation by one CA does not affect other CAs. Security follows by a simple hybrid-argument.

*Threshold Scheme.* Related to the prior idea is an extension to threshold-cryptography. Namely, one could require that at least $n$-out-of-$m$ servers need to participate in order to achieve robustness against offline servers.

## 5  Conclusion and Future Work

We have introduced the notion of CA-Assisted Signatures. These signatures enable the revocation of signing-rights if a secret is corrupted. This is achieved by letting a CA contribute to signature generation, vouching that the used public key was not revoked. Thus, signatures remain valid even after revocation of the certificate. Moreover, the CA can add timestamps, while neither the verifier nor the CA need to be online for verification. This has the additional benefit that verification requires less effort to check the validity of the signature. We furthermore propose various extensions increasing the privacy guarantees of our basic constructions.

Our construction does not pose any non-standard requirements to the signature scheme used by the user. In particular, existing signing infrastructures could thus easily be adapted to our design without the users having to change their key material.

## References

1. Abe, M., Okamoto, T.: Provably secure partially blind signatures. In: Bellare, M. (ed.) CRYPTO 2000. LNCS, vol. 1880, pp. 271–286. Springer, Heidelberg (2000)
2. Al-Riyami, S.S., Paterson, K.G.: Certificateless public key cryptography. In: Laih, C.-S. (ed.) ASIACRYPT 2003. LNCS, vol. 2894, pp. 452–473. Springer, Heidelberg (2003)
3. Ateniese, G., Chou, D.H., de Medeiros, B., Tsudik, G.: Sanitizable signatures. In: di Vimercati, S.C., Syverson, P.F., Gollmann, D. (eds.) ESORICS 2005. LNCS, vol. 3679, pp. 159–177. Springer, Heidelberg (2005)
4. Bellare, M., Namprempre, C., Pointcheval, D., Semanko, M.: The one-more-RSA-inversion problems and the security of Chaum's blind signature scheme. J. Cryptology **16**(3), 185–215 (2003)
5. Bellare, M., Neven, G.: Multi-signatures in the plain public-key model and a general forking lemma. In: CCS, pp. 390–399 (2006)
6. Benaloh, J.C., de Mare, M.: One-way accumulators: a decentralized alternative to digital signatures. In: Helleseth, T. (ed.) EUROCRYPT 1993. LNCS, vol. 765, pp. 274–285. Springer, Heidelberg (1994)

7. Bicakci, K., Baykal, N.: Server assisted signatures revisited. In: Okamoto, T. (ed.) CT-RSA 2004. LNCS, vol. 2964, pp. 143–156. Springer, Heidelberg (2004)
8. Boldyreva, A.: Threshold signatures, multisignatures and blind signatures based on the Gap-Diffie-Hellman-group signature scheme. In: Desmedt, Y.G. (ed.) PKC 2003. LNCS, vol. 2567, pp. 31–46. Springer, Heidelberg (2003)
9. Boneh, D., Ding, X., Tsudik, G., Wong, C.: A method for fast revocation of public key certificates and security capabilities. In: USENIX (2001)
10. Boneh, D., Gentry, C., Lynn, B., Shacham, H.: Aggregate and verifiably encrypted signatures from bilinear maps. In: Biham, E. (ed.) EUROCRYPT 2003. LNCS, vol. 2656, pp. 416–432. Springer, Heidelberg (2003)
11. Brzuska, C., et al.: Security of sanitizable signatures revisited. In: Jarecki, S., Tsudik, G. (eds.) PKC 2009. LNCS, vol. 5443, pp. 317–336. Springer, Heidelberg (2009)
12. Camenisch, J., Dubovitskaya, M., Enderlein, R.R., Lehmann, A., Neven, G., Paquin, C., Preiss, F.: Concepts and languages for privacy-preserving attribute-based authentication. J. Inf. Sec. Appl. 19(1), 25–44 (2014)
13. Camenisch, J., van Herreweghen, E.: Design and implementation of the idemix anonymous credential system. In: CCS, pp. 21–30 (2002)
14. Camenisch, J., Koprowski, M., Warinschi, B.: Efficient blind signatures without random oracles. In: Blundo, C., Cimato, S. (eds.) SCN 2004. LNCS, vol. 3352, pp. 134–148. Springer, Heidelberg (2005)
15. Camenisch, J., Lehmann, A., Neven, G., Samelin, K.: Virtual smart cards: how to sign with a password and a server. ePrint 2015, 1101 (2015)
16. Camenisch, J., Lysyanskaya, A.: Dynamic accumulators and application to efficient revocation of anonymous credentials. In: Yung, M. (ed.) CRYPTO 2002. LNCS, vol. 2442, pp. 61–76. Springer, Heidelberg (2002)
17. Chaum, D.: Blind signatures for untraceable payments. In: Chaum, D., Rivest, R.L., Sherman, A.T. (eds.) Advances in Cryptology, pp. 199–203. Springer, New York (1982)
18. Chow, S.S.M., Hui, L.C.K., Yiu, S.M., Chow, K.P.: Two improved partially blind signature schemes from bilinear pairings. In: Boyd, C., González Nieto, J.M. (eds.) ACISP 2005. LNCS, vol. 3574, pp. 316–328. Springer, Heidelberg (2005)
19. Cooper, D., Santesson, S., Farrell, S., Boeyen, S., Housley, R., Polk, W.: Internet X.509 Public Key Infrastructure Certificate and Certificate Revocation List (CRL) Profile. RFC 5280 (2008)
20. Derler, D., Hanser, C., Slamanig, D.: Revisiting cryptographic accumulators, additional properties and relations to other primitives. In: Nyberg, K. (ed.) CT-RSA 2015. LNCS, vol. 9048, pp. 127–144. Springer, Heidelberg (2015)
21. Desmedt, Y.G., Frankel, Y.: Threshold cryptosystems. In: Brassard, G. (ed.) CRYPTO 1989. LNCS, vol. 435, pp. 307–315. Springer, Heidelberg (1990)
22. Fischlin, M., Schröder, D.: Security of blind signatures under aborts. In: Jarecki, S., Tsudik, G. (eds.) PKC 2009. LNCS, vol. 5443, pp. 297–316. Springer, Heidelberg (2009)
23. Fischlin, M., Schröder, D.: On the impossibility of three-move blind signature schemes. In: Gilbert, H. (ed.) EUROCRYPT 2010. LNCS, vol. 6110, pp. 197–215. Springer, Heidelberg (2010)
24. Goldwasser, S., Micali, S., Rivest, R.L.: A digital signature scheme secure against adaptive chosen-message attacks. SIAM J. Comput. 17, 281–308 (1988)
25. Gutmann, P.: PKI: it's not dead, just resting. IEEE Comput. 35(8), 41–49 (2002)

26. Huang, X., Susilo, W., Mu, Y., Zhang, F.T.: On the security of certificateless signature schemes from Asiacrypt 2003. In: Desmedt, Y.G., Wang, H., Mu, Y., Li, Y. (eds.) CANS 2005. LNCS, vol. 3810, pp. 13–25. Springer, Heidelberg (2005)
27. Juels, A., Luby, M., Ostrovsky, R.: Security of blind digital signatures. In: Kaliski Jr., B.S. (ed.) CRYPTO 1997. LNCS, vol. 1294, pp. 150–164. Springer, Heidelberg (1997)
28. Krenn, S., Samelin, K., Sommer, D.: Stronger security for sanitizable signatures. In: Garcia-Alfaro, J., et al. (eds.) DPM and QASA 2015. LNCS, vol. 9481, pp. 100–117. Springer, Heidelberg (2016). doi:10.1007/978-3-319-29883-2_7
29. Mambo, M., Usuda, K., Okamoto, E.: Proxy signatures for delegating signing operation. In: CCS 1996, pp. 48–57 (1996)
30. Milles, D.L.: Time synchronization in DCNET hosts. Technical report, COMSAT Laboratories (1981)
31. Okamoto, T.: Efficient blind and partially blind signatures without random oracles. In: Halevi, S., Rabin, T. (eds.) TCC 2006. LNCS, vol. 3876, pp. 80–99. Springer, Heidelberg (2006)
32. Pedersen, T.P.: Non-interactive and information-theoretic secure verifiable secret sharing. In: Feigenbaum, J. (ed.) CRYPTO 1991. LNCS, vol. 576, pp. 129–140. Springer, Heidelberg (1992)
33. Pöhls, H.C., Samelin, K.: On updatable redactable signatures. In: Boureanu, I., Owesarski, P., Vaudenay, S. (eds.) ACNS 2014. LNCS, vol. 8479, pp. 457–475. Springer, Heidelberg (2014)
34. McDaniel, P., Rubin, A.D., Rivest, R.L.: Can we eliminate certificate revocation lists? In: Hirschfeld, R. (ed.) FC 1998. LNCS, vol. 1465, pp. 178–183. Springer, Heidelberg (1998)

# Sensor Captchas: On the Usability of Instrumenting Hardware Sensors to Prove Liveliness

Thomas Hupperich[1]([⊠]), Katharina Krombholz[2], and Thorsten Holz[1]

[1] Horst Görtz Institute for IT-Security (HGI),
Ruhr-University, Bochum, Germany
thomas.hupperich@rub.de
[2] SBA Research, Vienna, Austria

**Abstract.** A CAPTCHA is a challenge-response test often used on the Web to determine whether a Web site's visitor is a human or an automated program (so called *bot*). Existing and widely used CAPTCHA schemes are based on visual puzzles that are hard to solve on mobile devices with a limited screen. We propose to leverage movement data from hardware sensors to build a CAPTCHA scheme suitable for mobile devices. Our approach is based on human motion information and the scheme requires users to perform gestures from everyday life (e. g., *hammering* where the smartphone should be imagined as a hammer and the user has to hit a nail five times). We implemented a prototype of the proposed method and report findings from a comparative usability study with 50 participants. The results suggest that our scheme outperforms other competing schemes on usability metrics such as solving time, accuracy, and error rate. Furthermore, the results of the user study indicate that gestures are a suitable input method to solve CAPTCHAs on (mobile) devices with smaller screens and hardware sensors.

**Keywords:** CAPTCHAs · Motion-based liveliness test · Device sensors

## 1 Introduction

CAPTCHAs[1] (*Completely Automated Public Turing tests to tell Computers and Humans Apart*) are challenge-response tests used to distinguish human users from automated programs masquerading as humans. Due to the increasing abuse of resources on the Web (e.g., automated creation of web site accounts that are then used to perform nefarious actions), captchas have become an essential part of online forms and the Internet ecosystem. They typically consist of visual puzzles intended to be easy to solve for humans, yet difficult to solve for computers [17]. The same idea can also be applied to audio puzzles such that visually impaired persons can also prove that they are humans and not

---

[1] For better readability, we write the acronym in lowercase in the following.

© Springer International Publishing Switzerland 2016
M. Franz and P. Papadimitratos (Eds.): TRUST 2016, LNCS 9824, pp. 40–59, 2016.
DOI: 10.1007/978-3-319-45572-3_3

computer programs. In reality, however, these puzzles are often time-consuming and sometimes hard to solve for human users [6]. Furthermore, visual pattern recognition algorithms gradually improved in the last years and this makes automated captcha solving feasible. For example, Burzstein et al. [3,4] highlighted that due to the arms race between captcha designers and OCR algorithms, we must reconsider the design of (reverse) Turing tests from ground up. As such, there is a continous arms race to design captcha schemes that are secure against automated attacks, but still useable for humans.

In the last few years, mobile devices have become a primary medium for accessing online resources. While most web content has already been adjusted to smaller screens and touchscreen interactions, most captcha schemes still suffer from these usability constraints and are perceived as error-prone and time-consuming by their users: several studies demonstrated that captcha usability in the mobile ecosystem is still an unsolved challenge [3–6,15,20], According to Reynaga et al. [14], captchas are primarily evaluated on their security and limited usability work has been carried out to evaluate captcha schemes for mobile device usage. With the emerging proliferation of wearable devices such as smartwatches, it becomes inevitable to re-think user interactions with captchas in order to successfully tell humans and computers apart, without placing the burden on users that struggle with hard-to-solve visual or audio puzzles.

In this paper, we present *Sensor Captchas*, a captcha scheme designed for mobile devices. Based on previously published findings, we collected a set of design recommendations to tie our design decisions to. We propose motion features from hardware sensors as a novel input paradigm for mobile captchas. A user is expected to perform gestures from everyday actions which might either be know or imagined easily, such as for example *hammering* where the smartphone should be imagined as a hammer and the user has to hit a nail five times, or *drinking*, where a user is asked to drink from the smartphone, imagining it is a glass of water. Our approach is solely based on state-of-the-art sensors available in most smartphones and wearables such as gyroscope and accelerometer, and obviates the need for users to solve complex graphical puzzles on small screens.

We implemented a prototype of the proposed scheme and present a repeated measures user study to compare our approach to state-of-the-art visual captcha schemes (namely reCAPTCHA and noCAPTCHA[2]) as well as an innovative mechanism called *Emerging Image captcha* [18].

Our findings show that sensor data is a suitable input for captcha challenges with high success rate and low solving time when leveraging gestures. While some gestures are easier to solve than other movements, the overall rate of solving successes shows the feasibility of our approach. Users rated our captcha mechanism comparable to established captcha schemes and we are able to show a learning effect within the first 15 challenges.

In summary, we make the following contributions:

– We design an extensible captcha scheme using accelerometer and gyroscope data as user input and machine learning classification for challenge validation.

---

[2] noCAPTCHA is also referred to as *new reCAPTCHA* [9].

– Based on a prototype implementation of the proposed scheme, we conduct
  a thorough user study with 50 participants to evaluate the usability of our
  approach, including a survey for direct user feedback.
– We compare our approach to well-known, established captcha methods
  (reCAPTCHA and noCAPTCHA) as well as another innovative scheme
  (Emerging Images) regarding success rates, solving times, and user experi-
  ence.

## 2    Related Work

Captchas are a controversial topic discussed amongst researchers and practitioners. The main reason for this observation is the fact that captchas put a lot of
burden on a user, while they are often not reliable when it comes to distinguishing human users from automated programs. Many approaches have been
presented in scientific literature and by companies such as Google, but most of
these schemes are still susceptible to different types of attacks.

Bursztein et al. identified major shortcomings of text captchas and proposed
design principles for creating secure captchas [4]. They focus on interaction with
desktop computers and do not consider usability shortcomings of captcha interactions on mobile devices. Fidas et al. validated visual captchas regarding their
solvability based on empirical evidence from an online survey [6]. They found
that background patterns are a major obstacle to correctly identify characters,
but provide little to no additional security. Reynaga et al. presented a comparative study of different captcha systems and their performance when accessed
via a smartphone [14]. They argue that visual captchas are hard to solve on
mobile devices and that usability could be increased by limiting the number of
tasks and by presenting simpler and shorter challenges with little or no obfuscation. Furthermore, distraction from the main task should be minimized by
presenting unobtrusive captchas that are isolated from the rest of the web form.
These factors highlight the need to develop novel captcha schemes that overcome
the limitations of visual captchas. Reynaga et al. also conducted a comparative
user study of nine captcha schemes and provided a set of ten specific design
recommendations based on their findings [15]. Bursztein et al. reported findings
from designing two new captcha schemes at Google and presented findings from
a consumer survey [5]. Xu et al. [19] explored the robustness and usability of
moving-image video captchas (*emerging captchas*) to defeat the shortcomings
of simple image captchas and discussed potential attacks. Jiang et al. proposed
gesture-based captchas that obviates the need to type letters by using swipe
gestures and other touch-screen interactions additionally [12]. However, such
complex methods may state a high burden to users. Gao et al. proposed a captcha scheme utilizing emerging images as a game [7]. Such game-based captchas
are solved and validated client-side making them vulnerable to replay attacks.

reCAPTCHA and noCAPTCHA by Google Inc. are field-tested, established mechanisms [8]. However, both methods disclose unapparent downsides:
reCAPTCHA is used to digitalize street view addresses as well as books and

magazines. noCAPTCHA implements behavioral analysis and browser finger-printing. Information that is used for fingerprinting includes but is not limited to: installed browser plugins, user agent, screen resolution, execution time, time-zone, and number of user actions – including clicks, keystrokes and touches – in the captcha frame. It also tests the behavior of many browser-specific functions as well as CSS rules and checks the rendering of canvas elements [1]. While these information are used for liveliness detection and therefore fit the aim of captchas, it can also be used for thorough user tracking, raising privacy concerns [11].

## 3   Sensor Captchas

Modern mobile devices contain a multitude of hardware sensors, including accelerometers and gyroscopes which are accessible via Web techniques like Java-Script and HTML5. These sensors are so accurate that it is possible to detect steps of a walking person [16] and to distinguish between certain user actions [10]. As a main difference to existing captcha schemes, we utilize these hardware sensors as input channel for solving a challenge. The benefit of this input channel is that a user does not need to type text on a small softkeyboard on a smartphone, but he can use a simple movement to prove liveliness.

In practice, a Web site provider aims to distinguish a human user from an automated bot and therefore utilizes a captcha challenge. In our approach, this challenge is represented by a gesture a user has to perform. We explored possible gestures for such challenges as they need to satisfy several requirements:

- **Understandable:** Users need to be able to understand the challenges and what they are supposed to do immediately.
- **Accurate:** The challenge needs to enable a precise differentiation between human users and automated bots.
- **Deterministic:** The choice whether a human or a bot is currently visiting a Web site needs to be deterministic.
- **Solvable:** It must be possible to solve the challenge within a reasonable amount of time.

### 3.1   Gesture Design

In an early stage of our research, we chose very simple gestures like moving a device in a circle clockwise. While these movements were easy to understand by a user, it was hardly possible to precisely distinguish between gestures due to too much variance: we did not include any precise statements about size and speed of the movement, so users were not able to solve these challenges accurately. Learning from these findings, we chose five gestures for our user study which are derived from everyday actions a user might either know or imagine easily:

- **Hammering:** The smartphone should be imagined as hammer and a user has to hit a nail five times.
- **Bodyturn:** A user is challenged to turn all around counter-clockwise.

- **Fishing:** The smartphone should be imagined as fishing rod which is to cast.
- **Drinking:** A user is asked to drink from the smartphone, imagining it is a glass of water.
- **Keyhole:** The smartphone is an imaginary key which is to be put in a door lock and rotated left and right like unlocking a door.

Note that these gestures can be easily extended, e. g., by randomly choosing the number of times the "hammer" has to hit the imaginary nail or by taking a clockwise bodyturn into account. With such variations, more gestures are possible so that in a practical use not only five movements are available, but a great variety of different challenges can be designed. The gestures can be presented to users in different ways. For our prototype and user study, we described all gestures to perform in short texts. Pictures showing a drawing of a human performing the asked movement or even an animated image or a short video clip can alternatively present the challenge.

When a user performs a gesture, accelerometer and gyroscope readings are recorded and afterwards transferred to the Web server. On the server side, we use a machine learning classifier to determine whether the sensor data matches the challenged gesture. If the data can be classified as the demanded gesture, the captcha has been solved successfully. If it is rejected by the classifier or matches a wrong gesture, the captcha has failed. Using machine learning technology in our captcha scheme is based on the following observation: If a captcha is based on text input, the challenge text is generated first and held by the server. When the user enters the text, this input can be compared to the generated text immediately. In our scenario, there is no challenge data generated first which the user input can be compared to. It is not usable to generate three-dimensional acceleration data and challenge a user to perform exactly this movement with a smartphone. Hence, we need a decider which is capable of distinguishing characteristics of one movement from another and ultimately determine whether given data matches a specific gesture. A machine learning classifier is an appropriate mechanism for this task as it describes a classification problem.

## 3.2   Satisfaction of Requirements

We ground our captcha scheme in design principles suggested in existing scientific work on captcha usability, such as Reynaga et al. [14], Fidas et al. [6], and Bursztein et al. [3]. In the following, we present a collection of design principles and recommendations from these publications and argue how our design addresses these features.

### Challenges

- *Deploy one task only.* Optional features hinder usability on small screens where captcha solving is already more time-consuming than on desktop computers. Challenges should be designed with a one-task only focus.

- *Leverage complexity.* Visual puzzles suffer from an arms race between captcha providers and pattern recognition algorithms that sometimes even perform better than human beings. Although finding a more difficult problem in computer vision will increase the cognitive load on the user side, captchas need to be challenging and of a complex domain.
- *Using cognitive behavior.* Everyday life movements such as the one used for our challenges are capable of shifting captcha interactions to a domain beyond visual puzzles and touchscreen interaction. As the gestures are found in everyday life, we believe it is an easy task for humans to perform them, yet hard to fake for automated programs.
- *Strive for a minimalistic interface.* An interface should focus on the essential and be minimalistic. Our captcha challenges can be displayed and solved even from wearables such as smartwatches.

**Environment of Use**

- *Expect common conditions.* Features which may fail in commonly expected environmental conditions should be avoided. Our design fulfils this recommendation although the performance of gestures may be conspicuous.
- *Minimize load.* For our approach, bandwidth usage is minimized as challenge descriptions are provided verbatim. Also, the data transmitted to the server consists of raw sensor data, as the decision whether the captcha was solved directly is performed on the server side to prevent attacks on the client.
- *Rely on default software.* For correct operation, a scheme should not rely on technologies that cannot be assumed obligatory. Our implementation is based on JavaScript which is supported by standard mobile browsers.

**Engineering**

- *Ensure compatability.* To reach a majority of users, input mechanisms should be cross-platform compatible and not interfere with normal operations. Our approach is solely based on input from motion sensors which are state-of-the-art in smartphones and smartwatches.
- *Aim for high robustness.* Errors must not interfere with normal operations of the browser. Our scheme does not interfere with other operations.
- *Support isolation.* The captcha challenge should be separated from the rest of the Web form. Our captchas may even be shown on another site of a form.
- *Enable consistency.* Orientation and size of the captcha should be kept consistent with the rest of the web form. As our challenge description is text-based or image-based, its presentation can easily be adjusted.

**Privacy**

- *Maximize user privacy.* Additionally to the design principles listed above, we aim to spotlight user privacy. A user input should not be replaced by user fingerprinting as seen in [1]. Our goal is to propose a scheme that minimizes the impact on user privacy and works without collecting sensitive information on the users and their devices.

## 4   User Study

We implemented a prototype of the proposed scheme and conducted a comparative evaluation to assess the usability of our new captcha scheme against already existing solutions. In the following, we provide details on both aspects.

### 4.1   Design and Procedure

Our user study is divided into two phases: first, a preliminary study was carried out to determine a suitable time frame for gesture performance, the best parameters for the machine learning classifier as well as the ground truth for the main user study. Both phases are described in more detail below. Figure 1 illustrates the complete user study setup.

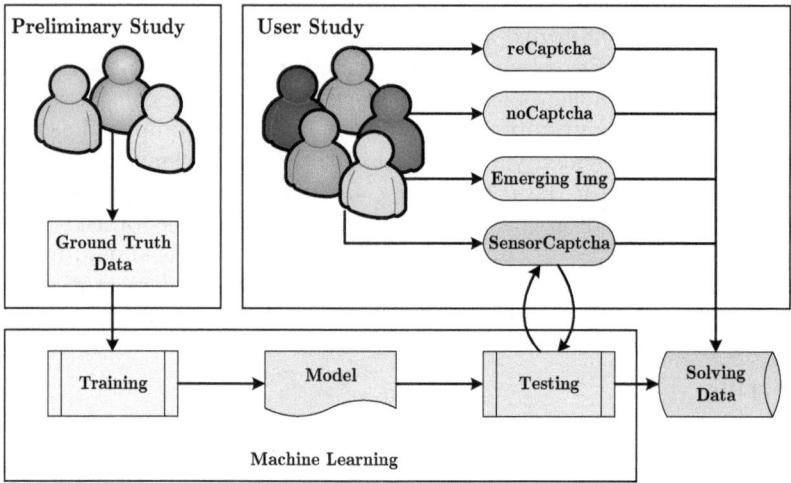

**Fig. 1.** User study setup

**Preliminary Study.** Sensor Captchas rely on motion input from hardware sensors and machine learning techniques to prove that the user is human. In order to train a model, we conducted a preliminary study. We built a data set of ground truth by instructing 20 participants to perform the movements and gestures described in Sect. 3. Then, we let them solve the challenges in a controlled environment under the following two conditions:

1. The challenges were not chosen randomly but assigned to the participants. Every user had to perform the same number of challenges. More precisely, every user performed every gesture three times.
2. We observed the users solving the challenges and instructed them if they made mistakes to ensure the correct performance.

The sensor data obtained in this preliminary study is used as ground truth for further processing. As the data collection was performed in a controlled environment and under the supervision of two experimenters, we assume that the gestures have been performed correctly.

To find the best-performing classifier, we conducted cross validations and classification experiments with algorithms from different families, including support vector machines, k-Nearest Neighbor, and different ensemble methods. Our results suggest that a *Random Forest* classifier performs best on our ground truth and thus we used this algorithm to generate a model that was then used in the actual user study.

**Main User Study.** We include three other captcha mechanisms besides Sensor Captchas in our main study: two schemes are well-known and commonly used in practice, while the other one is an experimental approach from a recent research paper:

1. *reCAPTCHA* is a well-proven text-based input mechanism. A user is asked to type words or numbers shown in an often distorted or blurred image.
2. *noCAPTCHA* is the field-tested successor of reCAPTCHA and challenges the user to select from nine images all these showing specific items, e. g., trees. It also instruments behavioral analysis.
3. *Emerging Images* relies on moving image recognition. A user has to type letters which are shown in an animated image series. This method has been proposed by Xu et al. [18].

While reCAPTCHA and noCAPTCHA are established mechanisms already used by Internet users and website providers every day, Emerging Images and Sensor Captcha represent scientific approaches and have not yet been deployed in a real-world environment.

We chose a repeated measures design for our lab study, i.e., every participant had to solve puzzles from every captcha scheme in a controlled environment at our university campus. It was important to us to observe sources of errors in order to improve our design. Each participant was asked to solve a minimum of 15 challenges per scheme. We designed our study to present the challenges in randomized order to reduce any bias or fatigue effects. As all participants were asked to solve captchas of all four types, we were able to gather comprehensive solving data, including the number of correctly solved captchas and failures as well as the amount of time needed to solve each captcha. As our implementation was written in JavaScript, the participants were encouraged to use their own devices to avoid bias and distractions from the study tasks due to unfamiliarity with the device. Even though we had two backup devices with us, all participants used their own devices.

After completing the captcha challenges, the participants filled out a short questionnaire (see Sect. 5.3 for a complete listing of these questions). In addition, one experimenter took notes in order to collect qualitative in-situ reactions and comments. This information was collected to understand particular difficulties and misunderstandings about the presented puzzles and the way of solving them. We believe these explorative findings are valuable to improve the usability of our captcha scheme.

## 4.2   Implementation

reCAPTCHA as well as noCAPTCHA are operated by Google Inc. and provide an API which we used to include these methods in our study. The Emerging Images technique has been provided and hosted by Gerardo Reynaga, School of Computer Science at Carleton University, Ottawa Canada for the duration of our test. We implemented our Sensor Captchas and a survey site from which the participants accessed the different captcha challenges and the questionnaire. The web site was implemented in JavaScript and contained a general information page and a separated page for every captcha method. Each of these pages contained a short description on how to solve this captcha and a start button. After tapping the start button, a form containing the captcha challenge and a submit button were displayed. For every captcha, we measured the solving time as duration between tapping the start button and tapping the form submit button. Hence we only measured the time it took the user to mentally process the captcha challenge and to input a correct solution. This way, we managed to measure the solving time irrespective of network delays, implementation issues and other technical factors. After a captcha challenge was completed, we stored the following information: A **name** every user could choose freely, the current **date**, the **captcha result** which is either success or failure, the **duration** a user needed for the solving attempt, and a **unique user key** which was generated automatically and stored in the browser's local storage as anonymous identifier.

reCAPTCHA and noCAPTCHA provide an API, so this information could be obtained and stored automatically except for one limitation: noCAPTCHA does not provide a way to check the result of a single challenge. If a challenge has not been solved correctly, the next challenge is displayed to the user automatically without triggering a Javascript event. Hence, it is not possible to record noCAPTCHA failures without interfering with Google's API and violating the way it works which may have voided results and measurements. As there is no API available for Emerging Images Captcha, we manually kept track of successes, failures, and solving durations and entered this data by hand.

Regarding Sensor Captchas, we additionally stored the following information: The **sensor data**, including accelerometer and gyroscope readings as arrays (of the dimensions $x$, $y$, and $z$ as well as $\alpha$, $\beta$, and $\gamma$), the **original challenge** which was displayed to the user, and the **classification result** which leads to a captcha success only if it matches the original challenge.

After tapping the submit button on the Sensor Captcha page, sensor events were measured for five seconds which we set as time frame to perform the gesture. We designed the gesture movements in such way that they are practical to perform within this time and tested every gesture beforehand. Our preliminary study showed that five seconds are a reasonable amount of time to make all required movements. Though, this parameter can be analyzed and adjusted in future studies. After this time, all data was submitted automatically, so that users did not have to tap another submit button in addition. The sensor data was sent to a socket parsing the data to our machine learning classifier, retrieving the classification result and finally storing all these information in the database. This functionalities were programmed in Python, implementing a Random Forest classifier from scikit-learn [2].

### 4.3   Recruitment and Participants

We recruited 50 participants between December 2015 and February 2016 at the university campus and a major computer security conference. Most participants were students at our university from different branches of study, including information technology, medicine, arts and science. While the youngest participant was 18 years old and the oldest 55, the majority was aged between 20 and 35 years; male and female in approximately equal shares. All participants were familiar with the purpose of captchas on websites and reported to have used established methods before. To comply with ethical guidelines from our university, we did not collect any personal identifiable information. We only collected information on age, gender and whether the participants had a background in information technology. Every session lasted about 20 min per participant and they were compensated for their time with a voucher of a major online shop.

## 5   Evaluation

In the following, we compare the different captcha schemes regarding successfull solving of challenges and amount of time needed to solve challenges. Concerning Sensor Captchas, we analyze the suitability of gestures as well as the survey included in our user study. Finally, we investigate whether a habituation effect can be asserted and shed light on the precision of our machine learning classifier.

### 5.1   Comparison of Mechanisms

To compare the solvability among all considered captcha mechanism, we measured the successes and failures. A success represents the correct solution of a captcha, while a failure represents a wrong input.

In our study, about 85 % of all reCAPTCHA challenges were successfully solved by the participants. As discussed in Sect. 4.2, it is not possible to catch success and failure cases of noCAPTCHA without interfering. Emerging Images seem to constitute a rather hard challenge, as only about 44 % of all challenges could be solved correctly. In contrast, Sensor Captchas achieve a high success rate: Of all provided gesture challenges, the participants were able to correctly solve about 92 % , making this mechanism to be reckoned with. These preliminary results of our study suggest that users were able to solve more Sensor Captchas correctly than challenges of any other type. Note that for Sensor Captchas, a failure may not only redound upon a wrong user input – namely not performing

**Table 1.** Success rates (SR)

| Mechanism | SR | Mean | SD |
|---|---|---|---|
| reCAPTCHA | 0.8463 | 0.8698 | 0.3356 |
| Emerging images | 0.4396 | 0.4491 | 0.4976 |
| Sensor captcha | 0.9160 | 0.4813 | 0.4997 |

SR = success rate,
SD = standard deviation

**Table 2.** Average solving times

| Mechanism | S | F | Total | Mean | SD |
|---|---|---|---|---|---|
| reCAPTCHA | 12.22 | 26.36 | 14.39 | 12.4260 | 18.5934 |
| noCAPTCHA | - | - | 26.99 | 24.1814 | 17.8862 |
| Emerging images | 21.91 | 24.29 | 23.24 | 26.1504 | 29.4114 |
| Sensor captchas | 12.35 | 8.85 | 12.05 | 12.2519 | 7.10444 |

S = successes, F = failures,
SD = standard deviation

the challenge gesture – but also upon a misclassification by our machine learning algorithm. This factor will be discussed below.

As described in Sect. 4.2, we measured the time users needed to solve every single challenge. Hence, we can analyze how much time is needed on average to succeed at every mechanism. Table 2 shows the average amount of time per mechanism and captcha result.

We observe that in general failures take more time for reCAPTCHA as well as Emerging Images. The reason for this lies probably in the way of user input: Users have to read and decipher letters or numbers first. Depending on the specific challenge, this may be difficult so that hard challenges are more likely to fail but also take more time. We observed these cases to annoy many users as they first needed to invest high effort to recognize the challenge's letters or numbers and then fail anyway. For Sensor Captchas, we can see a lower solving time for failures than for successes, indicating that users may have failed to solve the challenge because they did not read the description text carefully enough.

We found noCAPTCHA to take generally more time than reCAPTCHA, which may be explained by the fact that reCAPTCHA applies browser finger-printing first and then displays the challenge. Comparing the total time users were taken to solve captchas, reCAPTCHA is the fastest mechanism – probably because it is a practical method many users are already familiar with. Nevertheless, reCAPTCHA is directly followed by Sensor Captchas, suggesting that this approach is practicable and showing that users are able to perform the challenge's gestures in a reasonable amount of time. Please note that Sensor Captchas' solving time can be influenced by adjusting the time window for performing a gesture. We based an interval of five seconds upon our preliminary study but increasing this time would result in higher solving durations while decreasing could make it impossible to perform a gesture thoroughly.

Our study has a repeated-measures design, so every participant was exposed to every condition. Therefore, we analyzed our data with repeated measures analyses of variance (ANOVAs). Table 1 shows not only the success rates of the captcha mechanisms but also their mean and standard deviation of successes, represented by 1 for success and 0 for failure. We see that the mean of Sensor Captchas resides within the standard deviation of reCAPTCHA and vice versa. Hence, differences between these two schemes are statistically not significant and may represent random errors. In contrast, the correct solving rate of Sensor

Captchas is significantly higher as of the Emerging Images mechanism, meaning that even if the random error is considered, the succcess rate of Sensor Captchas is superior. Similar trends can be observed regarding the solving times of each mechanism in Table 2: There is no statistically significant difference between Sensor Captchas and reCAPTCHA regarding the time a user takes to solve a captcha. Though, the mean solving times of these two mechanisms are significantly lower compared to noCAPTCHA and Emerging Images. We can conclude that Sensor Captchas and reCAPTCHA can be solved faster than noCAPTCHA and Emerging Images, even if the random error is taken into account.

## 5.2   Gesture Analysis

After comparing Sensor Captchas to other captcha mechanisms regarding success rates and solving times, we aim to analyze the gestures in detail. We conducted experiments to ascertain which gestures are accurate to perform and which movements happen to be related to other gestures. Table 3 shows the solving rates and error rates per gesture. We see that `bodyturn` and `keyhole` challenges were in general solved correctly, meaning that the sensor events measured during a user's gesture performance could be matched to the challenged gesture. `Bodyturn` and `keyhole` were correctly solved by about 97 % and 96 % in total. For both, the highest mismatching was to the `hammering` gesture, meaning if a user input could not be related to the challenge, it was classified as `hammering`. For the `drinking` movement, still about 92 % of the challenges were solved correctly. The gestures `fishing` and `hammering` seem to be prone for errors: Of all `hammering` challenges, about 85 % could be solved correctly and in case of the `fishing` gesture only about 79 % . We also see that `fishing` and `hammering` are the least precise gestures as about 14 % of all `fishing` challenges were classified as `hammering` and about 5 % of all `hammering` challenges were mistakenly related to the `fishing` gesture. This confusion can be explained by the movement itself: For `hammering`, users had to move their devices in one axis up and down, so this gesture is not very complex. For `fishing` applies the same as this movement also involves only one axis and although there are differences like the number of accelerations (`hammering` requires several acceleration moves in order to hit the imaginary nail five times while the fishing rod is casted only once), this low complexity

**Table 3.** Solving rates and error rates per gesture

| Gesture | Categorized as | | | | |
|---|---|---|---|---|---|
|  | bodyturn | drinking | keyhole | fishing | hammering |
| Bodyturn | 0.9720 | 0.0 | 0.0 | 0.0 | 0.0279 |
| Drinking | 0.0 | 0.9174 | 0.0642 | 0.0091 | 0.0091 |
| Keyhole | 0.0065 | 0.0130 | 0.9608 | 0.0 | 0.0196 |
| Fishing | 0.0222 | 0.0444 | 0.0 | 0.7889 | 0.1444 |
| Hammering | 0.0162 | 0.0 | 0.0813 | 0.0487 | 0.8537 |

leads to confusion about these two gestures. For the same reason, the `fishing` gesture was sometimes classified as `drinking`, although this happened only in about 4 % of all fishing challenges. In about 8 % of all `hammering` challenges, the sensor data was related to the `keyhole` gesture. The reason for this might be that users may have slightly turned their phones while `hammering` their devices on an imaginary nail. This resulted in movements in the $z$ dimension which is an essential part of the `keyhole` gesture. The gestures `drinking`, `keyhole`, and `bodyturn` show only negligible errors and mistaken relations to other gestures. In general, only the `hammering` gesture yields potential for errors and should be excluded or enhanced in further studies. If this is fixed, the `fishing` gesture may presumably perform better as well because there will no confusion with the `hammering` movement any more.

### 5.3   Survey Results

As a part of our study, users had to participate in a survey, rating all four captcha mechanisms regarding nine aspects. We leveraged a ten-levelled Likert scale for every item, adopted and extended statements from previous research by Reynaga et al. [15] to allow a direct comparison to this work. In detail, we let the users rate the following statements (* represents inverted items):

– **Accuracy:** It was easy to solve the challenges accurately.
– **Understandability:** The challenges were easy to understand.
– **Memorability:** If I did not use this method for several weeks, I would still be able to remember how to solve challenges.
– **Pleasant:** The captcha method was pleasant to use.
– **Solvability\*:** It was hard to solve captcha challenges.
– **Suitability:** This method is well suitable for smartphones.
– **Preference:** On a mobile, I would prefer this captcha method to others.
– **Input Mechanism\*:** This method is more prone to input mistakes.
– **Habituation:** With frequent use, it get easier to solve the challenges.

Figure 2 reports the mean Likert scale responses from *strongly disagree* = 1 to *strongly agree* = 10. Also, the colors in the figure represent the scale, from red representing *strongly disagree* to green as *strongly agree*.

The established captcha mechanisms in our study – namely noCAPTCHA and reCAPTCHA – were in general rated high regarding accuracy, understandability, memorability, pleasant use, and suitability for mobile devices. Many users stated that they were familiar with these methods and therefore could easily solve the given challenges as the task was immediately clear. For understandability and memorability, we observe a low standard deviation among the ratings. In contrast, high standard deviation among participant ratings can be seen regarding the preferred captcha mechanism. This item holds a deviation of 2.99 for noCAPTCHA and 2.74 for reCAPTCHA, showing that users are at odds if they preferred these established methods which is substantiated by high standard deviation regarding input mistakes ("input mechanism") showing 2.67 for

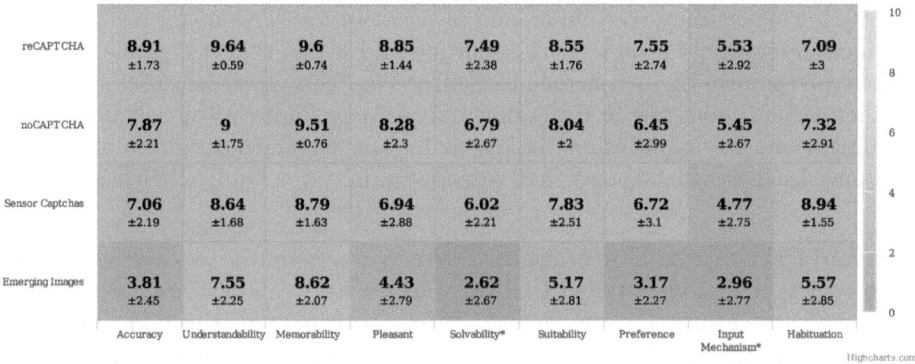

| | Accuracy | Understandability | Memorability | Pleasant | Solvability* | Suitability | Preference | Input Mechanism* | Habituation |
|---|---|---|---|---|---|---|---|---|---|
| reCAPTCHA | 8.91 ±1.73 | 9.64 ±0.59 | 9.6 ±0.74 | 8.85 ±1.44 | 7.49 ±2.38 | 8.55 ±1.76 | 7.55 ±2.74 | 5.53 ±2.92 | 7.09 ±3 |
| noCAPTCHA | 7.87 ±2.21 | 9 ±1.75 | 9.51 ±0.76 | 8.28 ±2.3 | 6.79 ±2.67 | 8.04 ±2 | 6.45 ±2.99 | 5.45 ±2.67 | 7.32 ±2.91 |
| Sensor Captchas | 7.06 ±2.19 | 8.64 ±1.68 | 8.79 ±1.63 | 6.94 ±2.88 | 6.02 ±2.21 | 7.83 ±2.51 | 6.72 ±3.1 | 4.77 ±2.75 | 8.94 ±1.55 |
| Emerging Images | 3.81 ±2.45 | 7.55 ±2.25 | 8.62 ±2.07 | 4.43 ±2.79 | 2.62 ±2.67 | 5.17 ±2.81 | 3.17 ±2.27 | 2.96 ±2.77 | 5.57 ±2.85 |

Highcharts.com

**Fig. 2.** Mean Likert-scores and standard deviations from survey

noCAPTCHA and 2.92 for reCAPTCHA. For some users, these captchas seem to work well and are easy to use. Anyway, other users are not comfortable with them and would not prefer these methods on mobile devices.

Although Sensor Captcha holds the highest solving rate, users are not accustomed to this mechanism which results in a generally lower rating compared to the established captcha methods reCAPTCHA and noCAPTCHA. Sensor Captchas keeps up with established mechanisms regarding accuracy, understandability, memorability, suitability, preference and input mechanism – differences of these ratings are smaller than one. Significant differences can be seen regarding the ratings "pleasant" which may be rooted in the fact that the participants were not used to Sensor Captcha and the gestures require movement of body(parts) which users may be uncomfortable with in public environments and "solvability". This is contradictory to the high solving rates and shows that users find it hard to solve Sensor Captchas although they were able to do so in most cases. The high rating of habituation shows that participants adjudge a high learnability to Sensor Captchas, hence long term studies may improve the perception of solvability as well. We also shed light on habituation aspects in the next section. The items of our questionnaire which were rated with a low value also show a high deviations: While "pleasant", "preference", and "input mechanism" show the lowest user ratings, the standard deviations are rather high with 2.88, 3.1, and 2.75. This shows that there is a wide array of user opinions and while some participants found Sensor Captcha not pleasant and would not prefer this mechanism, other users indeed stated the opposite and would prefer our mechanism to established captcha methods. Furthermore, the lowest standard deviation of 1.55 holds "habituation" which states that the majority of users think that continuous use would increase the solvability and easy-of-use of Sensor Captcha.

Emerging Images as another innovative captcha mechanism was rated well regarding understandability and memorability showing that users are familiar with text inputs and understand the task of typing letters from a sequence of images easily. Anyway, participants found it hard to solve these challenges, given a low rating of accuracy, solvability, and pleasant-of-use. This might be the reason why most users would not prefer this method and stated that it is prone to errors ("input mechanism"). In contrast to Sensor Captcha, users are not optimistic whether a continuous use of Emerging Images may improve the solvability and handling, though, "habituation" holds the highest standard deviation of 2.85 for Emerging Images which shows that some users may get familiar with it.

**Informal Participant Statements.** Participants were free to leave comments, so we could get a more detailed feedback on our study and scheme. Many users demanded animations for the description of gestures. As this may probably improve the understandability, accuracy, and solvability of Sensor Captchas, we will implement this feature in the future.

A few users stated that the chosen gestures were not suitable for everyday use. Indeed, for Sensor Captchas to evolve into an established captcha method, the available gestures need to be reassessed. We abstracted gestures from everyday actions because simple movements were prone to errors and misunderstandings (see Sect. 3). Still, casting an imaginary fishing rod may be imaginable but not an action users want to perform in public environments.

Some users stated that it is hard to solve text-based and image-based captchas – reCAPTCHA and noCAPTCHA – on a smartphones screen because it may be too small to comfortably display all images or the softkeyboard additionally to the challenge. This supports our original motivation for Sensor Captcha.

## 5.4    Habituation

According to the survey results, many users think that solving Sensor Captchas will get more and more comfortable and easy by using the scheme. Although the long term habituation to Sensor Captcha is left for future work, we investigate if users were able to improve their success rates during our user study. Like described in Sect. 4.1, every user tried to solve at least 15 Sensor Captchas. While only about 49 % of all participants were able to solve the very first Sensor Captcha correctly, we notice a clear trend that more gestures could be performed successfully the more captchas have been tried to solve. The average success rate among all users for the 15th Sensor Captcha is about 84 % which supports the assumption that users may probably habituate to this captcha mechanism fast. To test a possible correlation between the number of solving attempts and the number of successes, we calculate the Pearson correlation coefficient $\rho$. Taking all user data into account, $\rho = 0.7238$, which proves a strong positive linear relationship statistically and verifies that with increasing number of challenges the number of successes also increases in our user study.

## 5.5    Classification

There exist two possible factors for captcha failure: Not only humans may fail at solving a captcha challenge, but the machine learning classifier may fail at matching correct gesture data. To shed light on possible false classifications, we calculated precision and recall for different machine learning algorithms. In our scenario, a *false positive* is represented by the case that sensor data not belonging to a specific gesture will be accepted as correct solution for this gesture; in extreme case random sensor data is wrongly classified as correct solution to a challenge.

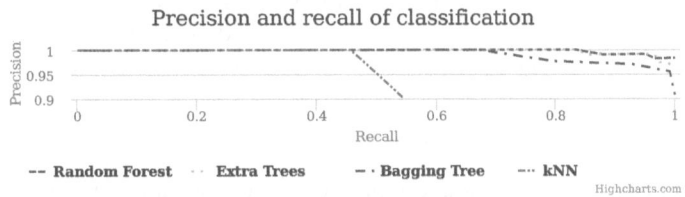

**Fig. 3.** Classification precision and recall

Consequently, if a correct sensor data input is mistakenly rejected by the classifier, this case states a *false negative*. Note that in context of captchas, false positives are worse compared to false negatives: If users were sporadically not recognized as human, they would have to solve a second captcha at worst. But if a bot was mistakenly accepted as human, it could circumvent the captcha protection. Correct classification of sensor data to the right gesture is a *true positive*, while a correct rejection of non-matching data constitutes a *true negative*. On this basis, we are able to calculate precision and recall of all data obtained in the user study. Figure 3 illustrates precision recall graphs of different classifiers which were to be considered.

Given the data set of our user study, including accelerometer and gyroscope data of all performed gestures, the classifiers *Random Forest, Extra Trees*, and *Bagging Tree* yield a very high precision in distinguishing the gestures. Only the *kNearestNeighbor* algorithm (testing $k = 1$, $k = 5$, $k = 10$) was not capable of precisely classifying the gestures. While this one achieves an AUC of only 0.7899, Bagging Tree achieved an AUC of 0.9917, Extra Trees of 0.9972 and finally Random Forest of 0.9989. This confirms our choice to implement a Random Forest classifier in our user study back end. As shown in Fig. 3, the classifier is capable of determining whether given sensor data satisfies a specific gesture at high precision. Hence, misclassifications are negligible in our study and we are able to ascribe most captcha failures to user input errors.

## 6   Discussion

The proposed mechanism meets the common requirements to captcha schemes: the main goal of telling computers and human apart by a challenge as simple as possible is achieved. We also satisfy common design principles for captcha methods as discussed in Sect. 3.2. In this section, we discuss security as well was potential limitations of our approach, and ideas for future work. Although our survey results indicate that users feel Sensor Captchas to be less accurate and solvable than established methods, our approach achieved the highest success rate and took users the least time to solve challenges. It thus might break the arms race in computer vision powered by more and more captcha mechanisms based on visual puzzles. The fact that the decision about success or failure is made server-side raises the bandwidth use in contrast to captcha schemes which work client-side only. However, the size of transferred sensor data is reasonable and deciding about a challenge's solution server-side is more secure. On average, the sensor readings of accelerometer and gyroscope take 5 KB in total.

## 6.1 Security Considerations

Basing liveliness determination on hardware sensor data enables new attack vectors aiming at data manipulating. An attacker may record sensor data and provide it as solution to a given challenge. As our captcha scheme currently supports five gestures only, a replay attack succeeds with a theoretic probability of 0.2 which needs to be reduced by more varieties of gesture challenges. Thus, even with such extensions, the entropy of our approach will not exceed the entropy of text-based captchas. A bot could solve Sensor Captcha challenges if correct input data is available for every single gesture and if the automated solver furthermore is able to recognize the challenge presented. As this applies to all common captcha schemes, it also applies to our approach. While an attacker may perform all gestures once and record the corresponding sensor data, the hardness of challenge recognition is essential for most captcha schemes. The security of text-based captchas especially relies on the assumption that the challenge is hard to identify. To harden a scheme against this attack vector, the way of presenting challenges could be randomly chosen to complicate automated detection.

Alternatively, an attacker could try to exploit the machine learning classification by replaying data of a different challenge than the presented. To test this behavior, we conducted a replay attack experiment choosing sensor measurements including accelerometer data and gyroscope data from the user study and attempt to solve a given challenge. We repeat this procedure 500 times to simulate such replay attacks under the same conditions like in our user study. Note that we do not use random sensor data but real-world sensor readings we obtained in our user study before. Leveraging completely random data may also be a possible scenario, but a less sophisticated attack. As a result, in two cases a sensor data replay of an original fishing challenge was misclassified as hammering leading to a false positive. One replay of a hammering gesture was accepted as solution to the keyhole challenge. As we already know, hammering tends to be misclassified (see Sect. 5), so diversifying this gestures may harden our system against this type of attack. All the other attacks – making a share of 99.4 % – were correctly rejected by our machine learning algorithm.

If a user's mobile is treated as untrusted or maliciously infected device it may falsify sensor data. This would enable to tamper user input used for solving the presented challenge. However, if malware is able to change the input – e. g., by manipulating system drivers requiring root access or by tampering the browser environment –, no captcha scheme can guarantee a correctly transferred input.

We designed our system in a way that the decision whether or not a captcha is solved successfully is made server-side. If it was made client-side like in game-based captchas [7], replay attacks might be more feasible as the attacker would only have to replay the decision instead of determining the challenge and provide previously recorded data for solving.

Finally, we focussed our studies on the general feasibility of sensor-based motion captchas and especially on usability aspects.

## 6.2    Limitations

Our work builds on existing captcha designs and lessons learned from previous studies. As we focussed on usability aspects of captchas, we assume that the implementations of our captcha schemes are secure and best-case implementations. A limitation of our prototype implementation is that it is a proof-of-concept and was first tested on users in the course of this study. Also the set of challenges our system provides is not sufficient to be resilient to replay attacks in practice.

For our comparative user study, we recruited participants around the university campus, hence our sample is biased towards this particular user group. Also, the participants solved the captcha puzzles in a controlled environment while an experimenter was present. We did not deploy our captcha scheme in the wild and therefore do not have data on the captcha performance in a real-world setting where users have to deal with environmental constraints. Also, we did not collect any evidence on whether the our scheme is applicable in all real-world situations, such as when a user performs a task on the phone while in a meeting. Due to the fact that sensor captchas require the user to move their device, they are potentially not applicable in some situations where a less obtrusive approach would be preferred by most users. We still believe that our results provide valuable insights to how users interact with the different types of captchas. We found that metrics like solving time, memorability, and error rate do not necessarily correspond to the perceived usefulness and user satisfaction.

## 7    Conclusion

In this work, we demonstrated that motion information from hardware sensors available in mobile devices can be used to tell computers and humans apart. Due to several limitations such as smaller screens and keyboards, traditional captcha schemes designed for desktop computers are often difficult to solve on smartphones, smartwatches, and other kinds of mobile devices. In order to tackle the challenges implied by these constraints, we designed a novel captcha scheme and evaluated it against already existing approaches found in the Internet ecosystem and in scientific literature. Our results indicate that sensor-based captchas are a suitable alternative when deployed on mobile devices as they perform well on usability metrics such as user satisfaction, accuracy, error rate, and solving time.

As our scheme requires users to perform gestures with a device in their hand, we plan to conduct a longitudinal field study to collect evidence on the feasibility of motion input in the wild (i. e., in situations where users are constrained by environmental conditions and unobtrusive interactions with their device) as well as involving wearables as input devices. For future work, we aim to iteratively improve the design and number of challenges. Although most gestures of user study were suitable, their movements need to be revised for everyday use and the entropy need to be increased by new gestures. Additionally, users would benefit from images or animations showing the challenge. Participants of our study agreed with Kluever et al. [13] that images and animations presenting a challenge are more enjoyable. Finally, conducting a long term study with participants using our mechanism regularly may confirm our findings on habituation effects.

# References

1. Inside ReCaptcha. https://github.com/neuroradiology/InsideReCaptcha. Accessed 01 Mar 2016
2. Buitinck, L., Louppe, G., Blondel, M., Pedregosa, F., Mueller, A., Grisel, O., Niculae, V., Prettenhofer, P., Gramfort, A., Grobler, J., Layton, R., VanderPlas, J., Joly, A., Holt, B., Varoquaux, G.: API design for machine learning software. In: ECML PKDD Workshop, pp. 108–122 (2013)
3. Bursztein, E., Aigrain, J., Moscicki, A., Mitchell, J.C.: The end is nigh: generic solving of text-based captchas. In: 8th USENIX Workshop on Offensive Technologies (WOOT 14) (2014)
4. Bursztein, E., Martin, M., Mitchell, J.: Text-based captcha strengths and weaknesses. In: Proceedings of the 18th ACM Conference on Computer and Communications Security, pp. 125–138. ACM (2011)
5. Bursztein, E., Moscicki, A., Fabry, C., Bethard, S., Mitchell, J.C., Jurafsky, D.: Easy does it: more usable captchas. In: Proceedings of the 32nd Annual ACM Conference on Human Factors in Computing Systems, pp. 2637–2646. ACM (2014)
6. Fidas, C.A., Voyiatzis, A.G., Avouris, N.M.: On the necessity of user-friendly captcha. In: Proceedings of the SIGCHI Conference on Human Factors in Computing Systems, pp. 2623–2626. ACM (2011)
7. Gao, S., Mohamed, M., Saxena, N., Zhang, C.: Emerging image game CAPTCHAs for resisting automated and human-solver relay attacks. In: 31st Annual Computer Security Applications Conference, ACSAC. ACM (2015)
8. Google Inc.: Introducing noCAPTCHA. http://goo.gl/x7N7qt. Accessed 01 Mar 2016
9. Google Inc.: reCAPTCHA – Easy on Humans Hard on Bots. https://www.google.com/recaptcha/intro/index.html. Accessed 01 Mar 2016
10. He, H.: HAR on Smartphones Using Various Classifiers (2013)
11. Hupperich, T., Maiorca, D., Kührer, M., Holz, T., Giacinto, G.: On the robustness of mobile device fingerprinting. In: Proceedings of the 31st Annual Computer Security Applications Conference, ACSAC. ACM (2015)
12. Jiang, N., Dogan, H.: A gesture-based captcha design supporting mobile devices. In: Proceedings of the 2015 British HCI Conference, pp. 202–207. ACM (2015)

13. Kluever, K.A., Zanibbi, R.: Balancing usability and security in a video captcha. In: 5th Symposium on Usable Privacy and Security, SOUPS. ACM (2009)
14. Reynaga, G., Chiasson, S.: The usability of captchas on smartphones. In: Security and Cryptography (SECRYPT) 2013 (2013)
15. Reynaga, G., Chiasson, S., van Oorschot, P.C.: Exploring the usability of captchas on smartphones: comparisons and recommendations. In: NDSS Workshop on Usable Security USEC 2015. NDSS (2015)
16. Sinofsky, S.: Supporting sensors in windows 8. http://blogs.msdn.com/b/b8/archive/2012/01/24/supporting-sensors-in-windows-8.aspx. Accessed 24 Apr 2016
17. Von Ahn, L., Blum, M., Hopper, N.J., Langford, J.: Captcha: using hard AI problems for security. In: Biham, E. (ed.) EUROCRYPT 2003. LNCS, vol. 2656, pp. 294–311. Springer, Heidelberg (2003)
18. Xu, Y., Reynaga, G., Chiasson, S., Frahm, J.M., Monrose, F., van Oorschot, P.: Security analysis and related usability of motion-based CAPTCHAs: decoding codewords in motion. IEEE TDSC **11**(5), 480–493 (2014)
19. Xu, Y., Reynaga, G., Chiasson, S., Frahm, J.M., Monrose, F., Van Oorschot, P.: Security and usability challenges of moving-object captchas: decoding codewords in motion. In: 21st USENIX Security Symposium, pp. 49–64 (2012)
20. Yan, J., Ahmad, E., Salah, A.: Usability of CAPTCHAs or usability issues in CAPTCHA design. In: Proceedings of the 4th Symposium on Usable Privacy and Security, pp. 44–52. ACM (2008)

# Runtime Integrity Checking for Exploit Mitigation on Lightweight Embedded Devices

Matthias Neugschwandtner[1,2](✉), Collin Mulliner[2],
William Robertson[2], and Engin Kirda[2]

[1] IBM Research Zurich, Rüschlikon, Switzerland
eug@zurich.ibm.com
[2] Northeastern University, Boston, USA

**Abstract.** Entering the age of the Internet of things, embedded devices
are everywhere. They are built using common hardware such as RISC-
based ARM and MIPS platforms, and lightweight open software components. Because of their limited resources, such systems often lack the
protection mechanisms that have been introduced to the desktop and
server world. In this paper, we present BINtegrity, a novel approach for
exploit mitigation that is specifically tailored towards embedded systems
that are based on the common RISC architecture. BINtegrity leverages
architectural features of RISC CPUs to extract a combination of static
and dynamic properties relevant to OS service requests from executables, and enforces them during runtime. Our technique borrows ideas
from several areas including system call monitoring, static analysis, and
code emulation, and combines them in a low-overhead fashion directly in
the operating system kernel. We implemented BINtegrity for the Linux
operating system. BINtegrity is practical, and restricts the ability of
attackers to exploit generic memory corruption vulnerabilities in COTS
binaries. In contrast to other approaches, BINtegrity does not require
access to source code, binary modification, or application specific configuration such as policies. Our evaluation demonstrates that BINtegrity
incurs a very low overhead – only 2 % on whole system performance,
– and shows that our approach mitigates both code injection and code
reuse attacks.

## 1 Introduction

Modern embedded devices are built using common hardware such as RISC-
based ARM and MIPS platforms and open software components such as Linux.
Thanks to their relatively high spread, constant uptime and common components, embedded devices have become an attractive target for attackers. Routers,
in particular, have been regularly abused as hosts for botnets in the past
years [3,18,19]. Similar to traditional desktop and server environments, embedded systems are attacked mostly through exploitation of software vulnerabilities
such as memory corruptions.

E. Kirda—Thanks to Secure Business Austria.

M. Franz and P. Papadimitratos (Eds.): TRUST 2016, LNCS 9824, pp. 60–81, 2016.
DOI: 10.1007/978-3-319-45572-3_4

Memory corruption vulnerabilities and attacks that exploit them remain one of the major issues in computer security [17, 22]. There is an ongoing arms race as defenders build new mitigations, and attackers discover ways to bypass these defenses. For example, Data Execution Prevention (DEP) was created to defend against code injection attacks. However, attack techniques such as generic code reuse (e.g., return-to-libc) and return-oriented-programming (ROP) were then developed that allowed attacks to be launched without the need to inject code. As a remedy for code reuse attacks, Address Space Layout Randomization (ASLR) was proposed. However, ASLR can also be bypassed if the attacker can leak addresses from a target process. Recent work [4, 13] started using hardware features to mitigate ROP attacks on desktop computers and servers running on the x86 platform.

Note that previous advancements on exploit mitigation focused mainly on desktop computers and servers, and have neglected securing embedded devices against software vulnerabilities. There is even a gap within the embedded systems world where CPUs for high-end applications contain security features such as DEP while the (cheaper and more common) low-end versions do not and thus leave the majority of embedded devices vulnerable to even simple attacks that have been eradicated in the desktop and server world.

This paper presents, BINtegrity, a practical, low-overhead system to mitigate memory corruption attacks that is specifically tailored towards embedded systems. Our approach aims to protect against state of the art attacks while still being practical. We specifically target platforms based on RISC architectures and systems where we only have access to program binaries.

The fundamental insight we gained from looking at previous work (Sect. 2) is the need to combine multiple techniques and aspects in a novel way to practically mitigate exploitation attempts. BINtegrity ensures that system calls are only invoked in a legitimate way by checking the runtime integrity of a program. Integrity means that the runtime state of a program has to be coherent with its binary executable. Coherence is given if the following conditions are met: (*i*) the invoked system call is actually used by the binary (*ii*) the system call arguments match the ones specified in the binary (*iii*) the observed call chain is reflected by the binary.

Our approach (Sects. 4 and 5) leverages several common design features found on all RISC CPUs to reconstruct part of the call chain and extract properties from a binary executable in an efficient way. To the best of our knowledge, we are the first to leverage these fundamental architectural features of RISC CPUs to build a security system. Our method is lightweight and allows our system to execute all operations at runtime.

BINtegrity is designed to be transparent to legacy binary code and works for arbitrary programs without requiring access to source code, prior training phases, or binary modifications. Note that previous approaches (e.g., intrusion detection based on system call monitoring and full control flow integrity) do not offer similar flexibility and are, thus, not practical for embedded systems. The only requirement for our approach is the presence of a kernel-based runtime component that – on-demand – extracts properties directly from program binaries and checks them against runtime behavior. Our technique guarantees that only system calls that are actually used by a program can ever be invoked by a corresponding process. BINtegrity enforces strong restrictions on *how* system calls can be invoked. When combined, these two features significantly reduce the attack surface available to code reuse attacks, and vastly limit the options for successful code injection attacks.

We built a prototype implementation (Sect. 6) of BINtegrity as an extension to the Linux operating system for the ARM and MIPS architectures and evaluated it on two common and popular off-the-shelf devices: a MIPS-based router, and an ARM-based smartphone. Our evaluation (Sect. 7) demonstrates that BINtegrity effectively mitigates code injection and code reuse attacks while incurring an extremely low performance overhead of only 2 %.

The paper makes the following contributions:

- We present a new practical method to efficiently extract and leverage process runtime information on RISC architectures. The extracted information is used to create and check properties against the program's binary file on disk.
- We propose a lightweight technique for restricting memory corruption attacks for COTS binary programs. Our system is the first to specifically target the RISC architecture leveraging some of its unique features.
- We developed a prototype implementation of this technique called BINtegrity as an extension to the Linux operating system for the ARM and MIPS architectures. The source code of BINtegrity is publicly available at www.bintegrity.org.
- We evaluated BINtegrity on two real-world systems, and show that our technique effectively defends against code injection and reuse attacks. We also show that it incurs a low performance overhead and, therefore, represents a practical, generic defense for embedded systems.

## 2   State of the Art

Mitigation of memory corruption attacks is a well-studied problem in literature. A wide range of approaches tackle the problem from various angles and at different stages during exploitation. Since preventing memory corruption in the first place is fairly difficult, most approaches focus on hindering an attacker in successful exploitation of a memory corruption vulnerability. After having corrupted the memory, the exploit has to redirect the control flow to either plain shellcode or a series of ROP gadgets. Basic defenses try to prevent shellcode injection or finding the desired code in memory while more advanced techniques such as Control Flow Integrity (CFI) aim at preventing malicious control flow redirection. Finally, an exploit has to invoke system calls to use functionality beyond pure computation. This fact led to a large body of research in the area of system call monitoring to detect malicious system calls.

*Basic Defenses.* Data execution prevention (DEP) [2], prohibits instruction fetch from data-only memory regions. While DEP proved to be an effective mitigation of straightforward code injection exploits, it relies on hardware support that is not necessarily available on embedded devices, depriving them of the benefits of this basic defense technique. Address space layout randomization (ASLR) places the text segments of a process at random memory locations. This probabilistic technique hinders the attacker in determining target addresses for code reuse attacks. The drawback of this technique is that unless the executable itself is compiled as a so-called PIE, randomization is limited to the dynamically linked libraries. In addition, the effectiveness of ASLR is limited on 32 bit platforms. Current deployments of ASLR also only perform randomization at program startup, which makes it less effective with long-running applications.

*Mitigating Code Pointer Corruption.* Code-Pointer Integrity [11] hides code pointers from being accessed by an attacker by storing them in a "safe", inaccessible memory region. While CPS, a relaxed variant of their solution, has relatively low overhead, it requires access to source code and is ineffective against attacks that do not require code pointer modifications [15].

*Control Flow Integrity.* The property of CFI [1] describes whether a program's execution flow has deviated from its intended path. Provided that it can be both measured and enforced to full extent, attacks based on control flow hijacking could be completely prevented. The problem with CFI is that solutions that can operate on binaries [25] have been shown to be too coarse grained to be effective [8]. Recent approaches use context-sensitive CFGs for higher precision [21], but achieve low-performance overhead only by relying on hardware features currently not present on embedded devices [6].

*System Call Monitoring and Policy Enforcement.* Early approaches on exploit mitigation entirely focused on the inspection of system call properties. Starting from writing policies for system call execution [14,20,23], these approaches eventually evolved to full-fledged mandatory access control systems such as SELinux[1] or AppArmor[2] that require a corresponding configuration effort.

A different line of work tries to detect anomalous system calls that would deviate from normal program behavior [7,10]. These systems rely on a runtime learning phase to model normal behavior. However, mimicry attacks [24] that hide their malicious system calls in a valid sequence or change the parameters to system calls have soon shown the limitations of such approaches. Recent work [16] claims to be resilient against mimicry attacks by working on extremely long execution paths.

---

[1] SELinux http://www.selinuxproject.org.
[2] AppArmor http://apparmor.net.

## 3   Threat Model

Our threat model covers memory corruption exploits such as buffer overflows on binary programs running on the device. We assume that the attacker has access to the target application, and that she can launch local or remote attacks against it. We note that in order to have an effect on the system, the attack code has to request operating system services at some point, i.e. perform a system call. Without being able to perform a system call, its possibilities are limited to pure computational tasks while operations like file or network I/O as well as process control are impossible.

In summary, we assume that:

– The operating system kernel and the underlying hardware are trusted, and have not been compromised by the attacker.
– The application binary on disk is trusted, and cannot be modified by the attacker. We assume the same holds true for the shared libraries used by the application.
– The process memory is *untrusted*, since the attacks we mitigate are based on memory corruption. We assume that the attacker might be able to execute a limited number of instructions without being detected. Also, we assume that the attacker has the ability to modify and overwrite arbitrary memory locations, including regions that contain executable code.

Based on our threat model, an attacker can manipulate the control flow of a process to the attacker's benefit through targeted memory manipulation. We do not cover memory corruption attacks that only change program data (e.g. file names in a write operation) and do not redirect control flow. This allows for two classes of attacks: *code injection* and *code reuse*. In case of code injection, the attacker introduces completely new code into memory and redirects control flow to it. Code reuse attacks on the other hand leverage code already existing in a process. They can operate at different levels of granularity, either targeting whole library functions (commonly referred to as "return-to-library") or small code chunks of the program that are stitched together (i.e., "gadgets").

## 4   Approach

Our goal is to create a *practical, efficient* and *effective* defense to mitigate exploitation of memory corruption attacks on RISC platforms for embedded systems.

We designed BINtegrity around the fact that code that has an effect on the system does so by making use of the operating system through system calls. The same principle is true for exploits. Hence, our approach is centered around system calls. Whenever a system call is invoked, we ensure that this is done in a legitimate way by checking the integrity of a program's runtime state. To this end, we extract several properties from the program's executable on disk that are relevant to the system call invocation at hand. We then compare these properties with the actual runtime state. In case the comparison succeeds, the program is allowed to perform the system call. Figure 1 shows a high-level overview of this process.

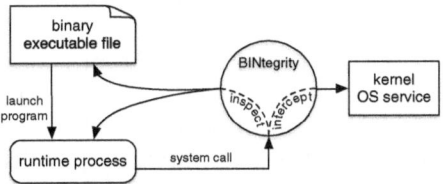

**Fig. 1.** A high-level overview of our approach. BINtegrity intercepts system calls and inspects both the runtime state and the binary executable image of a process. In case it detects a mismatch, the process is terminated.

The properties used in the comparison are extracted from the corresponding binary executable. Based on the origin of the last two items in the call stack before the system call invocation, we first check the existence of corresponding control flow instructions at the respective locations in the binary. We proceed by evaluating the targets of these control flow instructions and ensure that they match the call chain. As a next step, we compare the arguments of the system call with the instructions in the binary that precede the invocation and ensure that they do not contradict the actual arguments. Finally, we evaluate the import tables of the executables corresponding to the call stack, and ensure that all required import-export dependencies are indeed met. In case the runtime state's integrity has been violated, i.e. a mismatch is detected, the program is terminated.

The integrity checks based on these properties can effectively mitigate code injection and reuse exploits. To begin with, system call requests coming from injected code are predestined to originate from an unusual code location. Mitigating such attacks by checking code origins forces attacks to be constructed using only code reuse methods such as return-oriented-programming (ROP). In theory return-oriented programs are Turing-complete, but real-world ROP-based exploits are harder to construct since they require a significant higher skill level and more time. An attack that reuses existing code naturally comes from the right origin, but will have to differ in its control flow and function arguments to use system calls in a way that deviates from their regular invocation. By enforcing properties of the original code, BINtegrity restricts this most important step of code reuse attacks, thus effectively mitigating code reuse attacks.

For our design, we leverage common properties of RISC architectures. Specifically, we leverage the fixed-length instruction set to implement static analysis and code emulation in a very efficient way. Further, we utilize registers that are used during control flow transfer to efficiently construct a program's call chain. In contrast to related work, we do not rely on hardware features specific to certain processor families [4, 13, 26].

BINtegrity is transparent to existing applications, and can handle arbitrary binary programs. As a consequence, it does neither require access to source code nor binary instrumentation or any other pre-analysis stage. Finally, the on-demand fashion of BINtegrity ensures that it only causes overhead whenever a system call is actually invoked, making it applicable to existing device and software configurations.

Looking from a different angle, our approach provides functionality similar to policy enforcement systems such as SELinux and AppArmor. In contrast, though, BINtegrity provides this functionality implicitly as it does not require any policy configuration – restrictions are automatically derived from the binary.

## 5    Ensuring Runtime Integrity

In this section, we present how we check and enforce adherence of a program's runtime execution to its executable image with respect to system calls. The technique executes completely at runtime as a kernel extension for arbitrary program binaries on any RISC architecture that supports the equivalent of a link register. Ensuring the integrity comprises four steps: ($i$) identification of a *trusted application code base*; ($ii$) extraction of the *runtime state* at the time of a system call invocation; ($iii$) *invariant extraction* from the original executable image given the runtime state; and, *iv*) *invariant enforcement* to ensure integrity. Figure 2 depicts an overview of this technique. In the following, we describe each of its components.

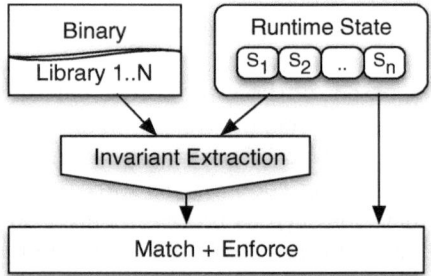

**Fig. 2.** Diagram depicting a high-level overview of ensuring runtime integrity. The key idea is to enforce security restrictions by matching a process' runtime state against invariants extracted from both the runtime state and facts from the corresponding executable image.

### 5.1    Trusted Application Code Base

The first requirement to ensure runtime integrity is to define a trusted application code base (TACB). This TACB refers to the program text of an application to be protected. The TACB is defined when a process is created by first allowing the runtime linker (e.g., ld.so on Linux) to load the executable image and any shared libraries it depends on into the process address space. At the point when control is transferred to the program itself, all mapped memory segments marked as executable – i.e., program text from the executable image and shared libraries – is taken as comprising the TACB.

## 5.2    Process Runtime State Extraction

Once a TACB has been established, the main part of the technique occurs at the time a system call is invoked. When a program invokes a system call and control transfers to the kernel, a runtime state is extracted from the process. This runtime state consists of the following information:

- The *return address* of the system call, which points to the successor instruction of the program call site. We denote it as $ret_{sc}$.
- The *link address*, which refers to the value that is stored in the LR (ARM) or RA (MIPS) register. This points to the successor instruction of the enclosing procedure call site before the system call invocation. We denoted it as $ret_{lr}$.
- The register that contains the system call number.
- All registers containing system call arguments.
- On MIPS, the jump target register.

Taken together, this state provides full information about the system call that is to be performed, its arguments, and a call chain of depth 2 in the program.

## 5.3    Invariant Extraction

Given a state, the next step of the technique is to extract invariants. These invariants are recovered by performing a lightweight static analysis of the program code referenced by the return and link addresses. We distinguish between two classes of actions performed during this procedure: (*i*) *code invariant extraction* refers to analysis of the executed instructions leading to the invocation of the system call, while (*ii*) *symbol invariant extraction* refers to resolution of the symbols for the last two entries in the program call chain.

*Code Invariant Extraction.* To derive control flow information and invariants, code invariant extraction uses a combination of static analysis and lightweight execution emulation. First, BINtegrity performs backwards disassembly from the offsets into the binary given by $ret_{(.)}$. Disassembly continues until either a control flow transfer instruction or a function prologue is found for the enclosing function $F(ret_{(.)})$. Starting from the point where backwards disassembly has stopped, BINtegrity emulates instruction execution. As an execution state, we use a lightweight abstraction consisting solely of registers. We note that on RISC architectures that traditionally provide a large number of registers, we did not find the lack of a memory abstraction to impair the effectiveness of this approach. Focusing on registers also limits the number of instructions that must be supported. Once the execution reaches $ret_{(.)}$, the current emulation state is collected; concrete values in this state are taken as state invariants. We also add the kind of control flow instruction that precedes $ret_{(.)}$, and attempt to derive its target in case it is an indirect call.

*Symbol Invariant Extraction.* Every program that uses an external library function needs some means to refer to that function. Executables refer to the functions they offer or use by means of symbols $S(F)$ encoded as simple character strings. The set of required functions are referred to as *imports $IM(E)$* of an executable $E$, while the set of available functions are the *exports $EX(E)$*. After loading the executable objects into memory, the linker matches all exports against the imports and resolves the symbols to actual addresses. Symbol invariant extraction resolves the symbol $S(F(ret_{(.)}))$ in the binary executable associated with $ret_{(.)}$ and looks up whether it is exported or imported by this binary. It then adds this information to the set of collected invariants.

## 5.4 Invariant Enforcement

Given the extracted runtime state and collected invariants, the final step is to check the collected invariants against the state. That is, the approach checks for contradictions that indicate violation of a safety condition. In particular, the technique checks the following properties:

1. Code provenance
2. Call chain integrity
3. System call argument integrity
4. Symbol integrity

For a runtime state to be accepted as safe, all of these properties need to be verified successfully. In the following, we describe each of them in detail.

*Code Provenance.* Code provenance enforces that only code from the TACB invokes system calls or their wrappers. Checks against the TACB are straightforward: both the system call *return address* as well as the *link address* have to point to code contained in the TACB to succeed – i.e., $ret_{sc} \in TACB \wedge ret_{lr} \in TACB$. The *link address* will either point to a location in the application binary, or to a location in one of the libraries that are used by the application. TACB checks are fast, as they do not require examination of the binary.

*Call Chain Integrity.* To check call chain integrity on $ret_{sc}$, we verify whether the preceding instruction $Pred(ret_{sc})$ is indeed an instruction that invokes a system call. Figure 3a shows the system call wrapper for the `write` system call, with the system call return address pointing to $ret_{sc}$. In addition, we compare the system call number that is stored in a dedicated register of the state to check whether the correct system call handler has been invoked. For call chain integrity on $ret_{lr}$, we check that $Pred(ret_{lr})$ is a branch instruction to begin with. Depending on whether the emulation step provides us with the target of the branch, we also ensure that only the corresponding function $F(ret_{sc})$ is called by $Pred(ret_{lr})$. In Fig. 3b this corresponds to the **bl** instruction calling the wrapper for **write**.

*Argument Integrity.* Argument integrity enforces that the parameters of a system call invocation from the runtime state matches the results of the emulation. Of course, this can only be enforced if invariants are recovered for those registers – that is, an assignment derived from a constant value must have been observed during emulation. A further requirement for performing this match is that the parameters are not changed by a system call wrapper $F(ret_{sc})$. Section 5.5 describes argument integrity in more detail.

*Symbol Integrity.* Symbol checks against the mapping established by the import and export tables of the code in the TACB prevent unauthorized use of functions. The intuition is that if a return address $ret_{(.)}$ falls into the address range of an exported function of an executable, the symbol of the function has to be imported by some other executable. More formally, given a call stack of depth $k$ with return addresses $ret_k, ret_{k-1}, \ldots$, two consecutive return addresses that point to different executables have to be linked by their exports, respectively imports.

$$\left. \begin{array}{c} ret_{k-j} \in E_a \wedge \\ ret_{k-j-1} \in E_b \wedge \\ E_a \neq E_b \end{array} \right\} \Rightarrow S(F(ret_{k-j})) \in \begin{array}{c} EX(E_a) \\ IM(E_b) \end{array} \tag{1}$$

Furthermore, if $ret_{k-j}$ is known and $S(F(ret_{k-j})$ is exported, but $ret_{k-j-1}$ is unknown, $S(F(ret_{k-j}))$ has to be imported by an executable that is not $E_a$.

$$S(F(ret_{k-j})) \in EX(E_a) \Rightarrow S(F(ret_{k-j})) \in IM(x), x \neq E_a \tag{2}$$

The runtime state provides us with $ret_{sc}$ and $ret_{lr}$, which are equivalent to the last two entries in the call chain before the system call invocations, $ret_k$ and $ret_{k-1}$. In the typical case, $ret_k$ will point to a system call wrapper in a library $E_a$, which is imported by and called from the main program executable $E_b$, with $ret_{k-1} \in E_b$. This allows us to enforce a strong match between two executables $E_a$ and $E_b$ based on Eq. 1. If this implication holds, we continue with inspecting $ret_{lr}$. If it points to the main executable, there is nothing more to check. However, $E_b$ might also be yet another library that provides some higher-level functionality. In case $F(ret_{lr})$ is exported as well, we can check it against the imports of all other mapped executables based on Eq. 2. In theory this could be an issue if $F(ret_{lr})$ is both exported and used internally by $E_b$, but not imported by any other executable. However, we did not encounter such a case in practice.

## 5.5   Function Call Arguments

A critical component of the execution emulation is deriving invariants on system call arguments. The specific idea is based on the observation that parameters to system calls are often composed of both static and dynamic values.

Dynamic values are often memory addresses, while static values often specify length values and flags. By extracting statically assigned arguments from the application binary and comparing them against observed values, it is possible to infer whether execution actually proceeded along the expected path through the binary to the system call invocation.

Figure 3 shows the instructions that are involved in a call to write. Figure 3a shows the system call wrapper in the libc (bionic) and Fig. 3b shows a call to write carried out in the application binary. The write system call takes three arguments. In our example, the first and third arguments are assigned statically, while the second argument is based on the content of another register. The second argument of write points to a buffer that holds the data that is to be written, while the first and third argument are a file descriptor (in this case, standard out) and the number of bytes that should be written.

During execution emulation we record static values for the first and third function argument because they were specified as constants in the executable image. These then become invariants that can be checked when that particular system call at that location in the executable is invoked. As a result no code reuse attack could abuse this write call to modify an arbitrary file. The second argument is marked as do-not-compare, as its value cannot be determined.

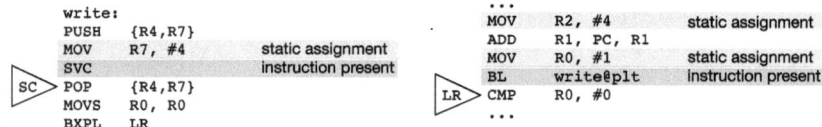

(a) System call wrapper for the write system call. From BINtegrity's point of view, the system call return address points to the successor of the system call instruction.

(b) Call to write in the application binary. From BINtegrity's point of view, the link return address points to the successor of the procedure call instruction.

**Fig. 3.** Example of critical code regions that are analyzed at runtime by our system.

Some system call wrappers perform more operations besides invoking the system call. If these additional operations include modifications of arguments passed from the application to the system call, our argument integrity check would fail. Our system takes this behavior into account, and analyzes the instructions preceding the system call instruction to determine if argument registers are modified. One example of a system call wrapper that modifies arguments before invoking the actual system call is the wrapper for open64 in uClibc compiled for MIPS. This wrapper modifies the second argument before invoking the system call by applying a bitmask to the second argument. In this case, our static analysis concludes that the second argument cannot be matched against the runtime state even if we are able to determine a statically assigned value in the application binary. The information about what arguments are modified by a system call wrapper is stored as part of the execution emulation procedure.

## 5.6   Dynamic Code Loading

While the TACB often does not change during execution, some processes do make use of interfaces like `dlopen` to dynamically load code. For this interface, an application can call `dlopen` to load a library, `dlsym` to resolve a function exported by that library, and invoke that function as any other. Internally, `dlopen` uses `mmap` and a small number of other system calls to load the library code into memory. BINtegrity handles dynamic code loading by tracking uses of `mmap`. Each time `mmap` is invoked by a process, our technique checks whether `dlopen` was called prior to calling `mmap`. This check is possible because of the invariant extraction mechanism we described above. If it is determined that `mmap` was executed on behalf of the `dlopen` function, the dynamically loaded library is added to the TACB.

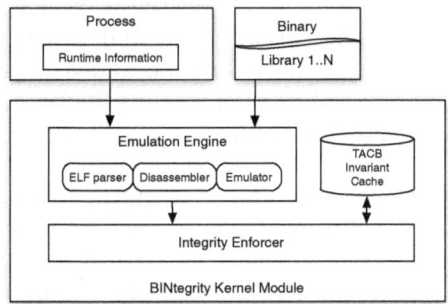

**Fig. 4.** Overview of the BINtegrity system.

# 6   The BINtegrity System

In this section, we present the BINtegrity prototype implementation, which is publicly available at www.bintegrity.org. BINtegrity is written as an extension to the Linux kernel, and is activated every time a process invokes a system call. The rationale behind this approach is that a program must always resort to services offered by the kernel to perform security critical actions such as file and network I/O, or to spawn new processes. Therefore, the system call boundary is an ideal location to collect process state information, and to enforce security policies.

## 6.1   Implementation

We developed BINtegrity as a loadable kernel module that is compatible with the Linux 3.x series. Since BINtegrity's operation has to be completely transparent to user mode programs, we do not introduce new techniques or modify existing ways to interact with the kernel. With support for different architectures in mind, we kept platform-specific code at a necessary minimum. That is, only components that require assembly-level support are platform-specific, and are easily ported to new architecture. Figure 4 shows an overview of BINtegrity's design, which is composed of the following.

*Emulation Engine.* The emulation engine contains all components that extract invariants from the program's runtime state and executable image on disk. This includes a parser for ELF files to infer symbol information, as well as a disassembler and instruction emulator for both the ARM and MIPS instruction set.

*TACB and Invariant Cache.* The per-process information BINtegrity maintains consists of the TACB and the invariant cache. The TACB keeps track of a process' memory pages that contain executable code, and serves as a reference when mapping addresses to binary files on the disk. The process of invariant extraction includes file parsing, disassembly, and instruction emulation – all relatively expensive operations. Therefore, we added a caching mechanism to our system that stores extracted invariants, thus limiting the number of actual extraction operations executed per process.

*Integrity Enforcer.* The integrity enforcer performs invariant checks and acts upon their result. It is a lightweight component, as it is the most frequently invoked part of BINtegrity. After checking code provenance, this component queries the invariant cache. If it does not contain the invariants for the current state, it invokes the emulation engine to produce them. Subsequently, the invariant checks are performed. In case any of them fail, the process is terminated.

*System Call Interposition.* System call interposition has been implemented as detour trampolines that invoke BINtegrity's main functionality before the system call handler is executed. BINtegrity intercepts execution immediately after the kernel's dispatcher has performed basic context-switch duties. As soon as all checks have passed successfully, the execution of the system call handler routine commences as usual. In case one of the checks fails, the task that issued the system call is terminated.

*Disassembler and Emulator.* The disassemblers in BINtegrity operate in a linear sweep fashion. They support the instruction sets of the MIPS32 and ARM architectures, including the Thumb and Thumb2 instruction sets. The instruction set supported by the code emulator is reduced to the subset that operates on registers and immediate values.

## 6.2   Integrity Checking Levels

In order to improve performance, BINtegrity only interposes on a subset of the system call interface. Some system calls are invoked more frequently and thus more sensitive to enforcement overhead. Furthermore, system calls such as `write` are used by virtually every program and therefore do not require symbol checks. In contrast, system calls such as `execve` are rarely called and thus heavyweight checking can be performed without an observable performance impact.

BINtegrity therefore implements three distinct integrity checking levels, with each level adding additional checks to the previous level. The lowest checking level is the TACB check. Here, we only perform code provenance checks for the *return address* and *link address* using our TACB. The second checking level adds the checks for call chain integrity as well as system call argument integrity. The third checking level adds symbol checking. Naturally, the checking level directly affects which invariants need to be extracted. For instance, if symbol checking is not enabled, less extensive file parsing has to be performed.

In our prototype, we selected 33 security critical system calls that are used by BINtegrity. Of these 33 system calls, we configured 11 for checking level 2, and 22 for checking level 3. Checking level 1 is not used by itself. The list of system calls we perform checks on are listed in Table 2. We note that assigning checking levels to system calls is the only configuration our systems needs.

### 6.3   Invariant Caching

Emulated execution requires a considerable effort: reading files from the disk, parsing ELF information, disassembling machine code, and actually emulating execution. These operations would incur a severe performance overhead if they were executed for every system call invocation. Therefore, we implemented a caching mechanism that stores extracted invariants such that they can be reused in an efficient way during enforcement.

In particular, invariants are cached for the *return address* and *link address* individually. Splitting up the caching improves memory efficiency as system call wrappers are likely called from many program locations, while the system calls themselves are usually only invoked from a comparably small number of locations.

## 7   Evaluation

In this section, we evaluate the security characteristics and performance of BINtegrity. For the performance, we both take a look at BINtegrity's internal workings as well as application-level benchmarks.

### 7.1   Security Evaluation

In the following, we describe why BINtegrity effectively defends against both code injection and code reuse attacks.

*Code Injection.* BINtegrity mitigates code injection attacks with early steps in the enforcement process. *Code provenance* checks of return and link addresses against the TACB prevent attackers from invoking system calls or their library wrappers from untrusted memory regions. *Call chain integrity* checking prevents the attacker from invoking system calls or library wrappers from memory areas that contain the application and library binary code, but have been overwritten with other code.

*Code Reuse.* BINtegrity restricts the capabilities of code reuse attacks from different angles. *Call chain integrity* checking defends against abusing indirect jump targets to invoke library wrappers. *System call argument integrity* checking prevents the attacker from manipulating arguments of code that invokes library wrappers with static function arguments. *Symbol integrity* checking prevents calls to library functions that are not used by the application binary itself.

Table 1 shows an overview of the attacks covered by BINtegrity compared to other defense mechanisms. While we do not prevent code reuse, we greatly limit code reuse attack capabilities to resort to library functions or system calls. In summary, we provide a more fine grained protection against code injection than both DEP (which relies on hardware features not available on many RISC platforms) as well as approaches that strictly enforce write-or-executable memory pages such as grsecurity[3]. In addition, we provide a restricted form of control flow integrity at the system call boundary without the need for recompilation of the source code or rewriting the binary, and can achieve this with less performance overhead.

**Table 1.** Attacks handled by various protection mechanisms. DS = data segment only, L = library only, G = gadget only

| Attack | DEP | ASLR | LBR | CFI | BINtegrity |
|---|---|---|---|---|---|
| Injection | ✓ (DS) | | | ✓ | ✓ |
| Reuse | | ✓ (L) | ✓ (G) | ✓ | (✓) |

*Case Studies.* OSVDB-86824 describes a buffer overflow vulnerability on the D-Link DIR-605L router. The router's web server that handles login data processes user-supplied POST data without sufficient checks. Hence, remote exploitation is possible, leading to full system compromise as the web server runs with root privileges. Proof-of-concept exploits [5] inject shellcode on the stack that spawns a remote shell. BINtegrity's code provenance checks detect and prohibit such behavior.

As another example, the recent CVE-2013-4659 describes multiple buffer overflow vulnerabilities on the ASUS RT-AC66U router. In particular, the ACSD service's command processing routine is vulnerable and, again, can be used

---

[3] GRsecurity http://grsecurity.net.

to completely compromise the router as the service runs with root privileges. Advanced proof-of-concept exploits [9] use code reuse techniques to first flush the data cache and subsequently invoke the `system` function in libc. As the latter function is not imported by the ACSD service binary, BINtegrity's symbol integrity enforcement effectively prevents this attack.

## 7.2 Performance

To evaluate BINtegrity's performance, we deployed it on a Samsung Galaxy Nexus (ARM) running Android and a Buffalo WZR-HP-G450H (MIPS) running OpenWRT. All results were obtained using the software (i.e., libraries and programs) as it was deployed on these systems. Table 2 lists all security-critical system calls with the integrity checking level that we used during the evaluation. For some less critical and frequently invoked system calls, we chose to only check for code integrity.

**Table 2.** Integrity checking levels used for the evaluation of BINtegrity.

| Checking level | System calls |
|---|---|
| Code integrity | creat, write(v), fork, sendfile, unlink, open, send, sendmsg, sendto |
| Code + Symbol integrity | execve, mmap, mprotect, ioctl, connect, socket, delete_module, init_module, symlink, chmod, chown, kill, reboot, accept, dup, pipe, socketpair, socketcall, ipc |

We first provide an insight into the cost of BINtegrity's internal operations before we evaluate BINtegrity's impact on these systems using benchmarks.

**Internal Operation.** The evaluation of BINtegrity's internal operation, specifically the invariant extraction, is based on both micro-benchmarks and real-world scenarios. For the micro-benchmark, we used lmbench's [12] system call latency measurement on the WZR-HP-G450H for the `write` system call. For the real-world scenarios, we picked two typical applications, a web server and a web browser, each running on a different system that is protected by BINtegrity. We had BINtegrity collect statistical data for each process running in the system. During a two-minute evaluation time period, the web server received two requests on a page, and the web browser loaded a single page to simulate a typical usage scenario.

*Invariant Extraction and Caching.* Invariant extraction is time consuming. It requires costly operations such as file parsing as well as disassembling and emulating code. To alleviate its impact on BINtegrity's performance, we attempted to reduce invariant extraction to a necessary minimum. On one hand, we allow

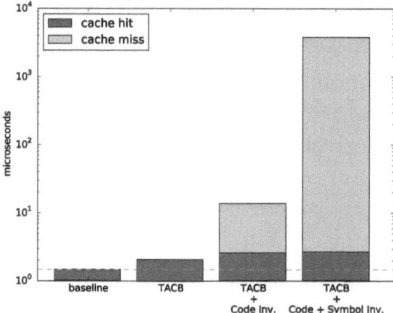

**Fig. 5.** Effect of invariant caching measured in system call latency. Once cached, checking invariants only incurs marginal overhead.

fine-tuning of BINtegrity to a specific platform's performance requirements by setting the checking levels. On the other hand, invariant extraction is only performed once per program state by caching its result. The drastic effect of caching is shown in Fig. 5. As can be seen, checks based on the results of the code invariants as well as both code and symbol invariants only add little additional overhead once they are cached.

*Frequency and Distribution of Invariant Extraction.* As mentioned before, the number of invariant extractions during program execution is critical to BINtegrity's performance. Table 3 shows how often code (for L2 checks) as well as code and symbol invariant extractions (for L3 checks) were performed. In spite of the complexity of the applications tested and the usage scenario, the numbers are quite low. In combination with caching, BINtegrity only has to carry out fewer than 100 performance-critical invariant extractions in each case.

**Table 3.** Number of invariant extractions executed for two typical applications. Args refers to the number of static argument assignments that were enforced.

| Invariant extractions | Code | Code + Symbol | Args |
|---|---|---|---|
| Android browser | 21 | 53 | 0 |
| Nginx web server | 19 | 24 | 10 |

Figure 6 shows the distribution of invariant extractions over time. We can see that a large number of extractions are executed at process startup, with the next spike occurring when the application first executes its main functionality. After a few seconds, the main code paths have been executed at least once. Hence, they do not require any further extractions during normal operation and, thus, unnecessary overhead is avoided.

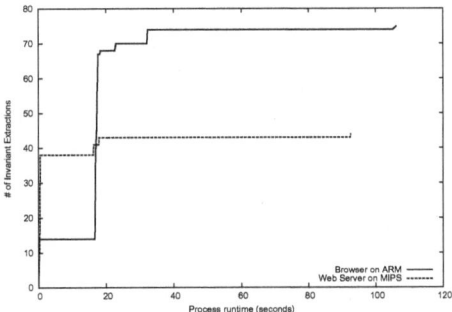

**Fig. 6.** Invariant extractions over the lifetime of two typical applications. For both applications, we show that extractions are executed at program startup and at the point where the application performs typical activity for the first time. After a code path has been executed once it causes no further extractions.

*Memory Overhead.* For each process in the system, BINtegrity reserves space to cache invariants for up to 257 code points. Every code point requires 40 bytes of storage for statistics that we use to measure our runtime performance. The memory requirement for this cache is 10 KB per process. During our evaluation, we never encountered more than 74 code points being cached for a process. The unused cache space provides enough storage to handle applications that require caching invariants for more code points while not wasting resources as the the overall memory usage is relatively small. We consider tuning the size of the cache as part of specializing BINtegrity for a specific platform. We further require a small amount of memory to store our per process TACB. The memory requirement for each TACB entry is 16 bytes. During our evaluation, we never encountered a process with more than 100 entries stored in its TACB, thus staying below 2 KB per process. In total, BINtegrity adds a memory overhead of around 12 KB for each process. This memory overhead is negligible if compared with the memory required through the use of shared libraries, some of which easily occupy a few hundred kilobytes.

**Benchmarks.** To measure BINtegrity's impact on system performance, we ran various benchmarks covering both specific metrics (e.g., disk I/O) and overall performance.

*Disk I/O.* For the disk I/O performance evaluation, we used Bonnie++, configured to use a filesize of 500 MB for access, and 16,348 files for creation/deletion benchmarks. Being platform independent, we ran it on both ARM and MIPS. For the ARM implementation, the worst-case overhead is 10 % for random seeks. On MIPS, the worst-case overhead is 20 % for block write operations.

*Network I/O.* For the WZR-HP-G450H, we used the Apache benchmark from a separate computer on the LAN to request a 128 KB document. The document was served by the default *nginx* installation running on the router. The average overhead measured over 1000 requests was 2.03 %.

*Whole-System Performance.* On the Galaxy Nexus Android phone, we used the popular AnTuTu benchmark[4] to measure performance overhead introduced by BINtegrity. The AnTuTu benchmark measures a variety of system components such as the Android runtime and the I/O subsystem. The benchmark result shows that BINtegrity only incurs an overhead of 1.2 % compared to the baseline.

# 8    Discussion and Limitations

In general, BINtegrity does not prevent code execution from arbitrary memory locations, but restricts the invocation of kernel services. Hence, BINtegrity mitigates attacks that interact with the operating system, but does not prevent attacks against the application logic itself. In the following, we discuss both how BINtegrity deals with certain code constructs and which aspects could hamper its effectiveness.

*Call Stack Depth.* The call stack BINtegrity relies on to extract data from the binary is only two levels deep. Undoubtedly, a deeper call stack would enable us to perform more thorough integrity checks. However, a deeper call stack would require keeping track of return addresses in the process' memory, which both contradicts our threat model and in addition slows down analysis.

A study of two lightweight C library implementations that are popular in the embedded world, uClibc and bionic, shows that only a relatively small subset of the library functions use indirection, i.e. call another function before invoking the system call (Table 4). Besides, these indirections can be removed entirely by recompiling the C library with inlining.

*Forward Emulation.* BINtegrity's effectiveness is determined by the information provided by the forward emulation. Some system call wrappers will degrade information on system call arguments by performing operations that our register-based code emulation cannot track. While for uClibc, the number of wrappers that modify might seem high, we note that only five out of them are security-critical. We plan to address this issue in future work by enhancing our static analysis with a lightweight memory model.

*Forging the Link Address.* An attacker who is aware of BINtegrity could try to set $ret_{lr}$ to another value. However, only valid values would pass all steps of the invariant enforcement, i.e. stemming from a correct origin, adhering to call chain integrity and argument integrity and be imported based on the rules of symbol integrity. If the attacker succeeds in finding such an address, she would lose control flow control after the function returns and thus be limited to a single function invocation.

---

[4] AnTuTu https://play.google.com/store/apps/details?id=com.antutu.ABenchMark.

**Table 4.** Characteristics of C library system call wrappers that degrade the detail level of the extracted invariants. The numbers were derived from the binaries we found on Android (Bionic) and OpenWRT (uClibc). Indirections can be reduced to zero by recompiling the library.

| System call wrappers | Bionic | uClibc |
|---|---|---|
| Total | 194 | 243 |
| Using indirections | 71 | 31 |
| Modifying arguments | 1 | 69 |

*Just-In-Time Compilation.* Just-In-Time (JIT) compilation, best known for speeding up Javascript and ActionScript, is rarely found on embedded devices. Although, in theory, JIT compiled code directly violates BINtegrity's fundamental idea of only executing code that is present in the binary on disk, BINtegrity does not break JIT. The reason is that JIT compiled code never directly interacts with the standard C library. At the same time, BINtegrity prevents JIT-ed code from direct interaction with the standard C library or the system call interface.

## 9  Conclusions

In this paper, we presented BINtegrity, a novel approach to exploit mitigation that is specifically tailored towards embedded systems that are based on common RISC architectures. BINtegrity works by extracting a combination of static and dynamic properties relevant to OS service requests from executables and enforcing them during runtime.

We leverage common properties of the RISC architecture to design and build an exploit mitigation system that is practical and low-overhead and thus lends itself specifically for the use in systems with limited resources.

## References

1. Abadi, M., Budiu, M., Erlingsson, U., Ligatti, J.: Control-flow integrity. In: ACM Conference on Computer and Communications Security (CCS) (2005)
2. Andersen, S., Abella, V.: Data Execution Prevention. Changes to Functionality in Microsoft Windows XP Service Pack 2, Part 3: Memory Protection Technologies (2004)
3. Baume, T.: Netcomm NB5 Botnet Psyb0t. http://baume.id.au/psyb0t/PSYB0T. pdf

4. Cheng, Y., Zhou, Z., Yu, M., Ding, X., Deng, R.: ROPecker: a generic and practical approach for defending against ROP attacks. In: Network and Distributed System Security Symposium (NDSS) (2013)
5. Heffner, C.: OSVDB 86824 Exploit. http://www.devttys0.com/wp-content/uploads/2012/10/dir605l_exploit.txt
6. Davi, L., Hanreich, M., Paul, D., Sadeghi, A.R., Koeberl, P., Sullivan, D., Arias, O., Jin, Y.: HAFIX: Hardware-assisted flow integrity extension. In: Proceedings of the Annual Design Automation Conference (2015)
7. Feng, H.H., Kolesnikov, O.M., Fogla, P., Lee, W., Gong, W.: Anomaly detection using call stack information. In: IEEE Symposium on Security and Privacy (Oakland) (2003)
8. Goektas, E., Athanasopoulos, E., Bos, H., Portokalidis, G.: Out of control: overcoming control-flow integrity. In: IEEE Symposium on Security and Privacy (Oakland) (2014)
9. Holcomb, J.: CVE-2013-465 Exploit. http://www.exploit-db.com/exploits/27133/
10. Kruegel, C., Mutz, D., Valeur, F., Vigna, G.: On the detection of anomalous system call arguments. In: Snekkenes, E., Gollmann, D. (eds.) ESORICS 2003. LNCS, vol. 2808, pp. 326–343. Springer, Heidelberg (2003)
11. Kuznetsov, V., Szekeres, L., Payer, M., Candea, G., Sekar, R., Song, D.: Code-pointer integrity. In: USENIX Symposium on Operating Systems Design and Implementation (OSDI) (2014)
12. McVoy, L., Staelin, C.: Lmbench: portable tools for performance analysis. In: USENIX Annual Technical Conference (USENIX ATC) (1996)
13. Pappas, V., Polychronakis, M., Keromytis, A.D.: Transparent ROP exploit mitigation using indirect branch tracing. In: USENIX Security Symposium (USENIX SEC) (2013)
14. Provos, N.: Improving host security with system call policies. In: USENIX Security Symposium (USENIX SEC) (2003)
15. Schuster, F., Tendyck, T., Liebchen, C., Davi, L., Sadeghi, A.R., Holz, T.: Counterfeit object-oriented programming: on the difficulty of preventing code reuse attacks in C++ applications. In: IEEE Symposium on Security and Privacy (Oakland) (2015)
16. Shu, X., Yao, D., Ramakrishnan, N.: Unearthing stealthy program attacks buried in extremely long execution paths. In: ACM SIGSAC Conference on Computer and Communications Security (CCS) (2015)
17. Szekeres, L., Payer, M., Wei, T., Song, D.: SoK: eternal war in memory. In: IEEE Symposium on Security and Privacy (Oakland) (2013)
18. Cymru, T.: SOHO Pharming (2014). https://www.team-cymru.com/ReadingRoom/Whitepapers/2013/TeamCymruSOHOPharming.pdf
19. Ullrich, J.: Linksys Worm The Moon (2014). https://isc.sans.edu/forums/diary/Linksys+Worm+TheMoon+Summary+What+we+know+so+far/17633
20. Vaughan, J.A., Hilton, A.D.: Paladin: Helping Programs Help Themselves with Internal System Call Interposition (2010)
21. van der Veen, V., Andriesse, D., Göktaş, E., Gras, B., Sambuc, L., Slowinska, A., Bos, H., Giuffrida, C.: Practical context-sensitive CFI. In: ACM Conference on Computer and Communications Security (CCS) (2015)
22. van der Veen, V., dutt-Sharma, N., Cavallaro, L., Bos, H.: Memory errors: the past, the present, and the future. In: Balzarotti, D., Stolfo, S.J., Cova, M. (eds.) RAID 2012. LNCS, vol. 7462, pp. 86–106. Springer, Heidelberg (2012)
23. Wagner, D., Dean, D.: Intrusion detection via static analysis. In: IEEE Symposium on Security and Privacy (Oakland) (2001)

24. Wagner, D., Soto, P.: Mimicry attacks on host-based intrusion detection systems. In: ACM Conference on Computer and Communications Security (CCS) (2002)
25. Zhang, M., Sekar, R.: Control flow integrity for COTS binaries. In: USENIX Security Symposium (USENIX SEC) (2013)
26. Zhou, Y., Wang, X., Chen, Y., Wang, Z.: ARMlock: hardware-based fault isolation for ARM. In: ACM Conference on Computer and Communications Security (CCS), November 2014

# Controversy in Trust Networks

Paolo Zicari, Roberto Interdonato, Diego Perna, Andrea Tagarelli[✉],
and Sergio Greco

DIMES, University of Calabria, Arcavacata di Rende, CS, Italy
{p.zicari,r.interdonato,d.perna,tagarelli,greco}@dimes.unical.it

**Abstract.** Given the increasing volume and impact of online social
interactions in various aspects of life, inferring how a user should be
trusted becomes a matter of crucial importance, which can strongly bias
any decision process. Existing trust inference algorithms are based on
the propagation and aggregation of trust values. However, trust opinions
are subjective and can be very different from one user to another. Consequently, inferred trust values can lose significance or even be unavailable
if there is a strong disagreement among the original values. In this work,
we discuss the trust controversy problem. We analyze to what extent
existing trust inference algorithms are robust with respect to controversial situations, and propose a novel trust controversy measure to support trust inference in controversial cases. Experimental results on real
world datasets demonstrate that controversial cases should be explicitly
taken into account and that the controversy level of inferred trust values
is highly related to the prediction error. Our trust controversy measure
can serve as an integrated and unsupervised estimator for trust inference
accuracy.

## 1 Introduction

The volume and importance of online social interactions have followed a strong
increasing trend in the last few years. Sharing of knowledge, personal information, experiences and opinions is nowadays a natural act, which occurs in several
everyday situations. Since they allow easy access to a massive crowd, online
social platforms are being exploited by individuals and companies for different
purposes, including marketing and political campaigns, personnel recruitment
and selection, public administration services, real-time support to customers
and so on. In all these contexts, the concept of trust becomes of crucial importance, since it implies interaction with and/or spreading of information towards
a large number of users. These may not be directly known by the initiator of the
process, which naturally has no control over the spreading process. From this
perspective, limiting the access to information and services to a subset of *trusted*
users is fundamental, e.g., for security reasons and brand protection purposes.

Several solutions have been proposed to address trust-related tasks in online
social contexts, such as trust ranking [3,11,15], trust prediction [6,7] and trust
inference [2,4]. Online social networks can be easily managed as trust networks,

© Springer International Publishing Switzerland 2016
M. Franz and P. Papadimitratos (Eds.): TRUST 2016, LNCS 9824, pp. 82–100, 2016.
DOI: 10.1007/978-3-319-45572-3_5

where trust edges can be retrieved directly or indirectly from users relation-ships [5,10]. In this context, trust inference methods are conceived to determine the level of trust between any pair of users not directly linked to each other in the network, which, in most real world situations, represents the great major-ity of all possible couples in a network. The mechanism behind trust inference algorithms is generally based on the propagation and aggregation of the original trust scores (i.e., trust values explicitly assigned by the users). However, trust is naturally subjective, because it is driven by personal experiences, prejudice, misunderstandings or circumstantial events. Consequently, trust values assigned to a specific target user can be very different from one to another, leading to inferred trust values which can lose significance or even be unavailable if there is a strong disagreement among the original values.

This paper focuses on the concept of *controversy* in trust networks. Whenever there is a strong disagreement among users, a controversial condition can arise and the trust inference process can become ambiguous. In literature [8,13,14], there have been some attempts to define controversy, but they have focused on the concept of controversial user rather than on the definition of controversial trust, i.e., defining as controversial a user who is judged by other users in very diverse ways. Though starting from similar observations, these works do not provide any technique to measure the level of controversy of an inferred trust value, which hence remains an open problem.

In this paper, we propose a novel measure for evaluating the level of contro-versy of an inferred trust. Our proposal is supported by an extensive analysis over existing trust inference methods [2,4], aimed at showing how these algorithms are not robust to controversial cases. In our setting, the concept of controversy in trust networks is related to the concept of reliability of trust inference, and radi-cally differs from tasks such as identification of controversial users, controversial items or controversial reviews. The proposed controversial score is designed to be a qualifier for the trust value inferred for a specific pair of nodes in a trust net-work, indicating how much agreement or disagreement is hidden in the inferred trust, under the hypothesis that high levels of controversy in the inferred trust values can make these values ambiguous and unreliable.

The rest of the paper is organized as follows. Section 2 overviews related work, Sect. 3 discusses several examples of controversial situation in trust networks, Sect. 4 presents our novel trust controversy measure, Sect. 5 presents experi-mental evaluation, Sect. 6 concludes the paper and provides pointers for future research.

## 2   Related Work

We organize discussion on related work into two parts: the first is devoted to trust inference algorithms, the second concerns existing definitions of controversy in trust contexts.

## 2.1   Trust Inference Algorithms

Trust inference is a well known task in the context of network analysis, and a variety of algorithms have been proposed in literature [12]. Trust inference algorithms are usually classified into two main categories: *local* trust methods and *global* trust methods. Given a trust network, local trust methods infer the trust from a source node to a sink node, i.e., the inferred local trust can be considered as an *edge* feature, since it represents the personalized opinion of one user with respect to another user. Conversely, global methods calculate a trust score (also referred to as *reputation*) for each user, i.e., the inferred trust is a *user* feature, which can be used to produce a trust-oriented global ranking of the users. In this work, we will focus on the analysis of local trust inference algorithms, since their personalized nature leads to more intuitive controversial cases, as we will discuss in Sect. 3. The analysis of controversial cases in global trust ranking scenarios is left as future work.

Local trust inference algorithms compute the trust by considering the different paths from a source node to a sink node, by defining a rule for trust propagation and a rule for aggregating the propagated trust values through the different available trust paths. In order to analyze the effects of controversy, two state-of-the-art local trust inference algorithms are taken as case in point: *TidalTrust* [2] and *TISoN* [4].

*TidalTrust* [2] is a local trust inference algorithm in which the trust between non-adjacent nodes is inferred by considering only shortest paths through trusted neighbors. Trust values are determined in the discrete range [0..10], where a trust value of zero means that no information is available about a specific trust relation. The trust from a source node to a sink node is calculated by calling a recursive trust function on the trusted neighbors, which terminates when the sink is reached. When the trust is back propagated to the source, it is averaged and rounded among the different trusted paths. As a refinement step, *TidalTrust* can filter paths based on a fixed edge-weight threshold (*thres*). The choice of selecting the shortest path derives from the hypothesis that reliability of trust values progressively decays proportionally to their distance from the source node. *TidalTrust* calculates the inferred trust $IT(X,Y)$ from the source node $X$ to the sink node $Y$ as in Eq. 1, where the trust is propagated and averaged only through the adjacent nodes which can effectively reach the sink.

$$IT(X,Y) = \frac{\sum_{\substack{K \in adj(X) \\ T(X,K) > thres}} T(X,K) \times T(K,Y)}{\sum_{\substack{K \in adj(X) \\ T(X,K) > thres}} T(X,K)} \tag{1}$$

*TISoN* (Trust Inference within online Social Networks) local trust inference model is proposed in [4]. In the Trust Paths Searching (*TPS*) step, a selection of the trust paths from a source node to a sink node is performed with respect to two criteria: the maximum allowed depth of the path, and the minimum threshold level allowed for the trust edges in the path. Among the *TPS* subset of selected paths, only the most trustable path (*MTP*) is used by a trust inference measure called $TIM$ to compute the inferred trust. The $MTP$ path is the strongest path, with the strength defined as a function of the path average (the average of the trust edges in the path), the path variance of the trust edges w.r.t. the average, and the path weight measured as the fraction between the length of the shortest path in $TPS$ and the length of the current path. Finally, the inferred trust is computed as a product of the direct trust obtained by the sink and the strength of $MTP$.

## 2.2   Controversy in Trust Contexts

Our work is, to the best of our knowledge, the first to address the problem of measuring the controversy level of inferred local trust values. Indeed, a couple of works exist which addresses the problem of controversy in trust contexts from perspectives different than ours.

In [8], a controversial user is defined as a user that is judged by others users in very different ways. In order to measure the controversy of a user in a trust network, only the in-neighbors of the user are taken into consideration. In this way, a single label of controversy value is assigned to each user. Two different definitions of controversy are given. In the first one, the controversy level of a user is defined as the number of users who disagree with the majority in issuing a statement about that user. Formally the controversy level is defined as the minimum between the number of trust evaluations and the number of distrust evaluations. In the second definition, a controversy percentage is calculated as the difference in the number of trust and distrust judgments with respect to the total number of judgments.

In [13], controversy was analyzed in the context of recommender systems, focusing on the formalization of the concept of Controversial Item (CI), i.e., an item which received a variety of high and low scores from its reviewing users. In order to identify CIs, the authors combine standard deviation of the ratings with a *level-of-disagreement* measure. This measure determines how often adjacent disagreeing scores in a certain time window appear w.r.t. the total number of received ratings, based on the intuition that different scores that are close to each other reflect less disagreement than different scores that are on opposite ends of the window. The authors then compare the performance of collaborative filtering and trust-enhanced recommendation algorithms for controversial and random items, also testing a combination of existing techniques in order to enhance coverage and accuracy performances. The same authors extended their work in [14], performing a similar analysis w.r.t. the concept of Controversial Review (CR), i.e., reviews which receive contrasting helpfulness rating.

It is straightforward to see that the existing definitions of controversy above discussed are both totally different from ours, and address totally different tasks. Indeed, the definition of controversy given in [8] is considered as a qualifier of the single user and not of the inferred trust evaluation (i.e., the task is the identification of *controversial users* and not of *controversial trust values*, as in our case). Moreover, it is based on a binary classification of statements in trust and distrust values (i.e., signed networks), while we take into account trust values in the continuous range [0,1]. The comparative studies in [13,14] are strictly tied to the specific domain of recommender systems, therefore the proposed level-of-disagreement measure is based on hypotheses which do not hold in our domain (e.g., closeness of disagreeing ratings of an item/review), making its use in our analysis inappropriate.

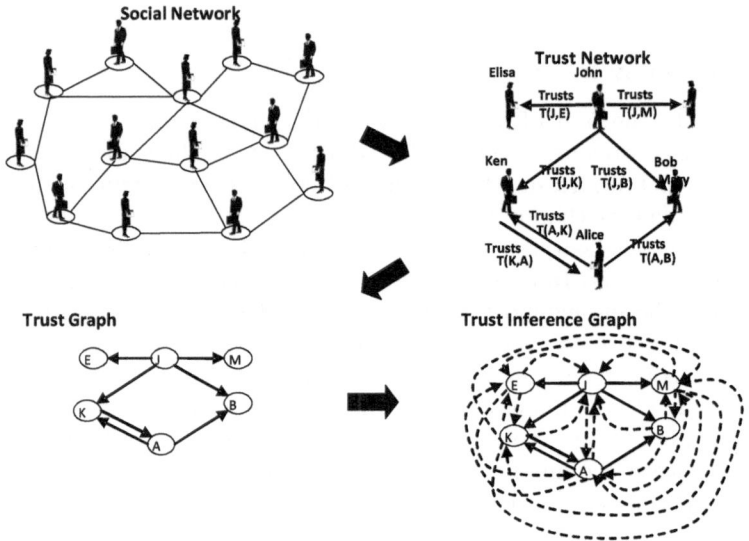

**Fig. 1.** Social network, trust network, trust graph

## 3   Controversy in Trust Networks

### 3.1   Modeling Trust Networks

Figure 1 shows the typical steps performed for modeling a trust network. The trust network extracted from the original social network can be represented as a directed graph $G = \langle V, E, T \rangle$, consisting of a set $V$ of $n$ nodes (users), a set of links (edges) that represent relations between couples of users, and the weighting function $T : E \rightarrow R$ for specifying the trust level corresponding to each edge. Then the trust network can be mathematically expressed as a square matrix $\mathbf{T}$ of size $n \times n$, here called trust matrix, where each generic element $T(i, j)$ is the level of trust from node $i$ to node $j$, with $i, j \in V$. Here we consider real trust values in the range $[0, 1]$, i.e., $T(i, j) \in [0, 1]$ $\forall (i, j) \in E$. $T(i, j) = 1$ means that the user $i$ fully trusts the user $j$, while $T(i, j) = 0$ means lack of trust.

A generic trust inference algorithm is represented by the function $IT(i, j)$ reported in Eq. 2. A trust inference algorithm calculates a trust value $t \in [0, 1]$ between two generic nodes $i$ and $j$ not directly connected in the trust network

$((i,j) \notin E)$. When a trust edge between nodes $i$ and $j$ exists in the network, the inferred trust assumes the same value of the trust weight, i.e., $IT(i,j) = T(i,j) \ \forall \, (i,j) \in E$. If there are no paths connecting the source node with the sink node, it is not possible to infer the trust, thus a placeholder value (e.g., $-1$) can be assigned in this case. Formally, $IT(i,j)$ is defined as:

$$IT(i,j) = \begin{cases} T(i,j) & \text{if} (i,j) \in E \\ -1 & \text{if there are no paths from } i \text{ to } j \\ t \in [0,1] & \text{if } (i,j) \notin E \end{cases} \qquad (2)$$

## 3.2  Controversial Cases in Trust Networks

A detailed analysis of controversial situations is here reported by presenting a set of controversy cases that can be originated by disagreement in trust networks. We will first describe a basic controversial situation, namely the *ToTrustOrNot-ToTrust* case, which serves as a simple introduction to the problem of controversy in trust networks. We will then discuss an *Asymmetric Controversy* case, which extends the previous one by taking into account paths of different length, leveraging the fact that considering the shortest paths as the most reliable may lead to ambiguous results in presence of controversial cases. Finally, we will discuss how taking into account trust values in the continuous range [0,1] leads to even more complex cases. We conclude with a discussion on how these controversial cases motivate the necessity of defining a clear and precise measure for determining the controversy level when inferring trust values in social networks.

**The *ToTrustOrNotToTrust* Case.** The basic controversial trust situation is here called *ToTrustOrNotToTrust* case. This case is shown in Fig. 2(a), where a node $A$ fully trusts both nodes $B$ and $C$ ($T(A,B) = T(A,C) = 1$), but nodes $B$ and $C$ have opposite trust opinions about node $Z$ ($T(B,Z) = 1$ and $T(C,Z) = 0$). The question: "Should $A$ trust $Z$ or should not?" remains an open problem if the answer depends solely on the recommendations from B and C. In any case, a reasonable average inferred trust value $IT(A,Z) = 0.5$ cannot be useful to take any

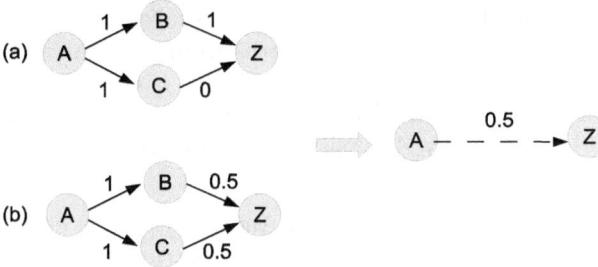

**Fig. 2.** The *ToTrustOrNotToTrust* case (a) and an uncontroversial case (b) which leads to the same trust inference value

decision, because it results from the aggregation of two opposite trust values. More-over, the inferred trust value would not be representative of the hidden controversial situation. In fact, the same value of trust inference could be derived in absolutely uncontroversial conditions, as in the example reported in Fig. 2(b), where both $B$ and $C$ trust $Z$ with the same trust level equal to 0.5 ($T(B, Z) = T(C, Z) = 0.5$). The two situations are completely different: in the first case there are two opposite opinions about the user $Z$ that reflect different experiences, while in the second case, the opinions by $B$ and $C$ are exactly the same, thus the inferred trust should be considered more significant, based on the fact that both $B$ and $C$ agree about $Z$.

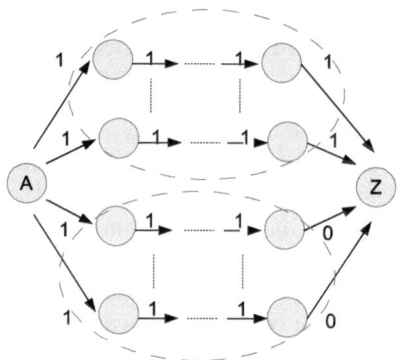

**Fig. 3.** The generalized balanced *ToTrustOrNotToTrust* case

This example let us consider that the inferred trust should be considered as more reliable when there is agreement among the recommender users, while ambiguity can be originated by disagreement. In the *ToTrustOrNotToTrust* case, node $A$ would not be able to infer any precise information about the trustworthiness of user $Z$, being only the opinions by user $B$ and user $C$ available. In the uncontroversial case, it would be trivial for user $A$ to infer that user $Z$ is *moderately* trustworthy (i.e., it has a trust value of 0.5 in the range [0,1]).

The basic example shown in the *ToTrustOrNotToTrust* case can be general-ized to take into account an arbitrary number of paths of any length between the source node $A$ and the sink node $Z$. The generalized case reported in Fig. 3 depicts a situation where several longer paths from the source $A$ to the sink $Z$ are grouped into two balanced opposite factions. It is easy to see that, as in the simple version of the *ToTrustOrNotToTrust* case, the ambiguity about whether or not $Z$ should be trusted by $A$ persists, as long as trust is equally propagated from the predecessors of $Z$ up to node $A$.

**The *Asymmetric Controversy* Case.** Another example of controversial sit-uation is shown in Fig. 4(a), namely the *Asymmetric Controversy* case (where the "asymmetry" refers to the presence of paths of different length). In this case, two opposite controversial paths exist from $A$ to $Z$, with different length. Since trust inference algorithms usually assume the shortest paths to be more reliable [2,4], in most cases only the trust opinion by node $B$ will be considered. As a consequence, $A$ will fully trust $Z$, even if there is a strong opposition from other trusted nodes.

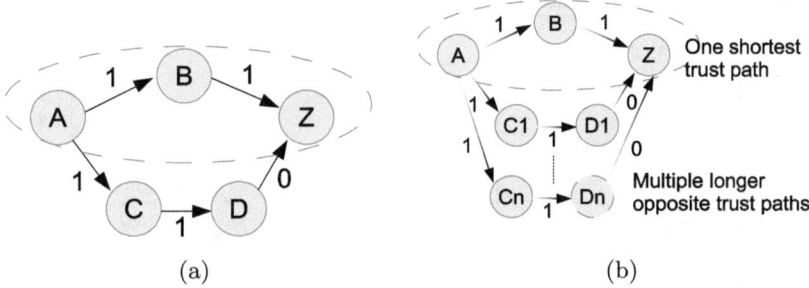

(a)                                                        (b)

**Fig. 4.** The *Asymmetric Controversy* case in its standard (a) and unbalanced (b) variants.

The problem is even more evident in the unbalanced variant of the case shown in Fig. 4(b). In this example, there is a majority of longer paths in contrast with a single shortest path. It is straightforward to note that if the trust decision is based solely on the shortest path, the presence of a majority of longer paths leading to opposite conclusions is completely neglected.

**Controversy in the Continuous Trust Range.** In real-world scenarios, unfolding of controversial situations may become critical, since often a user trusts his/her neighbors at different levels (i.e., the finer the scale, the greater the complexity of controversial situations to be managed).

Consider the trust network in Fig. 5(a), where trust values are in the continuous range [0,1]. The difference between the trust values $T(A, C)$ and $T(A, B)$ has a strong bias on the controversy level of the inferred trust $T(A, Z)$, i.e., the greater the gap between $T(A, C)$ and $T(A, B)$, the lower should be the level of controversy of $T(A, Z)$, since paths containing low trust values should have lower influence in the trust inference process.

A first naive solution to ease the interpretation of these situations corresponds to the introduction of a *trust threshold th*, above which a certain user can be considered trustworthy. Nevertheless, controversial situation can still arise. Take as case in point the networks in Fig. 5(b), where trust statements below the trust threshold $th$ are indicated with symbol $\leq th$. If the number of low trusted nodes with agreeing trust statements about node $Z$ increases, the inferred trust value $T(A, Z)$ can be considered more and more controversial, if it is based solely on the value of $T(B, Z)$ (as $B$ is the only node which receives a trust statement above $th$ by $A$).

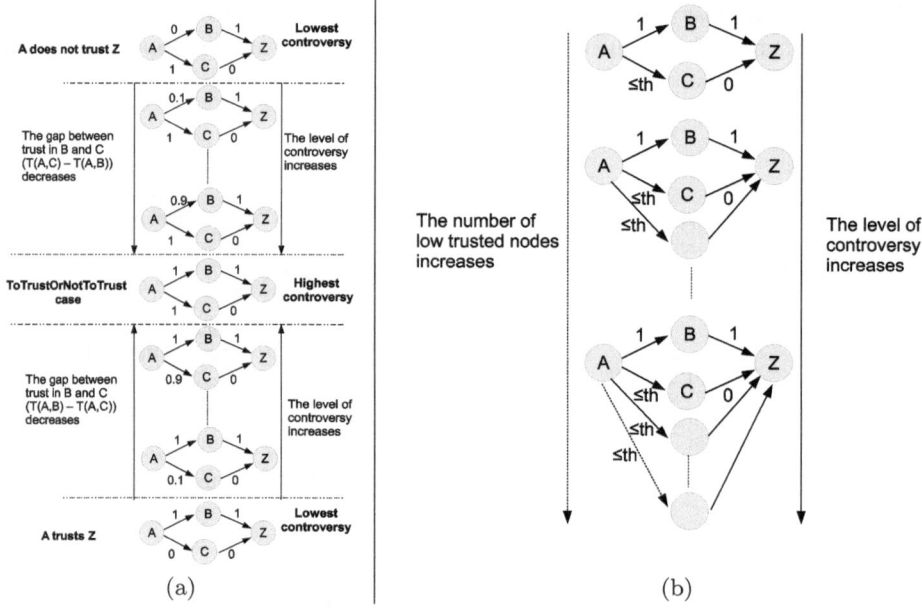

**Fig. 5.** Controversy in the continuous trust range (a) and controversy increasing with the number of low trusted nodes (b)

**Discussion.** The cases presented in this section highlight how the presence of controversial situations in a trust network leads to inferred trust values which can be counter-intuitive or poorly significant. Discovering and handling controversial situations is a challenging task which is worth studying, since inferring trust without taking into account controversy could result in misleading conclusions, thus having a considerable impact on several scenarios (e.g., negatively affecting a decision process). Based on these observations, in the following we introduce a measure for determining the controversy level, which can be used as an effective tool to assess the reliability of a trust inference process.

## 3.3    Trust Inference Algorithms in Controversial Conditions

We begin with a detailed analysis of the behavior of two state-of-the-art local trust inference algorithm, *TidalTrust* [2] and *TISoN* [4], in presence of controversial situations. For *TISoN* we use a uniform setting of the parameters, i.e., $\alpha = \beta = \gamma = 1/3$, as indicated by the authors in [4]. For this analysis, we take as case in point some of the examples of controversial situations discussed in Sect. 3.2: the *ToTrustOrNotToTrust* (Fig. 2(a)) case and the *Asymmetric Controversy* case in its simple (Fig. 4(a)) and unbalanced (Fig. 4(b)) variants.

In the *ToTrustOrNotToTrust* case (Fig. 2(a)), *TidalTrust* infers the trust $IT(A, Z)$ as:

$$IT(A, Z) = \frac{T(A, B) \times T(B, Z) + T(A, C) \times T(C, Z)}{T(A, B) + T(A, C)} \tag{3}$$

If node $A$ assigns equal trust to its two neighbors ($T(A, B) = T(A, C)$), the inferred trust can be calculated as:

$$IT(A, Z) = \frac{T(B, Z) + T(C, Z)}{2} \tag{4}$$

Let us consider that $A$ will take the decision to trust $Z$ only for inferred trust values above a fixed threshold $th$. This means that, whenever nodes $B$ and $C$ trust $Z$ with a difference $\pm\delta$ respect to the given threshold ($T(B, Z) = th \pm \delta$ and $T(C, Z) = th \mp \delta$), $A$ will not be able to take any decision whether to trust or not to trust $Z$, because the inferred trust $T(A, Z)$ is exactly equal to the threshold ($T(A, Z) = th$). The uncertainty of the *ToTrustOrNotToTrust* case naturally persists in its generalized version (Fig. 3), where a symmetric condition of opposite trust edges makes the inferred trust unreliable. In both the variants of the *Asymmetric Controversy* case (Fig. 4), *TidalTrust* takes into account only the shortest path (e.g., $Z$ would be trusted by $A$), thus neglecting the presence of a majority of longer paths which would lead to an opposite result (e.g., a majority of paths through trusted neighbors indicating that $Z$ should not be trusted by $A$).

The behavior of the *TiSoN* inference algorithm cannot univocally be determined in the *ToTrustOrNotToTrust* case (Fig. 2(a)). In fact, the two paths, $\{A, B, Z\}$ and $\{A, C, Z\}$ have the same strength, thus, the maximum is not unique and the inferred trust $T(A, Z)$ will depend on the specific implementation. In fact, the inferred trust will be calculated according to the selected maximum path strength (the first or the last occurrence of the maximum value). The same problem persists in its generalized variant (Fig. 3), which contains multiple controversial paths having the same value of maximum strength. It should be observed that inference algorithms like *TiSoN*, which are based on the search for the maximum strength, show high sensitivity to variations, which can cause instability and lead to critical situations. In controversial conditions, the sensitivity of the *TiSoN* algorithm is critically high. In fact, a minimum difference in the strength of different paths propagating opposite trust values has a strong bias in the final result, i.e., the trust will be inferred from the strongest path (ignoring the information coming from other paths showing significant strength, e.g., close to the maximum). In both the variants of the *Asymmetric Controversy* case (Fig. 4), where controversy resides in paths of different lengths, in the computation of the inferred trust by *TiSoN* there will be always a bias towards the shortest path. (Recall that path length is one of the three terms involved in the calculation of path strength, together with the average and variance of trust values in the path.)

## 4    A Novel Measure for Trust Controversy

Our analysis performed in Sect. 3 has demonstrated how controversial cases are quite common in trust networks, and how existing trust inference algorithms are not able to correctly handle these situations. Based on this observation, in this section we define a novel measure for determining the level of controversy associated with inferred trust values. The proposed measure is defined to support trust inference processes, by assessing the significance of inferred trust values.

The basic hypothesis here is that a measure for determining controversy should take into account how much nodes agree in their assigned trust statements opinions, being able to differentiate between values deriving from a common shared opinion and values deriving by disagreeing statements at different levels. To this aim, we define a trust controversy measure accounting for all paths propagating trust opinions from a source node $A$ to a sink node $Z$, and measuring the differences among all the propagated trust values.

Given a source node $A$ and a sink node $Z$, we define the mean trust $TM(A, Z)$ as the weighted average of the propagated trust from the predecessors of node $Z$ back to the source node, which is calculated as follows:

$$TM(A, Z) = \frac{\sum_{P_i \in Pred(Z)} IT(A, P_i) \times T(P_i, Z)}{\sum_{P_i \in Pred(Z)} IT(A, P_i)} \tag{5}$$

where $Pred(Z)$ is the set of predecessors of the node $Z$, $IT$ indicates inferred trust values and $T$ original trust weights.

According to Eq. 5, trust values assigned by the predecessors $P_i$ of node $Z$ are averaged by considering the inferred trust from the source node $A$ to the predecessor nodes $P_i$ as a weight. We define *Trust Controversy* $TC(A, Z)$ as the weighted variance of the inferred trust paths:

$$TC(A, Z) = \frac{\sum_{P_i \in Pred(Z)} IT(A, P_i) \times (T(P_i, Z) - TM(A, Z))^2}{\sum_{P_i \in Pred(Z)} IT(A, P_i)} \tag{6}$$

A small value of $TC(A, Z)$ indicates that the predecessors of node $Z$ agree in trusting $Z$ with a value close to the mean trust $TM(A, Z)$. Conversely, a high value of $TC(A, Z)$ indicates that the predecessors of $Z$ disagree. It should be noted that the deviation of the edge weights in each path $P_i$ from the mean trust $TM(A, Z)$ is here weighted based on its inferred trust $IT(A, P_i)$. Note that this definition of controversy takes into account the locality characteristic of trust inference algorithms, thus preserving the *personalized* fashion both in inferred trust values and in their associated controversy levels.

*Evaluation of Trust Controversy.* We will now show the behavior of the proposed Trust Controversy measure on the *ToTrustOrNotToTrust* case (Fig. 2(a)). This case is particularly representative, since the value of controversy of the inferred trust $IT(A, Z)$ is independent from the trust inference algorithm used to compute the trust (i.e., there are no inferred trust values in the paths from $A$ to $Z$). Based on Eq. 6, we have:

$$TM(A, Z) = \frac{T(A, B) \times T(B, Z) + T(A, C) \times T(C, Z)}{T(A, B) + T(A, C)} \tag{7}$$

$$\begin{aligned} TC(A, Z) = &\frac{T(A, B) \times (T(B, Z) - TM(A, Z))^2}{T(A, B) + T(A, C)} \\ &+ \frac{T(A, C) \times (T(C, Z) - TM(A, Z))^2}{T(A, B) + T(A, C)} \end{aligned} \tag{8}$$

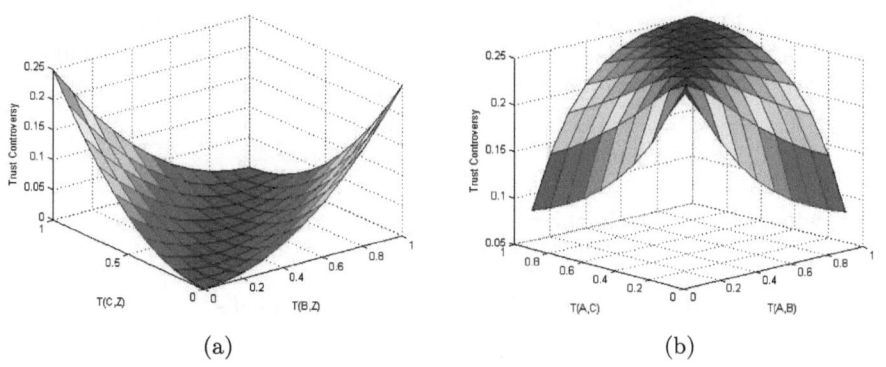

(a)                                    (b)

**Fig. 6.** Graph of the trust controversy in the *ToTrustOrNotToTrust* case when (a) $T(A, B) = T(A, C)$ and (b) $\delta = 0.5$ (maximum disagreement between $T(B, Z)$ and $T(C, Z)$)

Since the numerical value of $TC(A, Z)$ depends on the trust values in the network (i.e., edge weights), the variation of $TC(A, Z)$ with respect to the variation of these values is shown in Fig. 6. To ease readability of the plots, we fixed the value of a couple of parameters in each figure (i.e., $T(A, B)$ and $T(A, C)$ in Fig. 6(a), $T(B, Z)$ and $T(C, Z)$ in Fig. 6(b)). Figure 6(a) shows the values assumed by $TC(A, Z)$ for varying values of $T(B, Z)$ and $T(C, Z)$, for fixed equal trust values of $A$ towards its neighbors (i.e., $T(A, B) = T(A, C)$). As a first expected remark, $TC(A, Z) = 0$ when $T(B, Z) = T(C, Z)$ (which fully reflects our definition of controversy). Further observation can be drawn considering the following example. If we call $\mu$ the average between $T(B, Z)$ and $T(C, Z)$ (so that in this case $TM = \mu$), and $\delta$ the offset of $T(B, Z)$ and $T(C, Z)$ w.r.t. the central value $\mu$ (so that $T(B, Z) = \mu \pm \delta$ , $T(C, Z) = \mu \mp \delta$), the trust controversy $TC(A, Z)$ will be equal to the square of the offset, i.e., $TC = \delta^2$. In the case reported in Fig. 6(a) the most controversial condition happens when $A$ trusts equally $B$ and $C$ (i.e., $T(A, B) = T(A, C)$), but $B$ and $C$ completely disagree in their trust assignment to $Z$, i.e., $max(\delta) = (Tmax - Tmin)/2$ (where $Tmin$ and $Tmax$ are respectively the left and right extremes of the trust range, in our case $[0,1]$).

Figure 6(b) shows the values assumed by $TC(A, Z)$ for varying values of $T(A,B)$ and $T(A,C)$, with fixed $\delta = 0.5$ for $T(B,Z)$ and $T(C,Z)$ (i.e., maximum disagreement between $T(B,Z)$ and $T(C,Z)$). In this case $B$ and $C$ completely disagree with each other w.r.t. the trust assignment to $Z$, then the controversy reaches the maximum when $T(A,B) = T(A,C)$. The controversy decreases inversely proportionally to the difference between $T(A,B)$ and $T(A,C)$. Based on these observations, we can state that also in this case, the behavior of $TC(A, Z)$ fully reflects our desired concept of controversy.

*Normalized Trust Controversy.* From the previous analysis, we can find that when the trust range is $[0,1]$, $max(\delta) = 0.5$ and the maximum controversy is $TC(A, Z) = 0.25$, for any couple of nodes $(A, Z)$ in a directed network. To ease comparability and readability of *Trust Controversy* values we then define the *Normalized Trust Controversy NTC* as reported in Eq. 9:

$$NTC(A, Z) = \frac{TC(A, Z)}{((Tmax - Tmin)/2)^2} \tag{9}$$

so that, when trust varies in the range $[0,1]$, $NTC$ also varies in the same range.

## 5   Experiments on Social Network Datasets

The proposed trust controversy measure was evaluated through experiments conducted on real social networks. The subsequent experimental analysis is divided into two phases: (i) study of the relation between the proposed controversy measure and the performance of selected trust inference algorithms and (ii) analysis of the overall level of controversy in a trust network from a qualitative point of view. Details about the experimental setting will be discussed next.

### 5.1   Experimental Setting

For our experiments we selected three publicly available, directed weighted trust networks: Advogato, Residence hall [1] and Adolescent health [9]. The main structural characteristics of the evaluation datasets are summarized in Table 1. The Advogato network is a de-facto benchmark for trust analysis tasks, where

**Table 1.** Main structural characteristics of the evaluation network datasets

| Data | # nodes | # links | Avg. degree | Avg. path length | Cluster. coef. | Assortativ. |
|---|---|---|---|---|---|---|
| Adolescent Health | 2,539 | 12,969 | 10.216 | 4.52 | 0.142 | 0.251 |
| Advogato | 7,422 | 56,508 | 7.61 | 3.79 | 0.093 | −0.069 |
| Residence Hall | 217 | 2,672 | 24.627 | 2.33 | 0.304 | 0.096 |

edges are labeled according to three different levels of certifications (trust links), namely *master*, *journeyer*, *apprentice*; a user without any trust certificate is called an *observer*. We built our Advogato network dataset by aggregating the daily-snapshot graph files available at the www.trust\discretionary-let.org site, which cover the period Jan 1, 2008–Apr 2, 2014. For each link from user $u$ to user $v$, in the final aggregated graph we kept the last certification given by $u$ to $v$. Residence hall [1] is a directed network containing friendship ratings between 217 residents living in a residence hall located at the Australian National University campus. Nodes represent persons and edges represent the strength of friendship ties in the range [1..5]. Adolescent health is a directed network created from a survey that took place in 1994/1995. Each student was asked to list her/his 5 best female and her/his 5 best male friends. Nodes represent students and directed edges represent listed friendships, where higher edge weights indicate higher levels of interactions. Edge weights are in the range [1..6]. The edge weights (i.e., trust values) in the selected datasets were normalized in the continuous range [0, 1] for comparability reasons. Trust values inferred by *TidalTrust* and *TiSoN* algorithms (cf. Sect. 2) were taken as case in point to measure trust controversy. For *TISoN* we used a uniform setting of the parameters, i.e., $\alpha = \beta = \gamma = 1/3$, as indicated by the authors in [4]. For reasons of comparability and readability, we will always use the *Normalized Trust Controversy NTC* (Eq. 9) in our experiments.

As previously stated, we divided our experimental analysis into two phases. The first phase aims at studying to what extent the level of controversy of the inferred trust values are related to the performance of a trust inference algorithm, i.e., in terms of prediction error. The basic hypothesis here is that low levels of controversy in the inferred trust values should correspond to a lower prediction error rate, and vice versa (higher disagreement among the original trust values should lead to more ambiguous inferred trust values, and thus to an higher error rate). The focus of the first phase is then on the study of hidden relations between controversy and error in trust inference processes. In order to

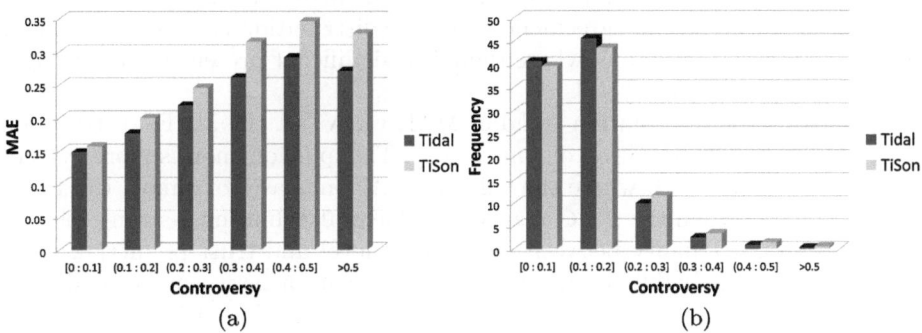

**Fig. 7.** Frequency vs. *NTC* (a) and MAE vs. *NTC* (b) distribution of trust edges in Advogato

measure the prediction error, we performed a classic leave-one-out evaluation method [4,5]: a random trust edge between two nodes $(A, B)$ is removed from the network, than the trust inference algorithm is used to calculate the inferred trust value $IT(A, B)$, than calculating the prediction error comparing $IT(A, B)$ to the original trust value of the removed edge $T(A, B)$. The process is then repeated for each edge in the network. The well-known *MAE* (Mean Absolute Error) measure is used to represent the prediction error of a set of trust edges in a trust network. The second phase is focused on the analysis of overall network controversy. This analysis aims at showing in detail how much a certain trust network is affected by controversial trust values, analyzing how there can be a relation between certain domains and an high trust controversy.

## 5.2   Results

**Frequency and MAE Distributions.** Figures 7, 8 and 9 show the histograms of Frequency vs. $NTC$ (left side) and MAE vs. $NTC$ (right side) distributions of trust edges for the Advogato, Residence hall and Adolescent health datasets, respectively. As regards the Frequency vs. $NTC$ histograms, the range of $NTC$ values was divided in intervals of size 0.1, where each bin represents the percentage of trust edges falling in the specific $NTC$ interval (so that all frequency values sum up to 100 %). In the MAE vs. $NTC$ histograms, we show the distribution of trust prediction error w.r.t. the level of $NTC$, i.e., the average error for the edges showing an $NTC$ in each specified interval.

It can be noted that the distribution trends of Frequency vs. $NTC$ are very similar for all datasets. Also, percentage of controversial trust edges decreases when the controversy level grows up, i.e., there are a very few edges showing an $NTC$ value over 0.5 in all datasets. More in detail, in Residence hall (Fig. 8(a)) there are no trust edges with $NTC$ higher than 0.3. It is worth noting that most of the trust edges have a relatively low value of controversy (i.e., below 0.1), while only a low percentage of trust edges are highly controversial. This phenomenon is also evident for Advogato (Fig. 7(a)), where more than 80 % of trust edges can be inferred with $NTC \leq 0.2$. This indicates that in these networks the trust edges are supported by a strong agreement. The edge distribution is more balanced for Adolescent Health (Fig. 9(a)), where there is a significant presence of trust edges in all the ranges for $NTC \leq 0.5$.

As regards the distribution trend of MAE vs. $NTC$, the MAEs distribution generally grows with the level of controversy. This phenomenon is more evident for Advogato (Fig. 7(b)), where the value of MAE increases of almost the 100 % (i.e., it doubles) when the $NTC$ reaches a value of 0.3, hinting a strong relation of inverse proportionality between controversy level and trust prediction accuracy. This analysis highlights an important correlation between the prediction error and the controversy measure. In fact, when the value of inferred trust is supported by the $NTC$ controversy level, extra information is revealed about how much the inferred trust is supported by the agreement from the network. This can serve as an integrated and unsupervised estimator for trust inference accuracy, e.g., using $NTC$ to estimate the average error on inferred trust values.

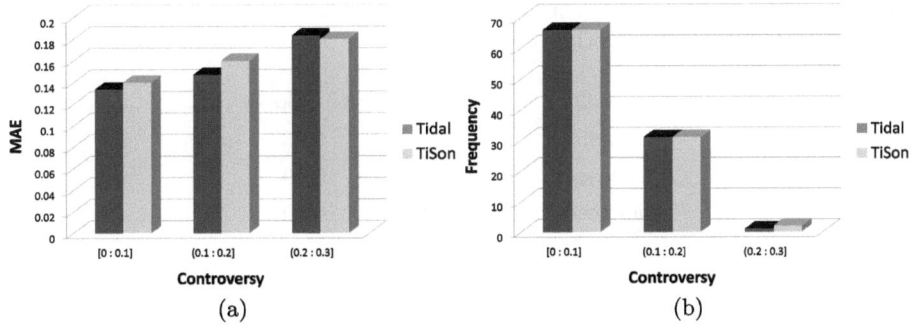

**Fig. 8.** Frequency vs. $NTC$ (a) and MAE vs $NTC$ (b) distribution of trust edges in Residence hall dataset

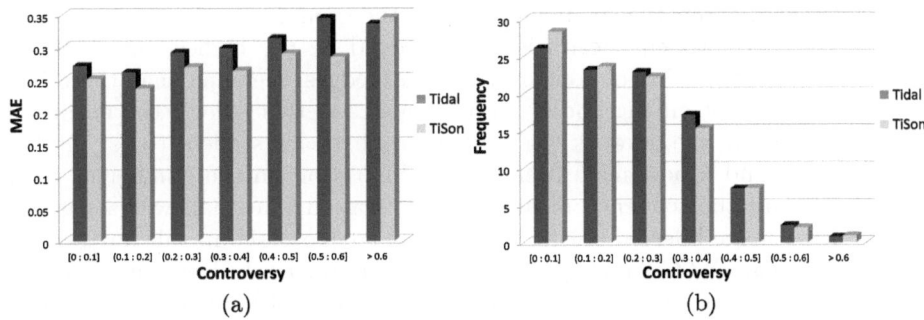

**Fig. 9.** Frequency vs. $NTC$ (a) and MAE vs $NTC$ (b) distribution of trust edges in Adolescent health dataset

**Overall Network Controversy.** Table 2 reports on the mean value of $NTC$ controversy of each trust network for different trust inference algorithms. The mean value of $NTC$ is an important indicator of the level of controversy in a trust network, which indicates the level of agreement in a group.

We observe that average $NTC$ values are relatively low in all datasets, with a minimum of 0.09 for Residence Hall and a maximum of 0.22 in Adolescent Health. However, this is not surprising, since we expect each network to contain a significant group of users on which there is a general trust agreement (as shown in the previous frequency distributions analysis). At the same time, the percentage of highly controversial trust values has a strong bias on the overall prediction error (as shown in the previous MAE distributions analysis): this suggests that trust controversy is worth studying to support trust inference and to gain a wider knowledge on the nature of a trust network.

As a first remark, it can be noted that mean $NTC$ values are very similar for *Tidal Trust* and *TiSoN* algorithms, indicating that different trust inference algorithms can lead to inferred trust values which are controversial at the same level. We also observe from Table 2 that mean $NTC$ values have a strong relation with the data domain and the original network structure. The Residence hall

**Table 2.** $NTC$ values on different trust networks, based on the trust values inferred by *TidalTrust* and *TiSoN* algorithms.

| Dataset | TidalTrust | TiSoN |
|---|---|---|
| Advogato | 0.12 | 0.13 |
| Residence Hall | 0.09 | 0.09 |
| Adolescent Health | 0.22 | 0.20 |

dataset shows a very low level of controversy, meaning that there is a very high level of agreement among the user nodes. This is probably due to the fact that it is related to a small group of individuals living at the same residence, indicating that a relatively small group with a high level of interaction tends to have similar trust judgments about the single members of the group.

Conversely, **Adolescent Health** is characterized by the highest mean $NTC$, with a wider distribution of controversial trust edges, meaning that there is a higher disagreement among nodes. Also in this case, this reflects the nature of the original group: the network was built by asking each student to list his/her 5 best female and 5 best male friends. The limitation on the number of trust statements, and the tendency of adolescents to group in small well-separated communities, make inferred trust values highly controversial in this dataset.

Finally, mean $NTC$ value on **Advogato** is also relatively low, which can be explained by the fact that it is a relatively big and active online community, focused on a specific topic (i.e., open source software). In this case, the very specific domain probably makes trust statements more homogeneous, i.e., when a community is focused on a specific topic, it is expected that each member of the community has a knowledge on the domain which allows him to give judgments with a certain level of objectivity. Moreover, the relatively high size of network should make trust inference algorithms more reliable (since the inferred trust is based on a greater amount of information).

# 6   Conclusions

In this work, we addressed the problem of controversy in trust inference algorithms, i.e., inferred trust values which are originated by discordant trust statements. We observed that several cases of controversial situations can be often found in trust networks and showed how existing trust inference algorithm cannot handle these cases correctly. We proposed a novel trust controversy measure to support trust inference in controversial cases. We conducted experimentation on three real world trust networks, which showed how the controversy level of inferred trust values is highly related to the prediction error, suggesting that our trust controversy measure can serve as an integrated and unsupervised estimator for trust inference accuracy. We also conducted a qualitative analysis based on the overall mean value of controversy of each network, finding evident relations between different data domains and controversy levels.

Since this is a first step towards the study of controversy in trust networks, several directions for future research remain open. First, based on the results of our qualitative analysis, we aim to study how the level of controversy can change when studied in community-based subnetworks, in order to highlight this social aspect in a specific group. Second, we would like to extend our analysis to a larger group of trust inference algorithms and trust network datasets, in order to confirm our findings about the hidden relation of trust controversy with different data domains and inference algorithms. Finally, it would be interesting to define a measure for trust controversy also in global trust ranking scenarios.

**Acknowledgements.** This work was partly supported by the Cyber Security Technological District funded within the Italian National Operational Programme for Research and Competitiveness 2007–2013 under grant number PON03PE_00032_1.

# References

1. Freeman, L.C., Webster, C.M., Kirke, D.M.: Exploring social structure using dynamic three-dimensional color images. Soc. Netw. **20**(2), 109–118 (1998)
2. Golbeck, J.A.: Computing and applying trust in web-based social networks. Ph.D. thesis, College Park, MD, USA (2005)
3. Gyöngyi, Z., Garcia-Molina, H., Pedersen, J.O.: Combating web spam with TrustRank. In: Proceedings International Conference on Very Large Data Bases (VLDB), pp. 576–587 (2004)
4. Hamdi, S., Bouzeghoub, A., Gancarski, A.L., Yahia, S.B.: Trust inference computation for online social networks. In: Proceedings IEEE International Conference on Trust, Security and Privacy in Computing and Communications (TrustCom), pp. 210–217 (2013)
5. Jiang, W., Wang, G., Wu, J.: Generating trusted graphs for trust evaluation in online social networks. Future Gener. Comput. Syst. **31**, 48–58 (2014)
6. Leskovec, J., Huttenlocher, D.P., Kleinberg, J.M.: Predicting positive and negative links in online social networks. In Proceedings of ACM Conference on World Wide Web (WWW), pp. 641–650 (2010)
7. Liu, H., Lim, E., Lauw, H.W., Le, M., Sun, A., Srivastava, J., Kim, Y.A.: Predicting trusts among users of online communities: an epinions case study. In: Proceeding ACM Conference on Electronic Commerce (EC), pp. 310–319 (2008)
8. Massa, P., Avesani, P.: Controversial users demand local trust metrics: an experimental study on epinions.com community. In: Proceedings of 20th National Conference on Artificial Intelligence, AAAI 2005, vol. 1, pp. 121–126 (2005)
9. Moody, J.: Peer influence groups: identifying dense clusters in large networks. Soc. Netw. **23**(4), 261–283 (2001)
10. Nepal, S., Sherchan, W., Paris, C.: STrust: a trust model for social networks. In: Proceedings IEEE International Conference on Trust, Security and Privacy in Computing and Communications (TrustCom), pp. 841–846 (2011)
11. Ortega, F.J., Troyano, J.A., Cruz, F.L., Vallejo, C.G., Enríquez, F.: Propagation of trust and distrust for the detection of trolls in a social network. Comput. Netw. **56**(12), 2884–2895 (2012)

12. Sherchan, W., Nepal, S., Paris, C.: A survey of trust in social networks. ACM Comput. Surv. **45**(4), 47:1–47:33 (2013)
13. Victor, P., Cornelis, C., Cock, M.D., Teredesai, A.: A comparative analysis of trust-enhanced recommenders for controversial items. In: Proceedings AAAI Conference on Weblogs and Social Media (ICWSM) (2009)
14. Victor, P., Cornelis, C., Cock, M.D., Teredesai, A.: Trust- and distrust-based recommendations for controversial reviews. IEEE Intell. Syst. **26**(1), 48–55 (2011)
15. Walter, F.E., Battiston, S., Schweitzer, F.: Personalised and dynamic trust in social networks. In: Proceedings ACM Conference on Recommender Systems (RecSys), pp. 197–204 (2009)

# Enabling Key Migration
# Between Non-compatible TPM Versions

Linus Karlsson[(✉)] and Martin Hell

Department of Electrical and Information Technology, Lund University,
P.O. Box 118, 221 00 Lund, Sweden
{linus.karlsson,martin.hell}@eit.lth.se

**Abstract.** We consider the problem of migrating keys from TPM 1.2 to the backwards incompatible TPM 2.0. The major differences between the two versions introduce several challenges for deployed systems when support for TPM 2.0 is introduced. We show how TPM 2.0 support can be introduced while still maintaining the functionality specified by TPM 1.2, allowing a smoother transition to the newer version. Specifically, we propose a solution such that keys can be migrated from TPM 1.2 to TPM 2.0, while retaining behavior with regard to e.g. authorization, migration secrets, PCR values and CMK functionality. This is achieved by utilizing new functionality, such as policies, in TPM 2.0. The proposed solution is implemented and verified using TPM emulators to ensure correctness.

**Keywords:** Trusted computing · TPM · Migration

## 1 Introduction

There are different versions of the TPM, which differ from one another in several ways. In this paper we consider TPM 1.2, introduced in 2003, and TPM 2.0 which was introduced in 2012. TPM 2.0 is not backwards compatible with TPM 1.2, but nevertheless TPM 2.0 chips are now available [4] and have started to ship in devices [5].

We consider the process of migrating from the TPM 1.2 generation chips, to the newer TPM 2.0. As new equipment comes with TPM 2.0 chips, we want to be able to move or copy keys from TPM 1.2 to the new chips, while still maintaining the same functionality. However, because of the lack of backwards compatibility, there is no such support built into the TPM specifications. This presents a problem when we would like to use the same keys even when moving to a newer TPM, for example to be able to decrypt previously encrypted data. In addition, we may want to continue to use these keys with the same functionality, despite the differences between the specifications.

The lack of backwards compatibility means that this migration has to be done manually. Keys have to be converted between different formats, and adapted to the different feature sets of the two standards. Some features in TPM 1.2 have no direct equivalent in TPM 2.0, but identical or similar behavior can be achieved

© Springer International Publishing Switzerland 2016
M. Franz and P. Papadimitratos (Eds.): TRUST 2016, LNCS 9824, pp. 101–118, 2016.
DOI: 10.1007/978-3-319-45572-3_6

by using new features of TPM 2.0. The goal of this paper is to give a solution for how to achieve this for all different key types and migration alternatives in TPM 1.2. As an example, in TPM 1.2 there is a concept of a *migration secret*, which authorizes the migration of a key to another TPM. This migration secret has no direct counterpart in TPM 2.0, but the same behavior can be implemented using functionality only available in the TPM 2.0 specifications. Another example is the use of Certifiable Migratable Keys (CMKs) in TPM 1.2, which also requires a non-trivial design by expressing the functionality as policies in TPM 2.0.

We describe a process which allows us to migrate keys from a TPM 1.2 to a TPM 2.0. We start by determining a set of requirements, and present a solution which performs migration according to the presented requirements. We start by implementing the equivalent functionality of TPM 1.2's migration secret in TPM 2.0, using constructions only available in the newest TPM version. We then look at keys bound to Platform Configuration Register (PCR) values, and present a way to handle the incompatibilities in key format between TPM 1.2 and TPM 2.0. We also present a solution for CMKs, such that equivalent behavior is achieved in both TPM versions. We do not consider the case of TPM 2.0 to 1.2 migration, since it is not likely that new TPM 1.2 equipment will be deployed once equipment with TPM 2.0 has been deployed.

The paper is organized as follows. Section 2 presents a brief overview of TPM 1.2 and 2.0. In Sect. 3 we present our goals and requirements. In Sect. 4 we describe our proposed solution for different relevant scenarios, which are then extended to the case of CMKs in Sect. 5. Section 6 describes the implementation. Finally in Sect. 7, we discuss some related work. Section 8 concludes the paper.

# 2   Overview of TPM 1.2 and TPM 2.0

This section will give a short introduction to TPM 1.2 and 2.0, with focus on issues related to key migration. For a complete review, consult the specifications [15,16].

## 2.1   Overview of TPM 1.2 and Certifiable Migratable Keys

A TPM 1.2 provides a key hierarchy of asymmetric keys. Keys can be of different types, for example storage keys, signing keys, or decryption keys (the last called binding key in TPM 1.2). Since the keys are asymmetric, they consist of two parts: one public and one private part. The private part of every key is encrypted with the public part of the parent key. Only a storage key can be the parent of another key.

Certain operations on the TPM, e.g. some commands related to migration, must only be performed by the TPM owner. These operations are authorized by proving knowledge of an *owner secret*, which is set when someone takes ownership of the TPM. To be able to use the private part of a key, e.g. to decrypt or sign data, the user must provide a *usage secret*. This secret is stored inside the key in the TPM, and can be unique for each key.

Copying keys between different TPMs is called *migration*, and was introduced in TPM 1.1 [13]. To authorize such an operation the TPM owner must first authorize the destination using the command `TPM_AuthorizeMigrationKey`. We note that the TPM owner can authorize any destination, thus making it possible to migrate the key to any TPM, or even to a keypair generated outside any TPM. In addition, the user performing the migration must prove knowledge of the *migration secret*, which is a secret set on key creation. If this secret is not known, the key is not migratable. This is verified during execution of `TPM_CreateMigrationBlob`, which outputs a data blob which can be transferred to the destination TPM. At the destination, the key can be loaded by `TPM_LoadKey2`, possibly after conversion by `TPM_ConvertMigrationBlob`.

In TPM 1.2, CMKs were introduced. Their migration is further restricted, such that instead of the migration secret above, an authorization from a trusted entity, called the Migration Selection Authority (MSA), is required. The MSAs are chosen at key creation time. During the migration, the MSA must approve the destination, either implicitly by migrating the key to the MSA itself, or by signing a ticket containing the destination. The signature is done using the private key of the MSA. By signing the ticket, the MSA approves the migration of the specified key to a specific destination. This signature is required by the source TPM to actually perform the migration.

## 2.2 Overview of TPM 2.0

In TPM 2.0 the asymmetric key hierarchy has been generalized, and has been replaced with an object hierarchy. Objects can be asymmetric or symmetric keys, or data blobs. The type of the object is determined by a set of flags on the object: *sign*, *decrypt*, and *restricted*. An object with the flags *decrypt* and *restricted* set is a storage key, since it can be used to encrypt and decrypt the private parts of child keys, and the *restricted* bit tells the TPM to operate only on data prepared by the TPM (for example keys). However, the storage keys in TPM 2.0 protect its child keys by using symmetric encryption instead of asymmetric. The symmetric key is derived from a seed included in the key itself. In addition to this, TPM 2.0 allows for a wide range of ciphers and algorithms, including different symmetric ciphers and hash functions.

In TPM 2.0, migration has been renamed to *duplication*. Indeed, this is a more appropriate terminology, since keys are not removed from the source when performing a migration. Instead the key will exist in both TPMs. There are two flags connected to the duplicability of a key: *fixedTPM* and *fixedParent*. A key with fixedTPM set can never leave the TPM, and can thus not be duplicated. The other flag, fixedParent, tells us if the key is fixed to its parent. If the flag is set, the key cannot be explicitly duplicated, but it may still be loaded in another TPM if it is possible to duplicate its parent.

Just like in TPM 1.2, use of the private part of a key requires a usage secret, but there is no direct equivalent of the migration secret. Instead, a more general authorization mechanism has been introduced in TPM 2.0, namely policies.

## 2.3    Policies in TPM 2.0

A major addition in TPM 2.0 is the introduction of policies. A policy can be used to authorize different operations on an object in the hierarchy. The policy is set at creation time, by including a value authPolicy in the object. This value is created by repeatedly hashing different values from different policy commands. Possible commands are for example policies based on time, signatures, or secret values. Different policies can also be combined using OR.

Before executing a command using the object, a policy hash must be built in a policy session. The session also includes context specific values which are checked during command execution, for example if we are authorizing duplication or usage of the object, or what authorization method to use. The resulting policy hash of the policy session is then compared to the authPolicy in the object to authorize the command execution.

In this paper we are mostly concerned with duplication and authorization. Thus, we are only interested in a subset of the different policy commands:

- TPM2_PolicyAuthValue requires the usage secret of the object being authorized, and does the authorization using a HMAC.
- TPM2_PolicyAuthorize allows us to modify an existing policy. A new policy is signed using the private key of an authority, and if this signature is valid, the policy is included in the policy session.
- TPM2_PolicyCommandCode limits the authorization to a certain command, for example to authorize duplication only. This is done by setting a *command code* in the current policy session.
- TPM2_PolicyDuplicationSelect limits the allowed destination parent when performing a duplication.
- TPM2_PolicyOR is a logical OR policy, true if the current policy hash matches any of the conditions in this policy.
- TPM2_PolicyPassword requires the usage secret of the object being authorized, and does the authorization using the password in clear.
- TPM2_PolicyPCR requires the PCRs (see Sect. 2.4) to have a specific set of values.
- TPM2_PolicySecret requires the usage secret of another object on the TPM.
- TPM2_PolicySigned requires a digital signature.

## 2.4    Platform Configuration Registers

Both TPM 1.2 and 2.0 have a number of Platform Configuration Registers (PCRs). Each PCR stores a hash value, which is created by repeatedly calling TPM_Extend or TPM2_Extend. The extend operation depends both on the previous PCR value, and on the new data. This can be used to store measurements of hardware configuration and software on the host. Keys in both TPM 1.2 and 2.0 can be bound to PCR values, such that the use of a key requires certain PCRs to be in a specified state. This ensures that such keys are only usable in a known environment. In addition, the PCR values can be read by using the commands TPM_PCRRead and TPM2_PCR_Read.

## 2.5  Comparing Migration in TPM 1.2 and TPM 2.0

From the descriptions above we see that when it comes to migration, there are several differences between the two TPM versions.

To perform a migration of a (non-CMK) TPM 1.2 key, the following criteria must be fulfilled:

1. The key must have been created with the key flag `migratable` set to TRUE.
2. The migration secret must be known.
3. The TPM owner must authorize the migration destination.
4. The usage secret of the parent key on the source TPM must be known.
5. The usage secret of the parent key on the destination TPM must be known.

In comparison, the following criteria must be fulfilled when migrating a TPM 2.0 key:

1. The key must have `fixedParent` CLEAR.
2. The command code of the policy session must be `TPM_CC_Duplicate`, i.e. the key must have a policy which allows for duplication.
3. The usage secret of the parent key on the source TPM must be known.
4. The usage secret of the parent key on the destination TPM must be known.

We first note the similarities, namely that for both TPM versions, the usage secret of the parent key on the source TPM must be known, such that the key to be migrated can be loaded into the TPM. In addition, the usage secret of the destination TPM's parent key must also be known, such that the key to be migrated can be added as a child key.

In TPM 1.2 there is an explicit flag which tells whether or not the key is migratable. This is not the case in TPM 2.0, where there are two flags which control the migratability of a key. If `fixedParent` is SET, then the key has a fixed parent, and cannot be migrated directly (however, it could still be migrated if its parent is migratable). If `fixedTPM` is SET, the key can never be migrated. We note that it is not possible to create a key with `fixedParent` CLEAR and `fixedTPM` SET, so a sufficient condition is that `fixedParent` is CLEAR.

Another difference is the authorization of the migration. In TPM 1.2 this is done by proving knowledge of the migration secret. In TPM 2.0, it is done with a policy session that authorizes the migration. We note that the policy session is a more generic approach, which supports multiple ways of authorizing the migration through the use of any policy command. The only requirement is that there exists a command in the chain of policy commands that explicitly sets the commandCode to `TPM_CC_Duplicate`, since duplication is a special authorization role in TPM 2.0.

Finally, we note that there is no requirement for owner authorization when performing a migration in TPM 2.0.

Looking at the migration of a CMK in TPM 1.2, the following criteria must be fulfilled:

1. The MSA must authorize the migration destination.

2. The TPM owner must authorize the migration destination.
3. The usage secret of the parent key on the source TPM must be known.
4. The usage secret of the parent key on the destination TPM must be known.

Compared to the non-CMK criteria described above, the migration secret criterion is replaced by the approval of the MSA. TPM 2.0 does not have the concept of CMKs, but the behavior can be implemented by the use of policies. Details will be presented later in Sect. 5.

## 3    Goals

We want to migrate a *migratable* key from a source TPM (TPM 1.2), hereafter called TPM$_S$, to a destination TPM (TPM 2.0), denoted TPM$_D$. The key to be migrated from TPM$_S$ to TPM$_D$ is denoted $K$.

If the source key is a CMK, then the migration must also be approved by an already existing trusted third-party, called the authority/MSA. This third party may, or may not, have a TPM module installed, but let's assume that this is the case, and call this party TPM$_A$.

When migrating a key between two TPMs of the same version (i.e. either $1.2 \rightarrow 1.2$, or $2.0 \rightarrow 2.0$) we can immediately import the binary migration blobs produced by the source TPM into the destination TPM. We can also be sure that all features are supported. However, when we do a migration from $1.2 \rightarrow 2.0$ the migration blob must be converted manually, taking into account the differences between the two versions.

We introduce a *conversion authority* which is a trusted entity that performs the actual binary conversion between 1.2 and 2.0, and denote this with TPM$_C$.

Introducing this trusted entity does not lower the security of our proposed solution. If the key $K$ is a CMK, there is already a trusted third-party (the authority/MSA). If a new, separate, conversion authority is undesirable, it would be possible to extend the MSA to also be the conversion authority.

In the case of a non-CMK, the source key owner is in full control of $K$. This means that the owner may migrate it to any destination, including a destination outside of a TPM. Thus the owner has full responsibility and opportunity to choose a trusted conversion authority. It is possible to have the conversion authority on either the source or destination, a separate third system is not required. Seeing the conversion authority as a separate entity does however provide a clear separation of concerns, and simplifies reasoning in this paper.

### 3.1    Requirements

We want our solution to maintain the same functionality with respect to authorization when moving from TPM 1.2 to TPM 2.0. Thus, if an entity is authorized to migrate or use a key at the source TPM, it should have the possibility and authorization to do so also at the destination TPM.

To maintain the functionality when moving between the different TPMs, we identify a number of requirements which must be supported by the conversion authority.

R1. Keep the same private and public part of the RSA key, such that it can be used to decrypt previously encrypted data, or create identical signatures.

R2. Keep the same authorization requirements for key usage.

R3. Keep the same authorization requirements for key migration.

R4. If a key requires a certain state (PCR values) of the TPM, the same state should be required after migration.

R5. Support all key types of the TPM 1.2, i.e., signing, decryption, and storage keys. Both non-CMK and CMK keys should be supported.

R6. Once migrated to a TPM 2.0, it should be possible (if authorized) to further migrate the key to another TPM 2.0.

R7. The migration should be deterministic, such that if the same key is migrated twice, the result at the destination TPM should be identical after both migrations.

The motivation for R7 is that when migrating a storage key in TPM 1.2 or TPM 2.0, its child keys are implicitly migrated as well, since they can just be loaded at the destination TPM with the respective Load-commands. This allows a hierarchy to be moved incrementally, simply by moving the child keys to the destination. However, when migrating keys between TPM 1.2 and 2.0, we will have to perform a conversion step. To be able to perform the migration incrementally at different occasions, the steps involved must be deterministic.

## 4    Migration Scenarios

We will look at the following different migration scenarios:

1. Migration of a simple, single, key from $TPM_S$ to $TPM_D$. Only signing keys and decryption keys, without considering PCR values.
2. Migration of a simple, single, key requiring specific values of the PCRs.
3. Migration of a storage key, including its child keys.
4. All of the scenarios above, for CMKs.

### 4.1    Signing or Decryption Key

In this case we want to migrate a signing or decryption key from $TPM_S$ to $TPM_D$. Clearly we must retain both the private and public portions of the key when migrating to $TPM_D$. Furthermore we assume that this key is the child key of the *storage root key* (SRK), but the steps will be identical for any parent key.

Because of the differences between TPM 1.2 and 2.0, both in functionality and in the actual binary migration blob format, we must do a conversion of the binary migration blob before importing it into $TPM_D$. This means that we cannot simply perform the migration to the SRK of $TPM_D$. If we did, the migration blob could only be decrypted by the destination TPM, which would also have to perform the actual conversion. This is not possible, since the conversion cannot be performed inside the destination TPM. Rather, we must use the previously introduced conversion authority, $TPM_C$. The conversion authority has its own RSA keypair, which will act as an intermediate destination during the migration.

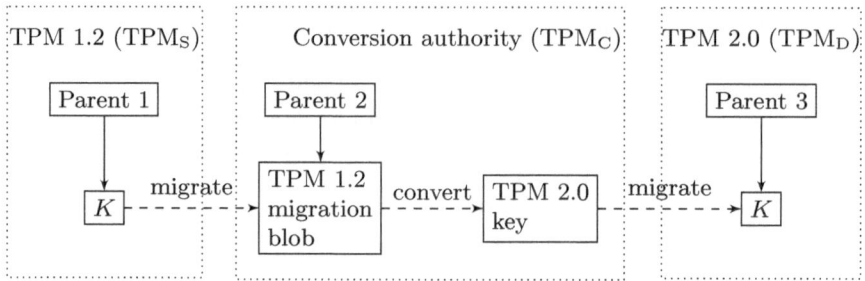

**Fig. 1.** Overview of migration using the conversion authority.

The outline of the conversion is as follows, also depicted in Fig. 1.

1. The owner of TPM$_S$, and the owner of $K$ authorize the migration of $K$ to TPM$_C$, by proving knowledge of the owner secret and migration secret respectively.
2. A migration blob is created by the command `TPM_CreateMigrationBlob`.
3. The migration blob is first decrypted by TPM$_C$, and then converted to a TPM 2.0-format, and migrated to the final destination TPM$_D$.
4. TPM$_D$ imports the migration blob and now has its own copy of $K$.

**Conversion.** The conversion authority will perform the conversion of the key. The following are some important steps in this process.

TPM 2.0 supports a wide range of hash functions, and each key has a property `nameAlg` which stores the algorithm for the key. We set `nameAlg` of the TPM 2.0 key to be SHA-1, since that is the only supported hash algorithm in TPM 1.2. After this, the `usageAuth` in the TPM 1.2 key (which is the SHA-1 hash of some secret) can be moved as-is to the TPM 2.0 formatted key.

Next, we want to move the public and private part of the source key. The public part of the key, which is simply a structure from the TPM 1.2 specification, must be sent separately to TPM$_C$, since it is not included in the migration blob. This contains the public modulus and exponent.

The private part of the key, which we obtained by manually decrypting the migration blob with the key of TPM$_C$, can be copied directly to the sensitive structure in TPM 2.0, since both TPM specifications states that the private part of RSA keys is one of the two RSA primes.

**Migration of the Migration Secret.** In TPM 1.2, each key has a migration secret, in addition to usage secret. If the value of this secret is *tpmProof*, no migration is possible since *tpmProof* is a value internal to the TPM. However, if the migration secret is the hash of a secret known to the user, migration is possible.

In TPM 2.0 there is no direct equivalent of the migration secret (called `migrationAuth`) in TPM 1.2. An analysis of the migration secret functionality provides the following four options.

1. Disallow any further migration, that is, once migrated to TPM 2.0, no more migrations will be possible. This violates requirement R6.
2. Always allow migration, that is, anyone can migrate the key. This violates requirement R3.
3. Only allow migration if the user knows the `usageAuth`. This can be implemented through a simple policy. However, this violates requirement R3.
4. Construct a more complex policy, which emulates the `migrationAuth` behavior of TPM 1.2.

Of these options, option 4 is the only one which fulfills our requirements, and most closely resembles the original behavior of TPM$_S$. Thus, when migrating $K$ to TPM$_D$, we wish to keep the same migration secret, such that only entities with knowledge of the migration secret can migrate the key further.

In TPM 2.0, migration authorization is performed using policies. Thus, to keep the same migration secret, we must find a policy scheme that mimics the behavior of TPM 1.2.

An initial thought may be to utilize the commands `TPM2_PolicyAuthValue` or `TPM2_PolicyPassword` command in combination with setting the command code with `TPM2_PolicyCommandCode(TPM_CC_DUPLICATION)`, which would allow migration to any destination as long as a secret is known. However, both `TPM2_PolicyAuthValue` and `TPM2_PolicyPassword` use the `authValue` of the key, which is the same secret which is required for regular usage of the key. This would correspond to our discarded option 3 in the list above.

In the general case, the migration and usage secret will be different, and thus these two policy commands do not offer a solution to our problem. Another possibility is to use `TPM2_PolicySecret`. This policy command uses the `authValue` of *another* entity in the TPM. Thus we could imagine a scenario where we could create a new, separate entity whose only purpose is to keep the previous `migrationAuth` as its own usage auth. In this way, we could create a policy with `TPM2_PolicySecret` which uses this extra entity.

However, we have chosen another approach, which somewhat mimics the scenario where we have an MSA that approves our migration. This makes our proposed solution more consistent when we later on start considering CMKs. The proposed solution is depicted in Fig. 2.

The `usageAuth` from our TPM 1.2 key is copied directly to the `authValue` field of the TPM 2.0 key. We also copy the `migrationAuth` from the TPM 1.2 key to the `authValue` field of a separate, newly created, signing key, called the *sibling* key ($K_{sib}$), on the TPM 2.0. Thus, to be able to create signatures using the sibling key, we must know the `authValue` of this key (which is the original `migrationAuth`).

Now, to control the migration of the key, we include a policy in the `authPolicy` field of the key $K$ at the destination TPM. We construct the policy

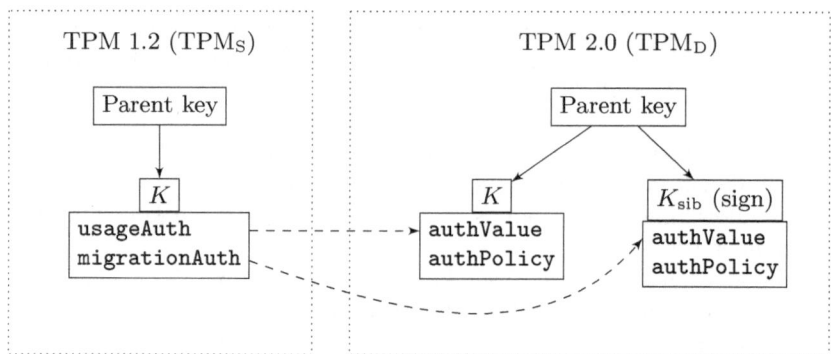

**Fig. 2.** Migration secret in TPM 2.0

such that a signature from the sibling key is required for a migration to succeed. To construct such a signature, the user clearly must have knowledge of the migration secret.

Constructing a policy which validates a signature can be done by using the policy command `TPM2_PolicySigned`. The policy will require the TPM user to present a signature from the sibling key (thus proving possession of the migration secret), and if valid, `TPM2_PolicyCommandCode(TPM_CC_Duplicate)` is used to authorize a migration to any destination, mimicking the behavior of TPM 1.2.

Furthermore, in the `authPolicy` field of the *sibling key* we include a policy which allows migration of the sibling key as long as the `authValue` is known. This allows us to migrate both the sibling key and $K$ to another TPM 2.0 destination, which fulfills requirement R6.

When creating $K_{\mathrm{sib}}$, care must be taken to ensure that we get a deterministic creation. Simply creating a new, random, RSA keypair would violate requirement R7, since every migration of $K$ would result in different $K_{\mathrm{sib}}$, and thus different `authPolicy` in $K$. Instead, we must base the generation of $K_{\mathrm{sib}}$ on $K$, to ensure that the generation is deterministic, yet unique for all keys. Assuming that the original private part of $K$, the pair of primes $(p, q)$, is random, we use a hash of $(p, q)$ as the seed to the prime number generator to construct new primes for the sibling key. This is similar to how TPM 2.0 generates primary objects (such as the SRK) using the primary seeds in the TPM. The process is depicted in Fig. 3. Since we assumed that the original $(p, q)$ were random primes, our derived seed can also be considered random, thus giving a deterministic, but still secure $K_{\mathrm{sib}}$. Clearly, if someone has knowledge of $(p, q)$ of $K$, they would be able to derive $K_{\mathrm{sib}}$, and authorize a migration. However, if $(p, q)$ of $K$ is already known, there is no reason for an attacker to do a migration, since the private part of $K$ is already compromised.

**Owner Secret.** In TPM 1.2 the TPM owner is also required to authorize the migration. However this is not the case in TPM 2.0. We propose a solution where

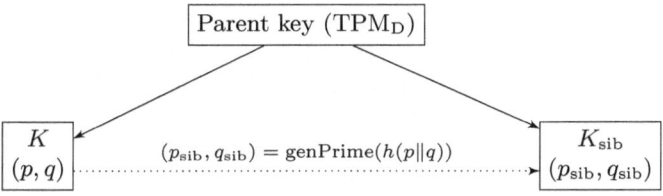

**Fig. 3.** Generating the primes for $K_{\mathrm{sib}}$ based on $(p, q)$ of $K$.

an extra signing key is introduced, similar to the sibling key above. However, different from the owner secret, this key is not unique per TPM, but rather per key. In a sense, it becomes an extra migration secret. It does deviate slightly from the behavior in TPM 1.2 since this owner signing key will have to be identical on all TPM 2.0 chips. The secret of the owner signing key is selected during the initial 1.2 to 2.0 migration, and the key will be created by the conversion authority. Just like for the migration key, the actual verification of the signature is done by including a TPM2_PolicySigned in the policy chain.

### 4.2 PCR Bound Keys

In TPM 1.2, key usage can be restricted such that both certain PCR values (through pcrSelection) and knowledge of the usageAuth is required. In TPM 2.0, this must be implemented through the use of policies. As can be seen in [16, Part 1, Annex A], this can be realized by combining the use of TPM2_PolicyPCR and TPM2_PolicyAuthValue. When converting the key to TPM 2.0-format, it is important to set the userWithAuth-attribute to CLEAR, since otherwise the user could circumvent the PCR requirement by only providing the authValue.

When migrating and converting from 1.2 to 2.0, the PCR values need to be moved from the pcrSelection structure and instead be included in the TPM2_PolicyPCR policy.

However, it is not possible for $\mathrm{TPM_C}$ to extract the PCR values from the TPM 1.2 migration blob. This is because the TPM 1.2 PCR structure present in the TPM 1.2 key only contains the hash over a structure containing multiple PCR values. The exact steps to calculate this hash is described in [15, Part 2, Sect. 5.4.1].

To be able to convert the PCR values to a format suitable for TPM 2.0, we would require access to each individual PCR value. In TPM 2.0 we will use the hash of the concatenation of all PCR values in the TPM2_PolicyPCR command, which is not the same structure that were used in TPM 1.2.

Thus, since we cannot extract each individual PCR value from the composite hash of the key in TPM 1.2, we cannot reconstruct a TPM 2.0 key bound to the exact same PCR values, at least not given only a migration blob. Therefore, the PCR values from $\mathrm{TPM_S}$ must be provided separately to the $\mathrm{TPM_C}$ during the conversion step.

A migration using TPM_CreateMigrationBlob does not require that the PCR values of the TPM are in the expected state. This means that we cannot be sure that reading PCR values using TPM_PCRRead returns the PCR values required to use the key. Instead, this must be verified by the conversion authority. Assuming that the PCR values, and the corresponding PCR index, are sent to the conversion authority, it can verify that these are indeed the correct values by calculating the hash in the same way as the TPM 1.2, and then compare it to the hash in the migration blob. If they match, $\text{TPM}_C$ can then use the PCR values when converting the key for TPM 2.0.

Assuming the correct PCR values are sent to the conversion authority, we can construct a policy using TPM2_PolicyPCR followed by TPM2_PolicyAuthValue, which when combined will require both the correct PCR values and the correct usage secret.

However, we must also combine this with the policy for migration authorization in Sect. 4.1, such that we both can have PCR requirements and migration requirements. This does not mean that a migration requires correct PCR values (this is not required in TPM 1.2 either), but that one of the two policy branches is satisfied.

Thus, we create a policy with two branches, combined with TPM2_PolicyOR, as in Fig. 4. Either of the two branches can be satisfied, if the left branch is satisfied, key usage is granted (if the PCR values are correct). If the right branch is satisfied, migration is authorized.

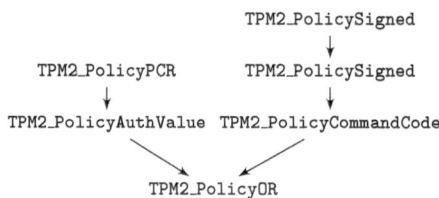

**Fig. 4.** Policy for PCR combined with migration authorization.

### 4.3   Key Hierarchies

Up until now, we have only considered the case where $K$ is either a signing or a decryption key. If $K$ is a storage key with child keys, we must be able to migrate the complete hierarchy as well.

Normally, when migrating keys either from 1.2 to 1.2, or from 2.0 to 2.0, there is no need to explicitly migrate the child keys. If the parent key is migrated and thus available in the destination TPM, all child keys can simply be loaded directly with TPM_LoadKey2 or TPM2_Load, using the same encrypted private part on both the source and destination, without any migration.

However, due to the difference in encryption and overall key storage format between 1.2 and 2.0, a more elaborate scheme is required when migrating a hierarchy from 1.2 to 2.0.

Recall that in TPM 1.2, the parent's public key is used to encrypt the child key's private part. Thus, asymmetric encryption is used. However, in TPM 2.0, symmetric encryption is used instead. The child key's private part is encrypted using a symmetric key derived from a *seed* in the parent key. Normally, this seed is generated upon key creation, and is based on data from the RNG in the TPM. However, due to requirement R7, we require a deterministic seed. Otherwise, subsequent migrations of the same hierarchy would yield different seeds, and child keys would be encrypted with different symmetric keys, even though they share the same parent.

When migrating a complete key hierarchy, we introduce extra requirements on our solution:

1. When migrating a hierarchy, only the migration secret of the hierarchy's root key should be required to migrate the root and all of its descendant keys.
2. It should be possible to migrate parts of a hierarchy at different occasions.

Assume the hierarchy of keys given in Fig. 5. If we want to migrate $K$, including its child keys C1 and C2, we first perform a migration of $K$ as usual, i.e. just like if it was a signature or decryption key. However, $TPM_C$ can see that $K$ is a storage key, and if this is the case we include a seed inside the TPM 2.0-version of the key.

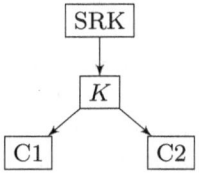

**Fig. 5.** Key hierarchy

We calculate the seed as $seed = \text{SHA1}(p\|q)$. The reason for using SHA-1 is because the seed must be of the same size as the `nameAlg` of the key, which is set to SHA-1 to be able to use the same `usageAuth` as in TPM 1.2.

When migrating a hierarchy, we also provide $TPM_C$ with the encrypted private parts of the child keys of $K$, which we wish to migrate to $TPM_D$. When $TPM_C$ receives this bundle of keys, it can use the private parts of $K$ to decrypt all the other encrypted private parts of the child keys. The child keys can then be converted to TPM 2.0-format, and re-encrypted using the symmetric key derived from the seed.

This approach will work for hierarchies of any depth. However, the hierarchy must be preserved inside the bundle, since $TPM_C$ must have access to the parent of a child key to be able to decrypt it. We can also migrate only parts of a deep hierarchy, as long as all relevant parents leading to $K$ are included.

When migrating keys in the hierarchy, their migration secret must be preserved just as before. This means that in addition to converted child keys, we will also get sibling keys for each converted child key. The sibling keys are placed so that they share parent with the key that they correspond to, see Fig. 6.

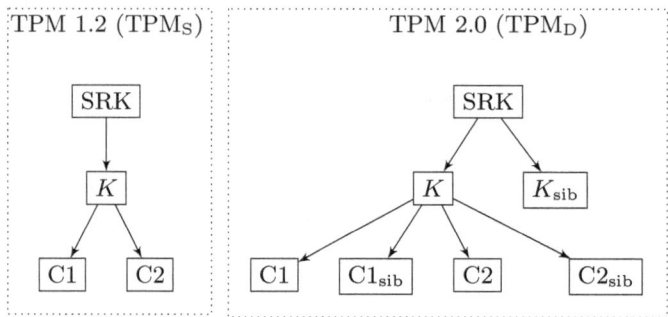

**Fig. 6.** Key hierarchy and sibling keys

## 5   Certifiable Migratable Keys

In TPM 1.2, a CMK can only be migrated with the approval of both the TPM owner and a third-party Migration Selection Authority (MSA).

In TPM 2.0, there is no direct equivalent of CMK, but the behavior can be achieved by using policies as in Fig. 7. TPM2_PolicyAuthorize allows us to replace the previous commands in the policy chain, in this case, it allows us to replace TPM2_PolicyDuplicationSelect with another destination, as long as we can present a valid signature of the policy hash. This signature is done by the authority (MSA in TPM 1.2 terminology).

In this way the MSA must approve the destination before any migration can be performed, and the approval is only valid for a specific destination.

**Fig. 7.** Policy for CMK.

A complication introduced by CMKs is that TPM 1.2 introduces restrictions on the place of CMKs in the key hierarchy. A CMK cannot be the child of a migratable key, nor can it be the child of another CMK. When we convert a CMK into TPM 2.0 format, we must ensure that these restrictions still hold. Otherwise we would violate requirement R3, since we would be able to further migrate the child CMK if we were authorized to migrate the migratable parent.

Thus, when migrating a CMK, we must ensure that the destination parent is not a migratable key. This is the responsibility of the MSA, and is not discussed any further.

We consider the three cases in the previous section, and construct the required policy for each case.

### 5.1   Signing or Decryption Key

When using CMKs, there is no migration secret that the key owner needs to present. In Sect. 4.1 we presented a solution where two TPM2_PolicySigned commands were included in the authPolicy of $K$. In the CMK case, we can remove one of the signatures, since there is no migration secret. This also means that no sibling key is required, we can consider the key of the MSA as our (remote) sibling key.

Since there is no built-in requirement in TPM 2.0 for the owner to authorize a migration, we introduced an owner signing key. This signature is still required in the CMK case.

We can do this by simply adding the TPM2_PolicySigned command to the end of the chain. Note that adding it to the start of the chain would make it possible for the authority to override the owner authorization, which we want to avoid. Thus the chain now look like in Fig. 8. TPM2_PolicyDuplicationSelect will set the command code to TPM_CC_Duplicate, so no explicit call to set the command code is required after TPM2_PolicySigned.

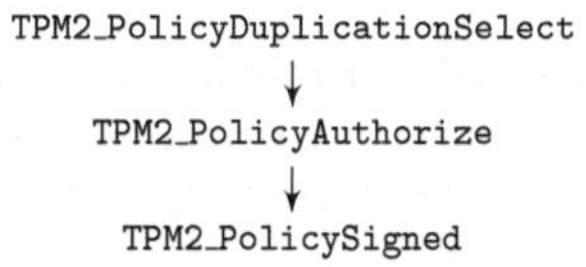

TPM2_PolicyDuplicationSelect

↓

TPM2_PolicyAuthorize

↓

TPM2_PolicySigned

**Fig. 8.** Policy for CMK, with owner authorization.

### 5.2   PCR Bound Keys

We start with the policy from the previous section, and add a PCR policy, similar to what we did in Sect. 4.2. Again, we get two different branches of the policy, one for usage, and one for migration, see Fig. 9. Just like before, either of the two branches can be satisfied. If the left branch is satisfied, key usage is granted (if the PCR values are correct). If the right branch is satisfied, migration is authorized, because TPM2_PolicyDuplicationSelect will set the correct command code for migration.

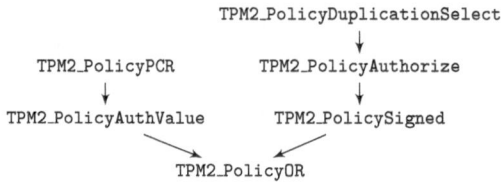

**Fig. 9.** Policy for PCR combined with migration authorization and CMK.

## 5.3   Storage Keys

Recall the restrictions on CMKs in the key hierarchy. A CMK may not have a migratable parent, neither a regular migratable key nor a CMK. The effect is the only possible key hierarchy which includes CMKs is a hierarchy where the root node is a CMK. This means that we can proceed as in Sect. 4.3, with the additional requirement that the root CMK key gets a policy just like in Sect. 5.1.

# 6   Implementation

To ensure that our conversion process works as intended, we have implemented all the above test cases, and verified their behavior. The TPMs have been emulated in software. For TPM 1.2, IBM's Software TPM version 4720 [3] has been used. For TPM 2.0, Microsoft's TPM2 Simulator version 1.1 [7] has been used.

To simplify the implementation, we have assumed the following:

- All TPM 1.2 keys are in the TPM_KEY12-key format.
- $K$ is 2048 bit RSA, two primes. Two primes and RSA is a requirement for migratable keys according to [15, Part 2, Sec. 10.7].
- The default RSA exponent $(2^{16} + 1)$ is used for all keys. For storage keys this is also required by the TPM 1.2 specification.

The TPM 1.2 specification in [15] has no defined formats on how to send migration packages between the different entities. It does, however, exist a specification [14] which describes an XML schema for supplying information about keys during the migration phase. This specification is, however, not fully updated for TPM 1.2, but rather based on TPM 1.1, and thus we have not used this XML-based approach in our implementation.

Instead, since our implementation was primary meant for testing and evaluation purposes, we have simply passed files with binary content between the different entities.

# 7   Related Work

While there are few widespread applications that rely on the functionality provided by the TPM, there are examples of existing pieces of software, and some other proposed use cases. From Microsoft we have both Bitlocker [6], used for full-disk encryption, and Virtual Smart Cards [8], which uses the TPM instead of physical smart cards to store private keys. Examples of proposed use cases for the newer TPM 2.0 are for example the use of TPM for tamper-proof logging [11], or the use of TPM 2.0 for electronic identities [9].

Related to the challenge of providing consistent behavior between the two TPM versions, in [2], the authors design a unified API which implements their functionality on both TPM 1.2 and 2.0. In contrast to this work, they consider the functionality for a certain use case, and then create two different and separate implementations, one for each TPM version, with no possibility of key migration between them.

The use of TPMs to provide trusted computing functionality within cloud computing is an area where there also has been development and research. In [10] the use of trusted computing in cloud platforms is discussed, and in [12] trusted snapshots of running virtual machines is discussed. Related to migrating keys between TPMs are ways of sharing keys between different TPMs. A cloud-based solution is proposed in [1].

## 8    Conclusions

We have proposed a solution to make it possible to move or copy key material from TPM 1.2 to TPM 2.0. Even though the two TPM versions differ significantly in functionality, and offer no backward compatibility, we have presented a design which allows the migration of keys between different versions, while still maintaining the same functionality. This allows users of the current TPM 1.2 version to start using the newer TPM 2.0 chips, still keeping the same encryption keys and functionality. In this way, previously encrypted data can be decrypted with the same set of authorization requirements as before. The required functionality was first identified and organized as a set of requirements. After this we looked at several different cases, where each case corresponded to different properties of the source key on the TPM 1.2.

We presented a way to provide the migration secret functionality of TPM 1.2 also in TPM 2.0. By introducing sibling keys and using policies, we can maintain the same authorization requirements in both TPM versions. We also handle migration of PCR bound keys from TPM 1.2 to TPM 2.0. Because of the differences in key format between the two versions, the migration requires PCR values to be sent to the conversion authority. The conversion authority can then verify the values against the source key before including them in the destination key. In addition to this, we showed how the TPM 1.2 CMK functionality can be expressed in terms of TPM 2.0 policies, and combined this with the previous results so that migration of all key types of TPM 1.2 are covered. Finally the different proposed solutions were implemented and tested using TPM emulators.

**Acknowledgments.** The authors would like to thank the anonymous reviewers for their helpful and valuable comments.

# References

1. Chen, C., Raj, H., Saroiu, S., Wolman, A.: cTPM: a cloud TPM for cross-device trusted applications. In: 11th USENIX Symposium on Networked Systems Design and Implementation (NSDI 14). USENIX Association, Seattle, WA, April 2014
2. Hell, M., Karlsson, L., Smeets, B., Mirosavljevic, J.: Using TPM secure storage in trusted high availability systems. In: Yung, M., Zhang, J., Yang, Z. (eds.) INTRUST 2015. LNCS, vol. 9565, pp. 243–258. Springer, Heidelberg (2016)
3. IBM: IBM's software trusted platform module. http://ibmswtpm.sourceforge.net/
4. Infineon: Infineon Advances Trusted Computing with New OPTIGA$^{TM}$ TPM Family: Security Chips Serve Industrial/Embedded Environments and Support Next Generation TPM 2.0 Firmware. http://www.infineon.com/cms/en/about-infineon/press/press-releases/2013/INFCCS201309-062.html
5. Infineon: Infineon Expands its Trusted Computing Expertise to Mobile Devices: OPTIGA$^{TM}$ TPM 2.0 Chips Secure Microsoft Surface Pro 3 Tablet. http://www.infineon.com/cms/en/about-infineon/press/press-releases/2015/INFCCS201502-026.html
6. Microsoft: BitLocker Drive Encryption Overview. https://www.microsoft.com/en-us/download/details.aspx?id=29076
7. Microsoft: TSS.MSR v1.1 TPM2 simulator. http://research.microsoft.com/en-US/downloads/35116857-e544-4003-8e7b-584182dc6833/default.aspx
8. Microsoft: Understanding and Evaluating Virtual Smart Cards, July 2014
9. Nyman, T., Ekberg, J.E., Asokan, N.: Citizen electronic identities using TPM 2.0. In: Proceedings of the 4th International Workshop on Trustworthy Embedded Devices, TrustED 2014, pp. 37–48. ACM, New York (2014)
10. Santos, N., Gummadi, K.P., Rodrigues, R.: Towards trusted cloud computing. In: Proceedings of the 2009 Conference on Hot topics in Cloud Computing. USENIX Association (2009)
11. Sinha, A., Jia, L., England, P., Lorch, J.R.: Continuous tamper-proof logging using TPM 2.0. In: Holz, T., Ioannidis, S. (eds.) Trust 2014. LNCS, vol. 8564, pp. 19–36. Springer, Heidelberg (2014)
12. Srivastava, A., Raj, H., Giffin, J., England, P.: Trusted VM snapshots in untrusted cloud infrastructures. In: Balzarotti, D., Stolfo, S.J., Cova, M. (eds.) RAID 2012. LNCS, vol. 7462, pp. 1–21. Springer, Heidelberg (2012)
13. Trusted Computing Group: Trusted Computing Platform Alliance (TCPA), Main Specification Version 1.1b, February 2002
14. Trusted Computing Group: Interoperability Specification for Backup and Migration Services, Specification Version: 1.0 Final, Revision 1.0, June 2005
15. Trusted Computing Group: TPM main specification, Version 1.2, Revision 116, March 2011
16. Trusted Computing Group: Trusted Platform Module Library Specification, Family "2.0", Level 00, Revision 01.16, October 2014

# Bundling Evidence for Layered Attestation

Paul D. Rowe[(✉)]

The MITRE Corporation, Bedford, MA, USA
`prowe@mitre.org`

**Abstract.** Systems designed with measurement and attestation in mind are often layered, with the lower layers measuring the layers above them. Attestations of such systems, which we call *layered attestations*, must bundle together the results of a diverse set of application-specific measurements of various parts of the system. Some methods of layered attestation are more trustworthy than others especially in the presence of an adversary that can dynamically corrupt system components. It is therefore important for system designers to understand the trust consequences of different designs. This paper presents a formal framework for reasoning about layered attestations. We identify inference principles based on the causal effects of dynamic corruption, and we propose a method for bundling evidence that is robust to such corruptions.

## 1    Introduction

Security decisions often rely on trust. Many computing architectures have been designed to help establish the trustworthiness of a system through remote attestation. They gather evidence of the integrity of a target system and report it to a remote party who appraises the evidence as part of a security decision. A simple example is a network gateway that requests evidence that a target system has recently run antivirus software before granting it access to a network. If the virus scan indicates a potential infection, or does not offer recent evidence, the gateway might decide to deny access, or perhaps divert the system to a remediation network. Of course the antivirus software itself is part of the target system, and the gateway may require integrity evidence for the antivirus for its own security decision. This leads to the design of layered systems in which deeper layers are responsible for generating integrity evidence of the layers above them.

A simple example of a layered system is one that supports "trusted boot" in which a chain of boot-time integrity evidence is generated for a trusted computing base that supports the upper layers of the system. A more complex example might be a virtualized cloud architecture. The virtual machines (VMs) at the top are supported at a lower layer by a hypervisor or virtual machine monitor. Such an architecture may be augmented with additional VMs at an intermediate layer that are responsible for measuring the main VMs to generate integrity evidence. These designs offer exciting possibilities for remote attestation. They allow for specialization and diversity of the components involved, tailoring the capabilities of measurers to their targets, and composing them in novel ways.

© Springer International Publishing Switzerland 2016
M. Franz and P. Papadimitratos (Eds.): TRUST 2016, LNCS 9824, pp. 119–139, 2016.
DOI: 10.1007/978-3-319-45572-3_7

An important fact about such layered systems is that the trustworthiness of the system is not simply a function of the evidence produced by measurement; the relative order of the measurement events is crucial. In particular, a strong intuition that is manifest in the literature is that it is better to build trust "bottom-up" by first gathering evidence for components lower in the system *before* they measure the higher level components. A measurer is more likely to be uncorrupted at the time it takes its measurements if this order is respected. This intuition for "bottom-up" measurement underlies many architectures, most notably trusted boot [9] and the integrity measurement architecture (IMA) [15]. In a companion paper [14] we characterize the guarantees provided by a bottom-up measurement scheme in the presence of an adversary that can dynamically corrupt system components. Namely, if an adversary successfully corrupts a target component $t$ without being discovered by measurements, then the adversary must have either performed a *recent* corruption of one of $t$'s immediate dependencies, or else the adversary must have corrupted one of $t$'s indirect dependencies *deeper* in the system. Thus bottom-up measurements confine undetectable corruptions to be either recent or deep. We schematize the main theorem of [14] in Eq. (1).

$$\text{Bottom-up measurement} \implies \text{Detectable, Recent or Deep} \tag{1}$$

Such a result is not enough, however. Since a remote appraiser cannot directly observe the order of measurements on a system, this information must be part of what is conveyed in the bundle of evidence during the attestation. In order to apply the result, the appraiser needs a way of inferring that the measurements were indeed taken bottom-up. If an adversary could make it look like measurements were taken in the desired order when they weren't then he could avoid the consequences of the theorem.

Much of the work on measurement and attestation relies on a Trusted Platform Module (TPM) to protect and report the evidence generated by measurement components. It is common to invoke the use of a TPM as sufficient for these purposes. Unfortunately, there are many natural ways to use a TPM that fail to accurately reflect the order of measurement. The ability of an adversary to dynamically corrupt components at runtime makes the problem all the more pronounced. This paper begins to address the issues surrounding the use of TPMs to bundle evidence in the presence of dynamic adversaries. We summarize our main contributions as follows:

1. We introduce a formalism for reasoning about the causal effects of dynamic corruption and repair of system components on the process of bundling measurement evidence for attestation using a TPM.
2. We prove correct a set of reusable principles for inferring the structure of system activity given that a certain structure of bundled evidence was produced by a TPM. Failure of these principles to prove some desirable property may indicate that the desirable property was not met.
3. We propose a particular method for using a virtualized TPM to bundle evidence, and we show (Theorem 2) that under some assumptions about the behavior of uncompromised components, a remote appraiser can infer that

either the measurements were taken bottom-up, or else the adversary performed a recent or deep corruption in the sense described above. Letting $\mathcal{Q}$ denote a set of quotes conforming to our method, we schematize this theorem in Eq. (2).

$$\mathcal{Q} \implies \text{Bottom-up, Recent, or Deep} \tag{2}$$

The first two contributions are quite general, and, we believe, could be applied to the design and analysis of many systems. The third suggests a particular design recommendation. It says, roughly, that if our recommendation is followed, then either the hypothesis of Eq. (1) is satisfied, or else its conclusion is satisfied. The particular assumptions required might limit its applicability. In particular, it assumes some flexible access control to TPM registers which is hard to achieve in physical TPMs. Thus it is naturally applicable to virtualized systems incorporating virtualized TPMs (vTPMs) [1] that could allow for such access control. Although no industry standard currently exists for securing vTPMs, architectural designs and specifications for such systems are beginning to emerge [2, 5, 12, 13].

**Paper Structure.** The rest of the paper is structured as follows. We begin in Sect. 2 by reviewing some basic facts about TPMs and introducing some notation. In Sect. 3 we build up some intuition about what types of inference an appraiser is justified in making and what types of problems can arise when using a TPM to bundle evidence from a layered system. Section 4 contains the description of our formal model which we will use to justify our intuitions. We develop our reusable principles and present our bundling strategy in Sect. 5, characterizing the guarantees provided by our strategy. We address related work in Sect. 6 before concluding.

## 2    Preliminaries

The results of this paper depend on some features of Trusted Platform Modules (TPMs). For reasons of space, a full review of the relevant features of TPMs is impractical. We present here only the most basic explanation of the notions necessary to proceed.

TPMs are stateful devices with a collection of platform configuration registers (PCRs) that contain information about the state of the system. These registers are isolated from the rest of the system and are thus protected from direct modification. They can only be updated in constrained ways, namely by *extending* a register or by *resetting* it. We explain below how this works. An additional restriction is imposed by a form of access control known as *locality*. This access control ensures that, for certain PCRs, only certain components with special privileges can extend or reset them. A TPM can also *quote* the state of a set of PCRs by emitting a digital signature over the contents of those PCRs. We will assume the signing key has not been compromised, as it never leaves the TPM unencrypted.

In order to describe how the state is updated and reported, we use elements of a term algebra. Terms are constructed from some base $V$ of atomic terms using constructors in a signature $\Sigma$. The set of terms is denoted $\mathcal{T}_\Sigma(V)$. We assume $\Sigma$ includes at least some basic constructors such as pairing $(\cdot, \cdot)$, signing $[\![ (\cdot) ]\!]_{(\cdot)}$, and hashing $\#(\cdot)$. The set $V$ is partitioned into public atoms $\mathcal{P}$, random nonces $\mathcal{N}$, and private keys $\mathcal{K}$.

Our analysis will sometimes depend on what terms an adversary can derive (or construct). We say that term $t$ is derivable from a set of term $T \subseteq V$ iff $t \in \mathcal{T}_\Sigma(T)$, and we write $T \vdash t$. We assume the adversary knows all the public atoms $\mathcal{P}$, and so can derive any term in $\mathcal{T}_\Sigma(\mathcal{P})$ at any time. We also assume the set of measurement values is public, so an adversary can forge acceptable evidence. We denote the set of potential measurement values for a target $t$ by $\mathcal{MV}(t)$.

We represent both the values stored in PCRs and the quotes as terms in $\mathcal{T}_\Sigma(V)$. Extending a PCR by value $v$ amounts to replacing its contents $c$ with the hash $\#(v, c)$. Resetting a PCR sets its contents to a fixed, public value, say rst. Since PCRs can only be updated by extending new values, their contents form a hash chain $\#(v_n, \#(..., \#(v_1, \mathsf{rst})))$. We abbreviate such a hash chain as $\mathsf{seq}(v_1, \ldots, v_n)$. So for example, $\mathsf{seq}(v_1, v_2) = \#(v_2, \#(v_1, \mathsf{rst}))$. We say a hash chain $\mathsf{seq}(v_1, \ldots, v_n)$ *contains* $v_i$ for each $i \leq n$. Thus the contents of a PCR contain exactly those values that have been extended into it. We also say $v_i$ is *contained before* $v_j$ in $\mathsf{seq}(v_1, \ldots, v_n)$ when $i < j \leq n$. That is, $v_i$ is contained before $v_j$ in the contents of $p$ exactly when $v_i$ was extended before $v_j$.

A quote from TPM $t$ is a term of the form $[\![ n, (p_i)_{i \in I}, (v_i)_{i \in I} ]\!]_{sk(t)}$. It is a signature over a nonce $n$, a list of PCRs $(p_i)_{i \in I}$ and their respective contents $(v_i)_{i \in I}$ using $sk(t)$, the secret key of $t$. We always assume $sk(t) \in \mathcal{K}$ the set of non-public, atomic keys. That means the adversary does not know $sk(t)$ and hence cannot forge quotes.

# 3   Examples of Weak Bundling

Before jumping into the technical details, we start with an example that illustrates some potential pitfalls of using TPMs for bundling evidence. Consider an enterprise that would like to ensure that systems connecting to its network provide a fresh system scan by the most up-to-date virus checker. The network gateway should ask systems to perform a system scan on demand when they attempt to connect. We may suppose the systems all have some component $A_1$ that is capable of accurately reporting the running version of the virus checker. Because this enterprise values high assurance, the systems also come equipped with another component $A_2$ capable of measuring the runtime state of the kernel. This is designed to detect any rootkits that might try to undermine the virus checker's system scan, for example by hiding part of the file system that contains malicious files. We may assume that $A_1$ and $A_2$ are both measured by a root of trust for measurement (rtm) such as Intel's TXT as part of a trusted boot process.

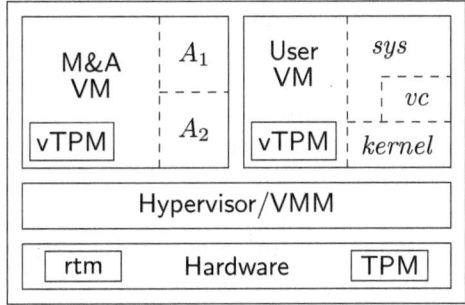

**Fig. 1.** Example Attestation System

Figure 1 is a notional depiction of an architecture supporting this use case. In this architecture, the primary user virtual machine (VM) hosts the *kernel*, the virus checker *vc* and the file system *sys*. A sibling VM hosts the two measurement components $A_1$ and $A_2$. These virtual machines are managed by some hypervisor that runs on the underlying hardware containing the root of trust for measurement (rtm). We have depicted a virtualized TPM (vTPM) for each VM while the hardware contains a physical TPM, although we might consider the possibility that the VMs only use the physical TPM. Such an architecture is reminiscent of those found, for example, in [4] or [2].

If the gateway is to appraise the system, it might expect the measurements to be taken according to the order depicted in Fig. 2 (in which time flows downward). The event of $o_m$ measuring $o_t$ is represented by $\mathsf{ms}_{o_c}(o_m, o_t)$, where we include the subscript $o_c$ only when it provides a clean runtime context for the measurer $o_m$. This order of events represents the intuitive "bottom-up" approach to measurement. It ensures that if *sys* is corrupted but not detected by the measurement event $\mathsf{ms}_{ker}(vc, sys)$ then the adversary must have either recently corrupted *vc* or *ker* or else he must have corrupted one of the more protected components $A_1$ or $A_2$ [14]. The att-start($n$) event indicates a moment in time in which the gateway chooses a random nonce $n$. "Recent" corruptions are those that occur after this event. The bullet after the first three events is inserted only for visible legibility, to avoid crossing arrows.

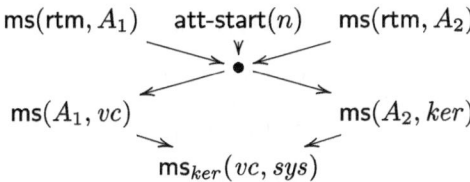

**Fig. 2.** Bottom-up order for measurement

Of course, the gateway cannot directly observe these events taking place. Rather, it must infer the order and outcome of measurements from evidence that is extended into a TPM and quoted for integrity protection. We now consider a couple natural ways one might think of doing this and point out some potential pitfalls in which the presence and order of the measurement events cannot be inferred from the quote structure.

**Strategy 1: A Single Hash Chain.** Since PCRs contain an ordered history of the extended values, the first natural idea is for all the components to share a PCR $p$, say in the physical TPM, each extending their measurements into $p$. The intuition is that the contents of $p$ should represent the order in which the measurements occurred on the system. To make this more concrete, assume the measurement events of $S_1$ have the following results: $\mathsf{ms}(\mathsf{rtm}, A_1) = v_1, \mathsf{ms}(\mathsf{rtm}, A_2) = v_2, \mathsf{ms}(A_1, vc) = v_3, \mathsf{ms}(A_2, ker) = v_4, \mathsf{ms}(vc, ker) = v_5$. Then this strategy would produce a single quote $Q = [\![\, n, p, \mathsf{seq}(v_1, v_2, v_3, v_4, v_5) \,]\!]_{sk(t)}$. To satisfy the order of Fig. 2, any linearization of the measurements would do, so the appraiser should also be willing to accept $Q' = [\![\, n, p, \mathsf{seq}(v_2, v_1, v_3, v_4, v_5) \,]\!]_{sk(t)}$ in which $v_1$ and $v_2$ were generated in the reverse order.

Figure 3 depicts an execution that produces the expected quote $Q$, but does not satisfy the desired order. Since all the measurement components have access to the same PCR, if any of those components is corrupted, it can extend values to make it look as though other measurements were taken although they were not. Since the bottom-up order of measurement was not respected, the conclusions from [14] cannot be applied. Indeed, neither of the corruptions in Fig. 3 are recent. It is also troublesome since the adversary does not need to corrupt the relatively deep components $A_1$ or $A_2$. The corrupted $vc$, having access to $p$ can extend the expected outcomes of measurement by $A_1$ and $A_2$ without those components even being involved.

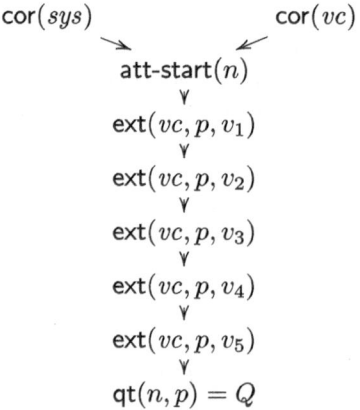

**Fig. 3.** Defeating Strategy 1

**Strategy 2: Disjoint Hash Chains.** The problem with Strategy 1 seems to be that PCR $p$ is a shared resource for many components of the system that should be trusted to varying degrees. The corruption of *any* component that can extend into the PCR can affect the results. This motivates a desire to separate access to the relevant PCRs, so that, in the extreme case, there is only a single component with the authority to extend each PCR. This could be done by making use of the virtualization architecture and vTPMs to ensure that each VM can only interact with its corresponding vTPM. Indeed, this separation may be much more natural for the architecture described above. The vTPM may further impose access control in the form of locality constraints for PCRs. Although locality is a relatively limited form of access control for physical TPMs, one opportunity provided by vTPMs is a more flexible notion of locality.

A natural next attempt given this assumption would be to produce three quotes, one from each (v)TPM over the set of PCRs that contain the measurement evidence. This would produce the quotes $Q_1 = [\![ n, p_r, \mathsf{seq}(v_1, v_2) ]\!]_{sk(t)}$, $Q_2 = [\![ n, (p_1, p_2), (\mathsf{seq}(v_2), \mathsf{seq}(v_3)) ]\!]_{sk(vt_1)}$, $Q_3 = [\![ n, p_{vc}, \mathsf{seq}(v_4) ]\!]_{sk(vt_2)}$. Figure 4 demonstrates that the appraiser is not justified in inferring a bottom-up order of measurement from this set of quotes. The problem, of course, is that, since the PCRs may be extended concurrently, the relative order of events is not captured by the structure of the quote. An adversary may thus be able to alter the order in which these events take place, taking advantage of the different order to avoid detection by measurement. For example he could repair a corrupted $vc$ just in time for it to be measured by $A_1$ so that it appears uncorrupted, when in fact it was previously corrupted when it performed its own measurement of $sys$.

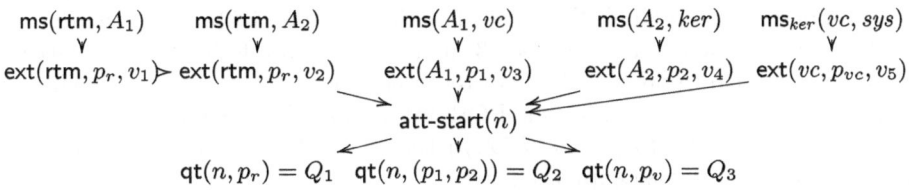

**Fig. 4.** Defeating Strategy 2

# 4 Attestation Systems

In this section we formalize the notions we used for the example in Sect. 3.

**System Architecture.** We start with a definition of attestation systems that focuses on the relevant dependencies among components.

**Definition 1.** *An* attestation system *is a tuple* $\mathcal{AS} = (O, M, C, P, L)$, *where $O$ is a set of objects (e.g. software components) with a distinguished element* rtm. *$M$ and $C$ are binary relations on $O$. We call*

$M$ *the* measures *relation, and*
$C$ *the* context *relation.*

$P = T \times R$ *for some set $T$ of TPMs and some index set $R$ of their PCR registers, and $L$ is a relation on $O \times P$.*

$M$ represents who can measure whom, so that $M(o_1, o_2)$ iff $o_1$ can measure $o_2$. rtm represents the root of trust for measurement. $C$ represents the kind of dependency that exists between $ker$ and $vc$ in the example from the previous section. In particular, the $vc$ depends on $ker$ to provide it a clean runtime context. We can thus capture the fact that a corrupted $ker$ can interfere with the $vc$'s ability to correctly perform measurements, for example by hiding a portion of the filesystem from $vc$. Many assumptions one might make about $M$ and $C$ affect the dynamics of corruption on the outcome of measurement. This current paper instead focuses on the bundling of evidence, and so we make only a minor assumption that $M \cup C$ is acyclic. This ensures that the combination of the two dependency types does not allow an object to depend on itself. Such systems are stratified, in the sense that we can define an increasing set of dependencies as follows.

$$D^1(o) = M^{-1}(o) \cup C^{-1}(M^{-1}(o))$$
$$D^{i+1}(o) = D^1(D^i(o))$$

So $D^1(o)$ consists of the measurers of $o$ and their context. Elements of $P$ have the form $p = t.i$ for $t \in T$ and $i \in R$. The relation $L$ represents the access control constraints for extending values into TPM PCRs. We assume each component in $O$ can only access a single TPM, so that if $L(o, t.i)$ and $L(o, t'.i')$, then $t = t'$. As discussed in the example of Sect. 3, it may be desirable to have a relatively strict access control policy $L$. We can represent the extreme case in which each component has access to its own PCR by adding the assumption that $L$ is injective. That is, if $L(o, p)$ and $L(o', p)$ then $o = o'$. Of course relaxations of this strict policy are also expressible.

**Events, Outputs, and Executions.** The components $o \in O$ perform actions on the system. In particular, as we have seen, components can measure each other, extend values into PCRs and the TPM can produce quotes. Additionally, an adversary on the system can corrupt and repair components with the aim of affecting the behavior of the other actions. Finally, an appraiser has the ability to inject a random nonce $n \in \mathcal{N}$ into an attestation in order to control the recency of events.

**Definition 2 (Events).** *Let $\mathcal{AS}$ be a target system. An event for $\mathcal{AS}$ is a node $e$ labeled by one of the following.*

a. *A measurement event is labeled by $\mathsf{ms}_{C^{-1}(o_2)}(o_2, o_1)$ such that $M(o_2, o_1)$. We say such an event measures $o_1$, and we call $o_1$ the target of $e$. When $C^{-1}(o_2)$ is empty we omit the subscript and write $\mathsf{ms}(o_2, o_1)$.*

b. An extend event *is labeled by* $\mathsf{ext}(o, v, p)$, *such that* $L(o, p)$ *and* $v$ *is a term.*
c. A quote event *is labeled by* $\mathsf{qt}(v, t_I)$, *where* $v$ *is a term, and* $t_I = \{t.i \mid i \in I\}$ *is a sequence of PCRs belonging to the same TPM* $t$. *We say a quote event reports on* $p$, *or is over* $p$, *if* $p \in t_I$.
d. An adversary event *is labeled by either* $\mathsf{cor}(o)$ *or* $\mathsf{rep}(o)$ *for* $o \in O \backslash \{\mathsf{rtm}\}$.
e. The attestation start *event is labeled by* $\mathsf{att\text{-}start}(n)$, *where* $n$ *is a term.*

*The second argument to extend events and the first argument to quote events is called the* input.

*An event* $e$ touches *object* $o$ *(or PCR* $p$*), iff* $o$ *(or* $p$*) is an argument or subscript to the label of* $e$.

*When an event* $e$ *is labeled by* $\ell$ *we will write* $e = \ell$. *We will often refer to the label* $\ell$ *as an event when no confusion will arise.*

A few observations about this definition: Measurement and extend events are constrained by the dependencies of the underlying system. So, for example, a component cannot extend a value into any PCR not allowed by the policy $L$. Notice that quote events have no component $o \in O$ as an argument. This is because (v)TPMs may produce quotes in response to a request by any component that has access to it. The only constraint on adversary events is that they do not affect the rtm. This is not essential, but it simplifies the statements and proofs of some theorems later on. We also do not consider the (v)TPMs as objects in $O$, so they are also immune from corruption. As for the $\mathsf{att\text{-}start}(n)$ event, since $n$ is randomly chosen, extend or quote events that incorporate $n$ must occur after $\mathsf{att\text{-}start}(n)$. We expect $\mathsf{ms}(\mathsf{rtm}, o)$ events not to occur after $\mathsf{att\text{-}start}(n)$ because they typically represent boot-time measurements of a system.

As we saw in the example from Sect. 3, an execution can be described as a partially ordered set (poset) of these events. We choose partially ordered sets rather than totally ordered sets because the latter unnecessarily obscure the difference between *causal* orderings and *coincidental* orderings. However, if we allow arbitrary posets of events we lose the causal structure. In particular, we need to ensure that in executions we can unambiguously identify (a) whether or not a component is corrupted at measurement and extension events, and (b) the contents of PCRs at extension and quote events. In the following, we thus impose two constraints on the posets of interest.

When no confusion arises, we often refer to a poset $(E, \prec)$ by its underlying set $E$ and use $\prec_E$ for its order relation. Given a poset $E$, let $e{\downarrow} = \{e' \mid e' \prec_E e\}$, and $e{\uparrow} = \{e' \mid e \prec_E e'\}$. Given a set of events $E$, we let $adv(E)$, $meas(E)$, $ext(E)$, and $qt(E)$ denote respectively the set of adversary, measurement, extension, and quote events of $E$. For any poset $(E, \prec)$ of events over attestation system $\mathcal{AS} = (O, M, C, P, L)$, let $(E_o, \prec_o)$ denote the substructure consisting of all and only events that touch $o \in O$. Similarly we define $(E_p, \prec_p)$ for $p \in P$.

**Definition 3 (Poset restrictions).** *We say* $(E, \prec)$ *is adversary-ordered iff for every* $o \in O$, $(E_o, \prec_o)$ *has the property that if* $e$ *and* $e'$ *are incomparable events, then neither* $e$ *nor* $e'$ *are adversary events.*

We say $(E, \prec)$ is extend-ordered *iff for every* $p \in P$, $(E_p, \prec_p)$ *has the property that if* $e$ *and* $e'$ *are incomparable events, then they are both quote events.*

Adversary-ordered posets ensure that we can unambiguously define the corruption state of a component at an event that touches it. Extend-ordered posets ensure that we can unambiguously identify the contents of a PCR at events that touch it. Both these claims require justification.

**Lemma 1.** *Let* $(E, \prec)$ *be a finite, adversary-ordered poset for* $\mathcal{MS}$, *and let* $(E_o, \prec_o)$ *be its restriction to some* $o \in O$. *Then for any non-adversarial event* $e \in E_o$, *the set* $adv(e{\downarrow})$ *(taken in* $E_o$*) is either empty or has a unique maximal element.*

This lemma (proved in [14]) ensures the following conditions are well-defined.

**Definition 4 (Corruption state).** *Let* $(E, \prec)$ *be a finite, adversary-ordered poset for* $\mathcal{MS}$. *For each event* $e \in E$ *and each object* $o$ *the* corruption state *of* $o$ *at* $e$, *written* $cs(e, o)$, *is an element of* $\{\bot, \mathsf{r}, \mathsf{c}\}$ *and is defined as follows.* $cs(e, o) = \bot$ *iff* $e \notin E_o$. *Otherwise, we define* $cs(e, o)$ *inductively:*

$$
cs(e, o) = \begin{cases}
\mathsf{c} & : e = \mathsf{cor}(o) \\
\mathsf{r} & : e = \mathsf{rep}(o) \\
\mathsf{r} & : e \in meas(E) \wedge adv(e{\downarrow}) \cap E_o = \emptyset \\
cs(e', o) & : e \in meas(E) \wedge e' \text{ maximal in } adv(e{\downarrow}) \cap E_o
\end{cases}
$$

*When* $cs(e, o)$ *takes the value* $\mathsf{c}$ *we say* $o$ *is* corrupt *at* $e$; *when it takes the value* $\mathsf{r}$ *we say* $o$ *is* uncorrupt *or* regular *at* $e$; *and when it takes the value* $\bot$ *we say the corruption state is* undefined.

The above definition also allows us to define the result of a measurement event. In this work, to simplify the analysis, we assume there are no false positives or negatives as long as the measurer and its context are uncorrupted. However, we assume a corrupted measurer (or its context) can always produce evidence indicating that the target of measurement is uncorrupted.

**Assumption 1 (Measurement accuracy).** *Let* $\mathcal{G}(o)$ *and* $\mathcal{B}(o)$ *be a partition for* $\mathcal{MV}(o)$. *Let* $e = \mathsf{ms}(o_2, o_1)$. *The* output *of* $e$, *written* $out(e)$, *is defined as follows.*

$$
out(e) = \begin{cases}
v \in \mathcal{B}(o_1) & cs(e, o_1) = \mathsf{c} \text{ and } \forall o \in \{o_2\} \cup C^{-1}(o_2) . cs(e, o) = \mathsf{r} \\
v \in \mathcal{G}(o_1) & \text{otherwise}
\end{cases}
$$

If $out(e) \in \mathcal{B}(o_1)$ we say $e$ *detects a corruption*. If $out(e) \in \mathcal{G}(o_1)$ but $cs(e, o_1) = \mathsf{c}$, we say the adversary *avoids detection at* $e$.

Assumption 1 can be used to reason in two ways. The first is to determine the result of measurement given the corruption states of the relevant components. It can also be used to infer the corruption states of some components given the corruption states of others and the result of measurement. That is, suppose we know the adversary avoids detection at $e = \mathsf{ms}_{C^{-1}(o)}(o, o_t)$. Then we can conclude that at least one member of $\{o\} \cup C^{-1}(o)$ is corrupt at $e$. This fact will be used in the proof of our main result.

**Lemma 2.** *Let $(E, \prec)$ be a finite extend-ordered poset for $\mathcal{AS}$, and let $(E_p, \prec_p)$ be its restriction to some $p \in P$. Then for every event $e \in E_p$, $ext(e{\downarrow})$ is either empty, or it has a unique maximal event $e'$.*

This lemma allows us to unambiguously define the value in a PCR at any event that touches the PCR.

**Definition 5 (PCR value).** *We define the* value *in a PCR $p$ at event $e$ touching $p$ to be the following, where $e{\downarrow}$ is taken in $E_p$.*

$$
val(e, p) = \begin{cases}
\mathsf{rst} & : ext(e{\downarrow}) = \emptyset, e = \mathsf{qt}(n, t_I) \\
\#(v, \mathsf{rst}) & : ext(e{\downarrow}) = \emptyset, e = \mathsf{ext}(o, v, p) \\
state(e', p) & : e' = max(ext(e{\downarrow})), e = \mathsf{qt}(n, t_I) \\
\#(v, state(e', p)) & : e' = max(ext(e{\downarrow})), e = \mathsf{ext}(o, v, p)
\end{cases}
$$

*When $e = \mathsf{ext}(o, v, p)$ we say $e$ is the event* recording *the value $v$.*

Lemma 2 and Definition 5 also allow us to determine the contents of a quote at a quote event. Recall that, to ensure the signature cannot be forged, we must assume the signing key is not available to the adversary.

**Definition 6 (Quote outputs).** *Let $e = \mathsf{qt}(n, t_I)$. Then its output is $out(e) = [\![n, (t.i)_{i \in I}, (v_i)_{i \in I}]\!]_{sk(t)}$, where for each $i \in I$, $val(e, t.i) = v_i$, and $sk(t) \in \mathcal{K}$ (the set of atomic, non-public keys). We say a quote $Q$* indicates a corruption *iff some $v_i$ contains a $v \in \mathcal{B}(o)$ for some $o$.*

Finally, we formally define executions of a measurement system.

**Definition 7 (Executions, specifications).** *Let $\mathcal{AS}$ be an attestation system.*

1. *An execution of $\mathcal{AS}$ is any finite, adversary-ordered, extend-ordered poset $E$ for $\mathcal{AS}$ such that whenever $e$ has input $v$, then $v$ is derivable from the set $\mathcal{P} \cup \{out(e') \mid e' \prec_E e\}$, i.e. the public terms together with the output of previous events.*
2. *A* specification *for $\mathcal{AS}$ is any execution that contains no adversary events.*

*We denote by $\mathcal{E}(S)$ the set of executions $E$ that contain $S$ as a substructure, and we say $S$* admits *$E$. When $S$ consists only of quote events outputting a set $\mathcal{Q}$ of quotes, we say $E$* produces *$\mathcal{Q}$. We sometime abuse notation and write $E \in \mathcal{E}(\mathcal{Q})$.*

We thus further restrict executions to ensure that all inputs to extension and quote events are derivable at the time of the event. This reflects natural limitations on the adversary that he cannot, for example, break cryptography.

# 5    Bundling Evidence for Attestation

When evaluating evidence from a set of quotes $Q$, the only information an appraiser has about the execution $E$ that produced them is that $E \in \mathcal{E}(Q)$. According to [14], the appraiser should have a "bottom-up" specification $S$ in mind, and she would like know whether $E \in \mathcal{E}(S)$. Thus, ideally, we could develop a strategy for bundling that would ensure $\mathcal{E}(Q) \subseteq \mathcal{E}(S)$, at least for bottom-up specifications $S$. However, this is too much to ask for in the presence of dynamic corruptions. If the adversary completely owns the system, he can always create an $E \in \mathcal{E}(Q)\backslash\mathcal{E}(S)$. The best we can do is ensure that it is difficult for the adversary to force the execution to be in $E \in \mathcal{E}(Q)\backslash\mathcal{E}(S)$. In particular, we will aim to force the adversary to perform corruptions in small time windows, or to corrupt deeper (and presumably better protected) components (so-called "recent or deep" corruptions). This section develops the core set of inferences for characterizing executions in $E \in \mathcal{E}(Q)\backslash\mathcal{E}(S)$, and proposes a particular strategy for bundling evidence relative to bottom-up measurements. The net result is that if an adversary would like to convince the appraiser the measurements were taken bottom-up when in fact they weren't, then he must perform recent or deep corruptions. That is, in order to avoid the hypothesis of the main result from [14] he must nonetheless subject himself to its conclusion!

## 5.1    Principles for TPM-based Bundling

For the remainder of this section we fix an arbitrary attestation system $\mathcal{AS} = (O, M, C, P, L)$. The proofs of these lemmas can be found in the appendix. Our first lemma allows us to infer the existence of some extend events in an execution.

**Lemma 3.** *Let $e$ be a quote event in execution $E$ with output $Q$. For each PCR $p$ reported on by $Q$, and for each $v$ contained in $val(e, p)$ there is some extend event $e_v \prec_E e$ recording $v$.*

**Lemma 4.** *Let $e \in E$ be an event with input parameter $v$. If $v \in \mathcal{N}$ or if $v$ is a signature using key $sk(t) \in \mathcal{K}$, then there is a prior event $e' \prec_E e$ such that $out(e') = v$.*

**Lemma 5.** *Let $E$ be an execution producing quote $Q$. Assume $v_i$ is contained before $v_j$ in PCR $p$ reported on by $Q$, and let $e_i$ and $e_j$ be the events recording $v_i$ and $v_j$ respectively. Then $e_i \prec_E e_j$.*

*Proof.* This is an immediate consequence of Definition 5.    □

**Corollary 1.** *Let $E$ be an execution producing quotes $Q$, and $Q'$ where $Q$ reports on PCR $p$. Suppose $Q'$ is contained in $p$ before $v$. Then every event recording values contained in $Q'$ occurs before the event recording $v$.*

These results form the core of what an appraiser is justified in inferring about an execution on the basis of a TPM quote $Q$. Notice that the conclusions are only about extend events, and not about measurement events. This is due to one of the fundamental limitations of a TPM: Its isolation from the rest of the system causes it not to have very much contextual information about the measurement events. We are therefore very careful in what follows to identify the additional assumptions we must make about components in order to justify the inferences about measurements we would like to make.

## 5.2    Formalizing and Justifying a Bundling Strategy

With these results in mind, we revisit the example of Sect. 3 to develop a strategy for bundling the evidence created by the measurers. In order to combine the benefits of the two strategies we considered, we are looking for a strategy that reflects the history of the events (in particular, their relative orders) while providing exclusive access for each component to its own PCR. The idea is to follow Strategy 2, but to ensure the evidence from lower layers is incorporated into the PCRs of the higher layers in a way that cannot be forged. This results in a layered, nested set of quotes of the following form.

$$Q_1 = [\![\, n, p_r, \mathsf{seq}(v_1, v_2) \,]\!]_{sk(t)}$$
$$Q_2 = [\![\, n, (p_1, p_2), (\mathsf{seq}(Q_1, v_3), \mathsf{seq}(Q_1, v_4)) \,]\!]_{sk(vt_1)}$$
$$Q_3 = [\![\, n, p_{vc}, \mathsf{seq}(Q_2, v_5) \,]\!]_{sk(vt_2)}$$

The quote $Q_1$ provides evidence that rtm has measured $A_1$ and $A_2$. This quote is itself extended into the PCRs of $A_1$ and $A_2$ before they take their measurements and extend the results. $Q_2$ thus represents evidence that rtm took its measurements before $A_1$ and $A_2$ took theirs. Similarly, $Q_3$ is evidence that $vc$ took its measurement after $A_1$ and $A_2$ took theirs since $Q_2$ is extended into $p_{vc}$ before the measurement evidence.

This quote structure is an instance of a more general strategy for bundling evidence from measurements that are taken bottom-up. The idea is that bottom-up measurements create temporal dependencies that reflect the $M$ and $C$ dependencies of the system. So each measurement agent $o$ extends a quote containing measurements of $M^{-1}(o) \cup C^{-1}(o)$ before extending the evidence it gathers. This is why we assume $M \cup C$ is acyclic; this strategy would not be well-defined otherwise.

We formalize this strategy by giving a criterion for recognizing when a set of quotes conforms to the strategy. But first, we must finally formalize the as-yet intuitive notion of bottom-up measurement.

**Definition 8.** *A measurement event* $e = \mathsf{ms}(o_2, o_1)$ *in execution $E$ is well-supported iff either*

i. $o_2 = \mathsf{rtm}$, *or*
ii. *for every $o \in D^1(o_1)$, there is a measurement event $e' \prec_E e$ such that $o$ is the target of $e'$.*

*When e is well-supported, we call the set of e' from Condition ii above the* support *of e. An execution E* measures bottom-up *iff each measurement event $e \in E$ is well-supported.*

**Bundling strategy criterion.** *Let $\mathcal{Q}$ be a set of quotes. We describe how to create a measurement specification $S(\mathcal{Q})$. For each $Q \in \mathcal{Q}$, and each $p$ that $Q$ reports on, and each $v \in \mathcal{MV}(o_2)$ contained in $p$, $S(\mathcal{Q})$ contains an event $e_v = \mathsf{ms}(o_1, o_2)$ where $M(o_1, o_2)$ and $L(o_1, p)$. Similarly, for each distinct $n$ in the nonce field of some $Q \in \mathcal{Q}$, $S(\mathcal{Q})$ contains the event $\mathsf{att\text{-}start}(n)$. Let $S_Q$ denote the set of events derived in this way from $Q \in \mathcal{Q}$. Then $e \prec_{S(\mathcal{Q})} e_v$ iff $Q$ is contained before $v$ and $e \in S_Q$. $\mathcal{Q}$ complies with the bundling strategy iff $S(\mathcal{Q})$ measures bottom-up.*

Using the results from the start of this section, we can prove that executions producing quotes that conform to the strategy contain a bottom-up extension structure that "shadows" the desired bottom-up measurement structure.

**Definition 9.** *Let $e = \mathsf{ext}(o, v, p)$ be an extend event in execution $E$ such that $v \in \mathcal{MV}(o_t)$ for some $o_t \in O$. We say $e$ is* well-supported *iff either*

i. *$o = \mathsf{rtm}$, or*
ii. *for every $o \in D^1(o_t)$ there is an extend event $e' \prec_E e$ such that $e' = \mathsf{ext}(o', v', p')$ with $v' \in \mathcal{MV}(o)$.*

*We call the set of such $e'$ the* support *of $e$. A collection of extend events $X$* extends bottom-up *iff each $e \in X$ is well-supported.*

**Lemma 6.** *Suppose $E \in \mathcal{E}(\mathcal{Q})$ where $S(\mathcal{Q})$ measures bottom-up. Then $E$ contains an extension substructure $X_{\mathcal{Q}}$ that extends bottom-up.*

*Proof.* Let $X_{\mathcal{Q}}$ be the subset of events of $E$ guaranteed by Lemma 3. That is, $X_{\mathcal{Q}}$ consists of all the events $e = \mathsf{ext}(o, v, p)$ that record measurement values $v$ reported in $\mathcal{Q}$. For any such event $e$, if $o = \mathsf{rtm}$ then $e$ is well-supported by definition. Otherwise, since $S(\mathcal{Q})$ measures bottom-up, Lemma 3 and Corollary 1 ensure $X_{\mathcal{Q}}$ contain events $e' = \mathsf{ext}(o', v', p')$ for every $o' \in D^1(o)$ where $e' \prec_E e$. Thus $e$ is also well supported in that case.  □

Unfortunately, based on the lemmas from the start of the section, this is as far as we can go. Those lemmas do not allow us to infer the existence of *any* measurement events based only on the existence of extension events. In fact, this seems to be an important fundamental limitation of TPMs. Due to their isolation from the rest of the system, they have virtually no view into the activities of the system. Rather, we must rely on the trustworthiness of the components interacting with the TPM and knowledge of their specified behavior to infer facts about the behavior of the rest of the system.

We thus identify two assumptions about the behavior of uncorrupted measurers that will be useful in recreating the desired bottom-up measurement structure from the bottom-up extend structure.

Our first assumption is that uncorrupted measurers extend measurement values for only the most recent measurement of a given target. This translates to the following formal condition on executions.

**Assumption 2.** If $E$ contains an event $e = \mathsf{ext}(o, v, p)$ with $v \in \mathcal{MV}(t)$, where $o$ is regular at that event, then there is an event $e' = \mathsf{ms}(o, t)$ such that $e' \prec_E e$. Furthermore, the most recent such event $e'$ satisfies $out(e') = v$.

Our second assumption is that when uncorrupted measurers extend a quote from a lower layer followed by measurement evidence it generates, it always generates the measurement evidence between those two extensions. This similarly translates to the following formal condition on executions.

**Assumption 3.** Suppose $E$ has events $e \prec_E e'$ with $e = \mathsf{ext}(o, Q, p)$ and $e' = \mathsf{ext}(o, v, p)$, where $Q$ contains evidence for $M^{-1}(o) \cup C^{-1}(o)$, and $v \in \mathcal{MV}(t)$. If $o$ is regular at $e'$ then there is an intervening event $e \prec_E e'' \prec_E e'$ such that $e'' = \mathsf{ms}(o, t)$.

The first assumption allows us to infer the existence of measurement events from extension events as long as the component is not corrupted. The second assumptions provides a way of inferring extra ordering information useful for reconstructing a bottom-up measurement structure.

The second assumption in particular is crafted to correspond closely to our proposed strategy for bundling evidence, and so we should not expect every architecture to satisfy these assumptions. While they may not be necessary for our purposes, we will show that they are jointly sufficient to guarantee that either the measurements were taken bottom-up, or else the adversary must have performed a recent or deep corruption relative to some component.

**Theorem 1.** *Let $E \in \mathcal{E}(\mathcal{Q})$ where $S(\mathcal{Q})$ measures bottom-up, and suppose it satisfies Assumptions 2 and 3. Suppose that $v_t \in \mathcal{G}(o_t)$ for each measurement value $v_t$ contained in $\mathcal{Q}$. Then for each extension event $e$ recording a measurement value, either*

*1. $e$ reflects a measurement event that is well-supported by measurement events reflected by the support of $e$.*
*2.  a.  some $o_2 \in D^2(o_t)$ gets corrupted in $E$, or*
 *b.  some $o_1 \in D^1(o_t)$ gets corrupted in $E$ after being measured.*

*Proof.* First note that we can immediately apply Lemma 6 to infer that the extension events represented by $\mathcal{Q}$ form a bottom-up extension structure. The rest of the proof considers an exhaustive list of cases, demonstrating that each one falls into one of Conditions 1, 2a, or 2b. The following diagram summarizes the proof by representing the branching case structure and indicating which clause of the conclusion (C1, C2a, or C2b) each case satisfies.

$$\bullet \xrightarrow{2} \bullet \xrightarrow{2} \bullet \xrightarrow{2} \bullet$$

$$1\downarrow \qquad 1\downarrow \qquad 1\downarrow \qquad 1\downarrow \qquad \searrow^{2}$$

$$C1 \qquad C2a \qquad C1 \qquad C2a \qquad C2b$$

Consider any extend event $e = \mathsf{ext}(o_1, v_t, p_1)$ of $X$ extending a measurement value for some $o_t \in O$. The first case distinction is whether or not $o_1 = \mathsf{rtm}$.

**Case 1:** Assume $o_1 = \mathsf{rtm}$. Since $\mathsf{rtm}$ cannot be corrupted, it is regular at $e$, and by Assumption 2, $e$ reflects the measurement event $\mathsf{ms}(\mathsf{rtm}, o_t)$ which is trivially well-supported, so Condition 1 is satisfied.

**Case 2:** Assume $o_1 \neq \mathsf{rtm}$. Since $X$ extends bottom-up, it has events $e_i = \mathsf{ext}(o_2^i, v_2^i, p_2^i)$ extending measurement values $v_2^i$ for every $o^i \in D^1(o_t)$, and for each $i$, $e_i \prec_E e$. Furthermore, by Corollary 1, there is an extend event $e_q = \mathsf{ext}(o_1, Q, p)$ with $e_i \prec_E e_q \prec_E e$ where $Q$ is a quote containing the values recorded at each $e_i$. Now either some $o_2^i$ is corrupt at $e_i$ (Case 2.1), or each $o_2^i$ is regular at $e_i$ (Case 2.2).

**Case 2.1:** Assume some $o_2^i$ is corrupt at $e_i$. Then there must have been a prior corruption of $o_2^i \in D^2(o_t)$, and hence we are in Condition 1.

**Case 2.2:** Assume each $o_2^i$ is regular at $e_i$. Then Assumption 2 applies to each $e_i$, so each one reflects a measurement event $e_i'$. In this setting, either $o_1$ is regular at $e$ (Case 2.2.1), or $o_1$ is corrupt at $e$ (Case 2.2.2).

**Case 2.2.1:** Assume $o_1$ is regular at $e$. Then since the events $e_q$ and $e$ satisfy the hypothesis of Assumption 3, we can conclude that $e$ reflects a measurement event $e' = \mathsf{ms}(o_1, o_t)$ such that $e_q \prec_E e' \prec_E e$. Thus, $e'$ is well-supported by the $e_i'$ events which are reflected by the support of $e$, putting us in Condition 1.

**Case 2.2.2:** Assume $o_1$ is corrupt at $e$. Since $o_1 \in D^1(o_t)$ one of the $e_i'$ is a measurement event of $o_1$ with output $v_1 \in \mathcal{G}(o_1)$ since $X$ only extends measurement values that do not indicate corruption. Call this event $e_*'$. The final case distinction is whether $o_1$ is corrupt at this event $e_*'$ (Case 2.2.2.1) or regular at $e_*'$ (Case 2.2.2.2).

**Case 2.2.2.1:** Assume $o_1$ is corrupt at $e_*'$. Since the measurement outputs a good value, some element $o_2 \in D^1(o_1) \subseteq D^2(o_t)$ is corrupt at $e_*'$. This satisfies Condition 1.

**Case 2.2.2.2:** Assume $o_1$ is regular at $e_*'$. By the assumption of Case 2.2.2, $o_1$ is corrupt at $e$ with $e_*' \prec_E e$. Thus there must be an intervening corruption of $o_1$. Since $e_*'$ is a measurement event of $o_1$, this satisfies Condition 1.    □

Theorem 1 guarantees that if there are no recent or deep corruptions, then we can infer the existence of a collection of measurement events reflected by the values in the quotes. It remains to show that this measurement substructure is precisely the one we want, namely that it is equal to $S(\mathcal{Q})$. Unfortunately, this may not be the case. $S(\mathcal{Q})$ may contain orderings that are not strictly necessary to ensure $S(\mathcal{Q})$ measures bottom-up. However, Assumption 3 can guarantee only that the orderings necessary to be bottom-up are present. For this reason we introduce the notion of the core of a bottom-up specification. The *core* of a bottom-up specification $S$ is the result of removing any orderings between measurement events $e_i \prec_S e_j$ whenever $e_i$ is not in the support of $e_j$. That is, the core of $S$ ignores all orderings that do not contribute to $S$ measuring bottom-up. We can then show that the measurement structure inferred from Theorem 1 is (isomorphic to) the core of $S(\mathcal{Q})$.

**Theorem 2.** *Let $E \in \mathcal{E}(\mathcal{Q})$ such that $S(\mathcal{Q})$ measures bottom-up, and let $S'$ be its core. Suppose that $\mathcal{Q}$ detects no corruptions, and that $E$ satisfies Assumptions 2 and 3. Then one of the following holds:*

1. $E \in \mathcal{E}(S')$,
2. *there is some $o_t \in O$ such that*
   a. *some $o_2 \in D^2(o_t)$ is corrupted, or*
   b. *some $o_1 \in D^1(o_t)$ is corrupted after being measured.*

# 6   Related Work

There has been much research into measurement and attestation. While a complete survey is infeasible for this paper, we mention the most relevant highlights in order to describe how the present work fits into the larger body of work.

Building on the early work of Trusted Boot [9], there have been numerous attempts to bring trust further up the software stack. Most notably, Sailer et al. [15] introduced an integrity measurement architecture (IMA) in which each application is measured as it is launched. More recently, this body of work on static measurement has been augmented with attempts to measure dynamic system properties that give a clearer picture of the current state of the system (e.g. [6–8,17]). Most of these focus on the low-level details of what to measure and how to implement it without considering how runtime corruption can affect the attestation process itself. In particular, it is common to invoke the use of Trusted Boot and IMA as a way to build a chain of trust from the hardware which the proposed measurement agent can extend. Our work could be applied to systems that incorporate these integrity measurers in order to better understand how they respond to dynamic corruption of the trusted computing base and measurement agents themselves.

We are not the first to discuss the dependencies that emerge in a layered system. Some work [10,16] builds on the notion of a tree of trust [11] to tease out a structure for the integrity evidence required of an attestation. The focus in these papers is on ensuring the integrity of the system can be correctly inferred from the structure of the evidence. While we focus on only a subset of the trust dependencies considered in, say, [10], they do not take full account of the effects dynamic corruption of components might have on the bundling of the evidence. Rather they explicitly bracket out the problem of guaranteeing the trustworthiness of the integrity information itself. An interesting line of future work would be to investigate the causal effects of dynamic corruption on the wider variety of dependencies they consider.

Layered dependencies are also implicit in the design of many systems intended to support attestation of their runtime properties. Coker et al. [4] present 5 principles for remote attestation and propose a layered system designed from those principles. They do not investigate the low-level structure of evidence that must be created in order to attest to the layered dependencies or how to bundle such evidence using the TPM. Cabuk et al. [3] present a hierarchical system with a software-based root of trust for measurement that is connected to a lower-level chain of trust rooted in hardware. They demonstrate the variety of hierarchical dependencies that can naturally arise and propose ways to manage this complexity. Finally, in [2], Berger et al. propose a way to manage the complexity of appraising systems with layered dependencies as the systems scale. In all of these examples, to the extent that runtime corruptions are considered seriously, the problem of understanding how such corruptions break the chain of trust is not examined. Within our formalism we should be able to represent all these systems and characterize the ways in which runtime corruptions can occur without being reflected in the final bundle of evidence. Particular designs may enable bundling strategies that are tailored to the design which require weaker assumptions than those we used in this paper.

## 7   Conclusion

In this paper we have developed a formalism for reasoning about layered attestations. Within the framework we have identified some potential pitfalls when using a TPM to bundle measurement evidence. These pitfalls arise due to a fundamental limitation of TPMs. Namely, by virtue of being isolated from the main system, TPMs have very limited contextual information about the events occurring on that system. This means further assumptions must be made about uncompromised components in order for an appraiser to infer desired behavior.

We also identified a core set of inference principles that can help system designers determine the consequences of a particular strategy for bundling evidence. Finally, we applied those principles to prove the robustness of a new layered approach to bundling evidence. We believe this new proposal gives easy to explain design advice. Namely, after identifying the temporal dependencies required for an attestation, the evidence should be extended into a TPM one layer at a time, ensuring the quotes from lower layers are incorporated into the quotes from higher layers as you go. This will remain robust as long as uncorrupted components can be trusted to take fresh measurements after receiving the results from below.

Although this proposal is most applicable to systems designed around the use of vTPMs, we believe the core idea illuminates the problems with certain naive ways of using a TPM to report evidence. In any case, we make no claims that this proposal represents a complete solution for all cases. Rather, we consider it the first attempt to seriously account for the possibility of runtime corruption during an attestation, and we would encourage others to develop complementary strategies. The formalism introduced here together with the inference principles would be a good way to evaluate such proposals.

**Acknowledgments.** I would like to thank Pete Loscocco for suggesting and guiding the direction of this research. Many thanks also to Perry Alexander and Joshua Guttman for their valuable feedback on earlier versions of this work. Thanks also to Sarah Helble and Aaron Pendergrass for lively discussions about measurement and attestation systems. Finally, thank you to the anonymous reviewers for helpful comments in improving the paper.

# A    Proof of Lemmas

The following is a proof of Lemma 3

*Proof.* By definition, the values contained in a PCR are exactly those that were previously extended into it. Thus, since ext events are the only way to extend values into PCRs, there must be some event $e_v = \mathsf{ext}(o, v, p)$ with $e_v \prec_E e$.    □

The following is a proof of Lemma 4

*Proof.* Definition 7 requires $v$ to be derivable from the public terms $\mathcal{P}$ and the output of previous messages. Call those outputs $\mathcal{O}$.

First suppose $v \in \mathcal{N}$. Since $v$ is atomic, the only way to derive it is if $v \in \mathcal{P} \cup \mathcal{O}$. Since $\mathcal{P} \cap \mathcal{N} = \emptyset$, $v \notin \mathcal{P}$, hence $v \in \mathcal{O}$ as required.

Now suppose $v$ is a signature using key $sk(t) \in \mathcal{K}$. Then $v$ can be derived in two ways. The first is if $v \in \mathcal{P} \cup \mathcal{O}$. In this case, since $v \notin \mathcal{P}$ it must be in $\mathcal{O}$ instead as required. The other way to derive $v$ is to construct it from the key $sk(t)$ and the signed message, say $m$. That is, we must first derive $sk(t)$. Arguing as above, the only way to derive $sk(t)$ is to find it in $\mathcal{O}$, but there are no events that output such a term.    □

We conclude with the complete proof of Theorem 2.

*Proof.* By Lemma 6, $E$ contains a substructure $X_Q$ of extend events that extends bottom-up. Thus by Theorem 1, Conditions 2a and 2b are possibilities. So suppose instead that $E$ satisfies Condition 1 of Theorem 1. We must show that $E \in \mathcal{E}(S')$. In particular, we construct $\alpha : S' \to E$ and show that it is label- and order-preserving.

Consider the measurement events $e_i^s$ of $S'$. By construction, each one comes from some measurement value $v_i$ contained in $Q$. Similarly, the well-supported measurement events $e_i^m$ of $E$ guaranteed by Theorem 1 are reflected by extend events $e_i$ of $E$ which are, in turn, those events that record each $v_i$ in $Q$. We need to show that $e_i^s = e_i^m$ for each $i$ (i.e. that the labels agree), and that the orders among the $e_i^s$ are reflected by corresponding orders among the $e_i^m$.

Consider first the label of $e_i^s$. It corresponds to a measurement value $v_i$ contained in some $p_i$ of $Q$. So $e_i^s$ is labeled $\mathsf{ms}(o, o')$ where $M(o, o')$, $v_i \in \mathcal{MV}(o')$, and $L(o, p_i)$. The event $e_i^m$ also corresponds to the same $v_i$. Lemma 3 ensures that $e_i = \mathsf{ext}(o, v, p_i)$ with $L(o, p_i)$, and so the measurement event it reflects is $e_i^m = \mathsf{ms}(o, o')$ with $M(o, o')$ and $v_i \in \mathcal{MV}(o')$. Thus $e_i^s$ and $e_i^m$ have the same label.

We now show that if $e_i^s \prec_{S(\mathcal{Q})} e_j^s$ then $e_i^m \prec_E e_j^m$. The former ordering exists in $S'$ because some quote $Q \in \mathcal{Q}$ is contained in $p_j$ before $v_j$ and $v_i$ is contained in $Q$, and because $e_i^s$ is in the support of $e_j^s$. By Corollary 1 $e_i \prec_E e_j$ and $e_i$ is in the support of $e_j$ and therefore Theorem 1 ensures that the measurements they reflect are also ordered, i.e. $e_i^m \prec_E e_j^m$.

Finally, consider any events $e = \mathsf{att\text{-}start}(n)$ in $S'$. They come from nonces $n$ found as inputs to quotes $Q \in \mathcal{Q}$. By Lemma 4, $E$ also has a corresponding event $e^*$ with $out(e^*) = n$. Since $\mathsf{att\text{-}start}(n)$ events are the only ones with output of the right kind, $e^* = \mathsf{att\text{-}start}(n)$ as well. Thus we can extend $\alpha$ by mapping each such $e$ to the corresponding $e^*$. The rules for $S(\mathcal{Q})$ say that $e \prec_{S(\mathcal{Q})} e'$ only when $Q$ has $n$ in the nonce field, and $Q$ occurs before the value recorded by $e'$. In $E$, $e^*$ precedes the event producing $Q$ (by Lemma 4) which in turn precedes $e'$ by Lemmas 4 and 5. Thus the orderings in $S(\mathcal{Q})$ involving $\mathsf{att\text{-}start}(n)$ events are also reflected in $E$. □

# References

1. Berger, S., Cáceres, R., Goldman, K.A., Perez, R., Sailer, R., van Doorn, L.: vTPM: virtualizing the trusted platform module. In: Proceedings of the 15th USENIX Security Symposium, Vancouver, BC, Canada, July 31–August 4, 2006 (2006)
2. Berger, S., Goldman, K.A., Pendarakis, D.E., Safford, D., Valdez, E., Zohar, M.: Scalable attestation: a step toward secure and trusted clouds. IEEE Cloud Comput. **2**(5), 10–18 (2015)
3. Cabuk, S., Chen, L., Plaquin, D., Ryan, M.: Trusted integrity measurement and reporting for virtualized platforms. In: Chen, L., Yung, M. (eds.) INTRUST 2009. LNCS, vol. 6163, pp. 180–196. Springer, Heidelberg (2010)
4. Coker, G., Guttman, J.D., Loscocco, P., Herzog, A.L., Millen, J.K., O'Hanlon, B., Ramsdell, J.D., Segall, A., Sheehy, J., Sniffen, B.T.: Principles of remote attestation. Int. J. Inf. Sec. **10**(2), 63–81 (2011)
5. Cucurull, J., Guasch, S.: Virtual TPM for a secure cloud: fallacy or reality? Universidad de Alicante (2014)
6. Davi, L., Sadeghi, A.-R., Winandy, M.: Dynamic integrity measurement and attestation: towards defense against return-oriented programming attacks. In: Proceedings of the 4th ACM Workshop on Scalable Trusted Computing, STC 2009, Chicago, Illinois, USA, 13 November 2009, pp. 49–54 (2009)
7. Kil, C., Sezer, E.C., Azab, A.M., Ning, P., Zhang, X.: Remote attestation to dynamic system properties: towards providing complete system integrity evidence. In: Proceedings of the 2009 IEEE/IFIP International Conference on Dependable Systems and Networks, DSN 2009, Estoril, Lisbon, Portugal, 29 June–2 July, 2009, pp. 115–124 (2009)
8. Loscocco, P., Wilson, P.W., Aaron Pendergrass, J., Durward McDonell, C.: Linux kernel integrity measurement using contextual inspection. In: Proceedings of the 2nd ACM Workshop on Scalable Trusted Computing, STC 2007, Alexandria, VA, USA, 2 November 2007, pp. 21–29 (2007)
9. Maliszewski, R., Sun, N., Wang, S., Wei, J., Qiaowei, R.: Trusted boot (tboot). http://sourceforge.net/p/tboot/wiki/Home/
10. Namiluko, C., Martin, A.: Provenance-based model for verifying trust-properties. In: Katzenbeisser, S., Weippl, E., Camp, L.J., Volkamer, M., Reiter, M., Zhang, X. (eds.) Trust 2012. LNCS, vol. 7344, pp. 255–272. Springer, Heidelberg (2012)

11. Lo Presti, S.: A tree of trust rooted in extended trusted computing. In: Proceedings of the Second Conference on Advances in Computer Security and Forensics Programme (ACSF), pp. 13–20 (2007)
12. Xen Project. http://www.xenproject.org
13. QEMU. http://wiki.qemu.org
14. Rowe, P.D.: Confining adversary actions via measurement. In: Proceeding of the 3rd International Workshop in Graphical Models for Security, GraMSec 2016 (in press)
15. Sailer, R., Zhang, X., Jaeger, T., van Doorn, L.: Design and implementation of a TCG-based integrity measurement architecture. In: Proceedings of the 13th USENIX Security Symposium, San Diego, CA, USA, 9–13 August 2004, pp. 223–238 (2004)
16. Schmidt, A.U., Leicher, A., Brett, A., Shah, Y., Cha, I.: Tree-formed verification data for trusted platforms. Comput. Secur. **32**, 19–35 (2013)
17. Wei, J., Calton, P., Rozas, C.V., Rajan, A., Zhu, F.: Modeling the runtime integrity of cloud servers: a scoped invariant perspective. In: Proceedings of the Second International Conference in Cloud Computing, CloudCom 2010, November 30–3 December 2010, Indianapolis, Indiana, USA, pp. 651–658 (2010)

# An Arbiter PUF Secured by Remote Random Reconfigurations of an FPGA

Alexander Spenke[1], Ralph Breithaupt[2], and Rainer Plaga[2(✉)]

[1] Hochschule Bonn-Rhein-Sieg, 53757 Sankt Augustin, Germany
[2] Federal Office for Information Security (BSI), 53175 Bonn, Germany
rainer.plaga@bsi.bund.de
https://www.h-brs.de
https://www.bsi.de

**Abstract.** We present a practical and highly secure method for the authentication of chips based on a new concept for implementing strong Physical Unclonable Function (PUF) on field programmable gate arrays (FPGA). Its qualitatively novel feature is a remote reconfiguration in which the delay stages of the PUF are arranged to a random pattern within a subset of the FPGA's gates. Before the reconfiguration is performed during authentication the PUF simply does not exist. Hence even if an attacker has the chip under control previously she can gain no useful information about the PUF. This feature, together with a strict renunciation of any error correction and challenge selection criteria that depend on individual properties of the PUF that goes into the field make our strong PUF construction immune to all machine learning attacks presented in the literature. More sophisticated attacks on our strong-PUF construction will be difficult, because they require the attacker to learn or directly measure the properties of the complete FPGA. A fully functional reference implementation for a secure "chip biometrics" is presented. We remotely configure ten 64-stage arbiter PUFs out of 1428 lookup tables within a time of 25 s and then receive one "fingerprint" from each PUF within 1 ms.

**Keywords:** Strong Physical Unclonable Functions (PUFs) · Biometrics of chips · Silicon biometrics · Field programmable gate arrays

## 1 Introduction

"Physical unclonable functions" (PUFs) are innovative hardware devices that shall be hard to reproduce physically because their functionality depends on variance in the production or configuration process (e.g. in dopant levels) [2,14]. They promise to enable qualitatively novel security mechanisms e.g. for authentication and key generation and distribution and have consequently become an important research area of hardware security [17,21,22].

Secure authentication of a chip when its responses are obtained from a remote location, i.e. when its physical properties cannot be directly examined, is an important security objective. In order to reach this objective, the chip's functionality

© Springer International Publishing Switzerland 2016
M. Franz and P. Papadimitratos (Eds.): TRUST 2016, LNCS 9824, pp. 140–158, 2016.
DOI: 10.1007/978-3-319-45572-3_8

must be unclonable not only physically but in general ("mathematical unclonability" [8]). This property is highly desirable e.g. for chips in banking cards and passports, but has proven to be very difficult to ensure against well-equipped attackers on the authentication secrets in chips [19]. Mathematical unclonability with PUFs can be reached with so called "strong PUF" which possesses a number of challenge-response (C-R) pairs that is so large that an attacker with temporary access to the PUF cannot evaluate them all. PUF constructions with an exponentially large number of C-R pairs have been constructed, e.g. the arbiter PUF [2]. It has proved possible to construct models of such PUFs based on a relatively small number of C-R pairs by using machine-learning programs [15,16,20]. With such a model, a simple piece of software can emulate the remote PUF, thus breaking its security, completely. It is the major aim of our contribution to present a qualitatively novel solution to this fundamental vulnerability of strong PUFs. The origin of the problem is that the true information stored in arbiter PUFs is not exponentially large but relatively small. The attacker only has to determine the relative delays of all stages in order to build a complete model. If we estimate that the delay in one stage can be quantified by 1 byte even an XOR PUF with 10 arbiter PUFs and 128 stages each has a true information content only about 1.3 kbyte. It is true that this information is harder to extract than information stored in a conventional unsecured memory. But because it is a straightforward exercise to construct simple models in which this information appears as parameters it proves to be too easy to extract it. Hence we need to require a qualitatively more difficult extraction methodology and to increase the amount of stored information in the form of manufacturing variations scalable and by a large factor.

The basic idea to meet this requirement is to employ a "second challenge" which specifies how the PUF is to be reconstructed with a subset of gates of an FPGA chip. If the power of this subset is large enough, there is an super-exponentially large number of possible PUF constructions, whose properties the attacker cannot all learn. Even if the attacker is in physical possession of the chip on which the PUF will be realized, she thus remains deprived of the possibility to examine the PUF which is finally used for authentication.

The security mechanism we employ for authentication is to compare a string of single bit responses from a PUF, its "fingerprint", with a previously recorded one from the same PUF. We prefer this "chip biometrics" to authentication methods based on secret keys, because it does not require to store any helper data for error correction on the chip or to select challenges based on properties derived from the chip. These practices reveal information about properties of the PUF. Such information has been shown to allow very effective learning attacks on the PUF employed in the authentication [1]. Because our security mechanism is to deprive the attacker of any chance to learn anything about the authenticated PUF, it reaches its full security potential.

Reconfigurable PUFs have been proposed before. Katzenbeisser et al. [4] and Lao and Parhi [5] studied architectures in which the challenge-response behaviour is changed without modifying the PUF itself. Lao and Parhi [5] also proposed constructions in which the underlying PUF is modified in its properties.

Zhang and Lin [23] presented a scheme against replay attacks in which PUFs are completely reconfigured on 16 different locations on an FPGA. Gehrer and Sigl [3] reconfigured PUFs on an FPGA repeatedly to generate keys efficiently. Majzoobi et al. [9] suggested the use of a "one time PUF" realized as a reconfigured arbiter PUF on an FPGA that is used for a single authentication as a measure against man in the middle attacks. Reconfiguration was not used as a measure against machine-learning attacks before.

*Contribution.* Our main contribution is a highly practical and efficient PUF based authentication system that we hope reaches a security level that rivals the best alternative technologies for authentication. Our contributions and insights are:

1. We develop a qualitatively new security mechanism that prevents in principle that an attacker with temporary direct access to the FPGA has access to the PUF that is later used for authentication. We thus present a strong PUF immune to all machine learning attacks presented up to now in the literature.
2. We demonstrate that, contrary to widespread belief, an FPGA based arbiter PUF with delay stages based on switched multiplexers offers a viable and simple alternative to the more complex constructions based on delay lines that have programmable lengths;
3. For the first time we employ a machine learning program as a tool for the quantitative characterization of properties of arbiter PUFs, rather than only for predicting its responses;
4. We completely avoid all risks from attacks on helper data or specially selected subsets of challenges by strictly only using challenges that are random relative to the chip for which they are chosen and employing no error correction (i.e. we perform a true "biometrics of the chip").

*Structure.* In Sect. 2 we supply the necessary background information on components of our PUF construction and methods used for the characterization of our PUF. Section 3 presents first our arbiter PUF design and then our authentication architecture. The results of an experimental characterization of our implementation are presented in Sect. 4. The discussion in Sect. 5 analyses the security of our construction and Sect. 6 concludes.

## 2    Background

### 2.1    Arbiter PUFs

An arbiter PUF [1,2,7] consists of a chain of N pairs of multiplexers (with an "upper" and "lower" multiplexer) through which pass two signals that started at the same time. Each multiplexer pair is controlled by one bit of a challenge of N bits. If the challenge bit is 0 the upper (lower) signal is passed through the upper (lower) multiplexer and if the challenge bit is 1 the upper (lower) signal is passed through the lower (upper) multiplexer. The response bit is 0 (1) if the lower (upper) signal arrives first at an arbiter at the end of the chain.

**Construction of Arbiter PUFs on FPGAs.** The construction of arbiter PUFs faces the demand to balance out crossing times for the two paths averaged over the manufacturing induced fluctuations [10,13]. On FPGAs the detailed routing on the fabric usually has to be balanced. Compared to PUF implementations in ASICs, where routing is done by fixed circuit path connections, routing in FPGAs has much more influence on the path delays. Due to their flexible design, a complex switching matrix is used to connect the logic elements to each other. Hence the routing delay is mostly defined by the number of switches involved and much less by the process variances of the gates. While it proved possible to roughly balance the delay within and among the delay stages by placing them symmetrically, the delays to the first delay stage and from the last stage to the arbiter turn out to have imbalances due to a different routing that are always at least an order of magnitude larger than the one due to manufacturing variance [13]. If this demand is not met, the responses are no longer unique to the individual PUF because the routing differences are of course the same on different chips[1] for the same PUF. Two solutions to this timing problem have been found. The first one is to configure the lookup tables typically provided by FPGAs as programmable delays lines instead of multiplexers and to tune an individual arbiter PUF by placing delay elements only in one of the paths so that it is perfectly balanced [10,11]. The other is to duplicate the PUF on different slices of the FPGA and to compare the output of these PUFs with identical routing ("double arbiter PUF") [7]. It seems difficult to apply these solutions to our basic approach of an arbiter PUF whose delay stages are placed at random positions of the FPGA fabric. The former would require to balance each individual arbiter for the large number of PUFs that need to be constructed. The latter solution is not applicable if the PUF must be distributed over a considerable fraction of the FPGA fabric as necessary for our approach. We therefore present another solution to the routing problem in Sect. 3.1.

**Learning Attacks on Arbiter PUFs.** The simplest topological timing model of an arbiter PUF is the following [20]. The parameters $\delta_0$ and $\delta_1$ are the differences in delay time between the multiplexers of one pair for a challenge bit of 0 and 1 respectively. The total delay time of in a n-stage arbiter PUF $\Delta D_n$ is then given as:

$$\Delta D_n = \omega^T \Phi \tag{1}$$

Here $\Phi$ a vector with the challenge bits as entry and $\omega$ is the following recursive parameter:

$$\omega_1 = \delta_{0,1} - \delta_{1,1}$$
$$\omega_i = \delta_{0,i-1} + \delta_{1,i-1} + \delta_{0,i} - \delta_{1,i}$$
$$\omega_{n+1} = \delta_{0,n} - \delta_{1,n} \tag{2}$$

---

[1] Below "chip" will be a shorthand our FPGA and "PUF" for one instance of our arbiter PUF construction.

Here i in $\delta_{0,i}$ stands for the i-th delay stage. It is possible to employ programs for machine learning to estimate the vector of $\omega$ values. The estimate is often good enough to predict the response values of an arbiter PUF which is then completely broken as a strong PUF because it can be emulated with a piece of software. We used a learning program based on logistic regression together with the RPROP optimization (Sect. 3 in Tobisch and Becker [20]), to analyse our implementation. Because the meaning of $\omega$ is not intuitive we calculated the time difference of the delay difference of the upper and lower path for a challenge bit 0 and a challenge bit 1 in each delay stage i:

$$\Delta\delta_i = \delta_{0,i} - \delta_{1,i} \tag{3}$$

This set of all $\Delta\delta_i$ quantifies the functionality of the arbiter PUF. We obtained $\Delta\delta_i$ by setting all $\delta_{0,i}$ to 0. Then we inferred 64 $\Delta\delta_i$ values and the value of $\delta_{0,64}$ from Eq. (2). $\Delta\delta_i$ remains dimensionless, because the absolute values of the delay times have no influence on the responses.

## 2.2    Chip Biometrics

Here we authenticate chips with a protocol that is roughly analogous to protocols for biometric authentication, e.g. with a fingerprint. A "basic protocol" was discussed and realized with several types of ASIC-based PUFs by Maes [8]. This protocol consists of two phases, enrolment and verification. During the enrolment phase the verifier records a subset of responses to randomly chosen challenges (analogous to a subset of biometric features chosen) for each chip to be deployed and stores them in a database together with an ID that identifies the chip. During the verification a chip in the field sends its identifier to the verifier. The verifier sends one of the stored challenges. The chip determines the response to the challenge and sends it to the verifier. The chip is verified if this response differs by less bits than a verification threshold t from the response stored in the database.

According to Maes the main drawback of the basic protocol is that it can only be employed in PUFs which cannot be cloned mathematically, i.e. which functionality cannot be cloned in principle. Our main contribution is such a PUF, and therefore we will present a realization of the basic protocol in Sect. 3.2. Rather than inventing a new nomenclature (like e.g. "FPGA signature") we continue to use the term "fingerprint" for our authenticating characteristic, but keep the quotation marks to emphasize that this merely expresses the conceptual similarity to biometrics.

## 2.3    The Smartfusion2 Chip

We used the SmartFusion2 SoC from Microsemi Corp. for our project [12]. It combines a 166 MHz ARM Cortex M3 microprocessor, a system controller for a variety of hardware tasks and interfaces, embedded non-volatile memory (eNVM) and an FPGA fabric on the same chip. Because our construction needs both a microprocessor and FPGA fabric this SoC is ideally suited, because the housing of these components on the same chip eliminates many possible attack vectors among these components. We used SmartFusion2 M2S-FG484 SOM starter kits from Emcraft Systems for our investigations. The FPGA of this starter kit has 12084 "logic units" each of which consists of a look-up table (LUT) with four inputs, a flip-flop and a carry signal from the neighbouring logic element. While most of the characterizations of our implementation was performed in JTAG programming mode, the authentication was also tested in the so called "in-system" programming mode (ISP) in which the microprocessor receives data from an interface (e.g. Ethernet and USB) and transfers it to the system controller which then programs the FPGA and/or the eNVM.

## 3    Design of a Biometric Authentication System Based on Remote Random Reconfiguration

### 3.1    Design of a Random Arbiter PUF

In our implementation we realized an arbiter PUF with 64 delay stages. We first present our solution to the problem of balanced timing announced in Sect. 2.1. From a set of randomly chosen challenges we simply selected those challenges for which the delay-time difference between the two signals happens to be close to 0 fortuitously. We call these challenges "m-challenges" (m for metastable). We employed two methods:

1. We selected challenges with metastable responses (i.e. responses that flip between 0 and 1 when the same challenge is repeatedly applied) on a "reference chip" that will never leave the customer's security lab.
   For the m-challenges the delay difference induced by routing and by manufacturing variance exactly balance on the reference chip. Therefore on other chips the m-challenges will also lead to delay times that are expected to be balanced up to time differences induced by manufacturing variance.
2. We modelled the reference chip with the machine-learning model explained in Sect. 2.1. We then used this model to calculate the predicted delay difference d for a given challenge. Then we selected those challenges for which d was smaller then a maximal bound b.

These two methods did not select the same challenges (i.e. our learning program was not precise enough to always predict the challenges leading to metastability). When we chose b $= 0.2^2$ the sets selected by the two different methods had about equal power and were both suitable for the selection of m-challenges for production. Figure 2 illustrates the distribution of delay-time differences and the selection of the bounded sample.

---

[2] The upper limit has no units because one cannot measure the absolute delay times with machine learning programs.

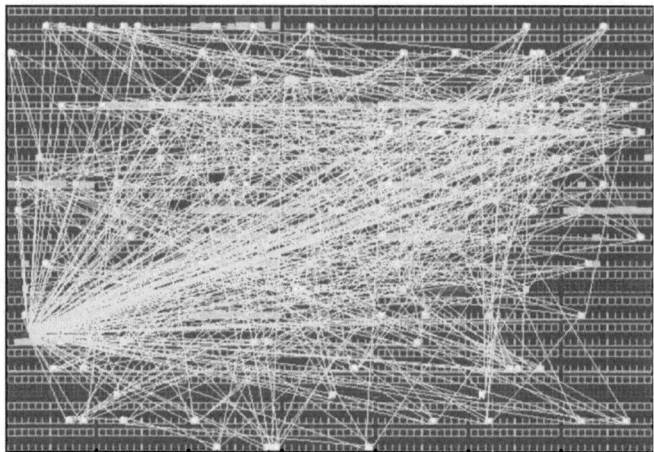

**Fig. 1.** Layout of arbiter PUF #1 on the region of 1428 logical units on the FPGA. The positions of the LUTs used to implement the multiplexers for the delay lines and the interconnections between them are displayed.

Our construction is non-ideal because it just balances the routing delays (these delays will be referred to as "routing induced delay" below) with the delays due to manufacturing variance ("manufacturing induced delay").

In order to allow for a very large number of possible arbiter PUF constructions we selected a region of the FPGA fabric which includes of $84 \times 17 = 1428$ lookup tables. We chose only a small subset of all available lookup tables to make our scheme practical: the rest of the FPGA could still be used for other purposes. The 128 lookup tables used for the 64 delay stages of our arbiter PUF are selected randomly from this set. The positions of the selected LUTs are stored in the "core-cell-constraint" file. Figure 1 displays the layout of random PUF #1.

The decision of the response was performed in an arbiter which was not realized as a flip-flop but with a LUT that evaluates the response R as (U AND L) OR (U AND R), where U and L are the signal from the upper and low path of the arbiter PUF. This construction yields a more symmetric and less temperature dependent response of the arbiter. The VHDL code of our arbiter PUF is given in the appendix.

### 3.2 Architecture and Protocol of Authentication System

Our authentication system works analogous to conventional biometrics and Maes' basic protocol [8] (see Sect. 2.2). In the enrolment phase a set of reference templates, consisting of the responses to a number of arbiter-PUF random layouts as "2nd challenges", together with 100 randomly chosen m-challenges, is determined and stored in a data base. Both these challenge-response pairs and the random layouts the PUFs must be kept secret. The number of 2nd-challenge/100 m challenge pairs must be sufficiently large for the intended

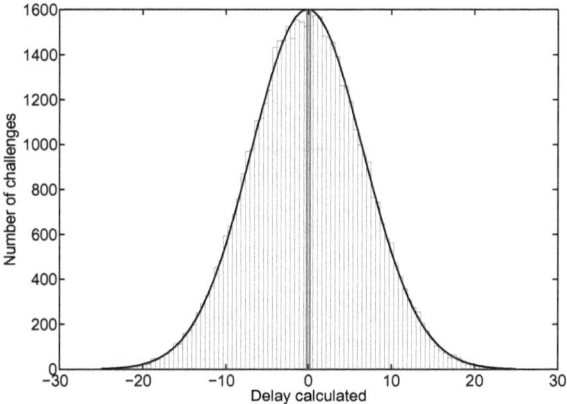

**Fig. 2.** The distribution of delay times calculated with a learning program for 50000 randomly chosen challenges. The delay times are dimensionless because the responses do not depend on the absolute speed of the signals that determine them. The full curve is a Gaussian fit to the data which has a mean value of $-0.15$ and a standard deviation of 6.78. The region marked in red (light shaded) indicates the challenges that were chosen as "m-challenges" because they lead to a small delay between the paths of the arbiter PUF. (Color figure online)

application for the chip authentication. Creating and maintaining such a database before the deployment of the chip is a significant effort.

When a chip in the field is to be authenticated, two challenges are sent:

1. A novel type of challenge, which consist of the compiled VHDL code that determines the configuration of the FPGA. This challenge, which always has a size of 556 kbyte for our FPGA[3], is transferred by the M3 microprocessor to the system controller which then programs the FPGA within a time of at most $28\,\text{s}$[4].
2. 100 conventional 64 bit long m-challenges that decide the multiplexers' settings. The 100 responses are defined to be the "fingerprint" of the chip and are sent to the authenticating party. It took about $10\,\mu\text{s}$ to obtain a single response to an m-challenge.

This procedure is sketched in Fig. 3. It is identical to Maes' basic protocol except that instead of challenge-response pairs, 2nd-challenge and m-challenge-response pairs have to be sent. The authenticating party calculates the Hamming distance between the template and the "fingerprint". Only if this Hamming distance is smaller than a certain threshold t, the chip is authenticated.

Both the novel and the m-challenge are analogous just to the information on which part of the human body (e.g. which finger) is to be used for authentication.

---

[3] The SmartFusion2 chip does not support a partial reconfiguration of the FPGA.
[4] With JTAG programming the total programming cycle took $25\,\text{s}$.

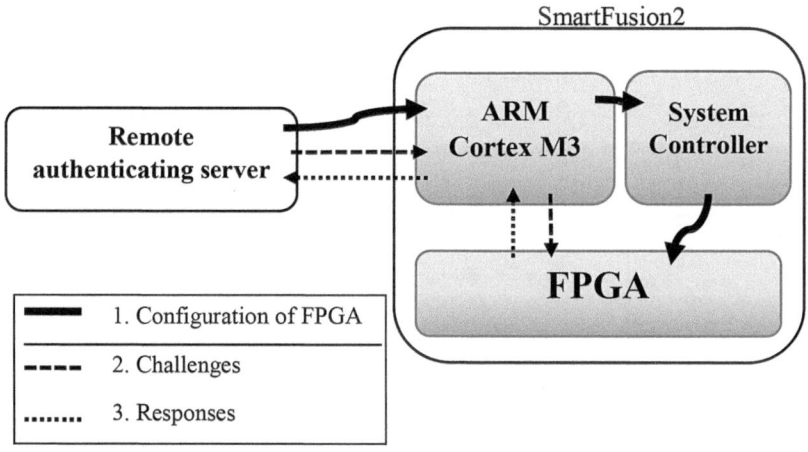

**Fig. 3.** Authentication procedure of a SmartFusion2 chip.

# 4     Experimental Results of Tests with the Implementation

## 4.1     Characterization of Arbiter PUFs

We characterized the properties of ten different randomly placed arbiter PUFs in a climate chamber at different temperatures. Firstly we verified that our construction is really a functional arbiter PUF:

1. By applying the learning program discussed in Sect. 2.1 in order to test if our designs can be modelled as arbiter PUFs which show manufacturing variances.
2. By directly testing if m-challenges that lead to metastable responses on the reference chip do mostly not lead to metastability bits in other chips instances due to manufacturing variance.

Figure 4 shows the difference of delay differences of the 64 stages of ten arbiter PUFs obtained with about 20–30 iterations of their machine-learning program. One recognizes that, as expected, the difference of delays differences vary strongly among the PUFs because the routing depends strongly on the random positions of the delay stages on the FPGA fabric. We succeeded to predict the responses to random challenges with an error rate of about 1.4 %. Figure 5 shows the difference of delay differences (see Eq. (3)) of the 64 stages of one randomly placed arbiter PUF in three different chips, relative to the mean of the delay differences. Even though we are sure that the derived delay differences are correct, because they enable a correct prediction of responses, we did not achieve a deeper understanding of their distribution, e.g. of the surprisingly strong correlation of the delay values in consecutive stages[5]. The inter-chip differences in Fig. 5 are mainly due to manufacturing variance. Their mean absolute values were found to be a

---

[5] We will argue below (Sect. 5) that the difficulty of understanding the routing enhances the security of our design by obfuscation.

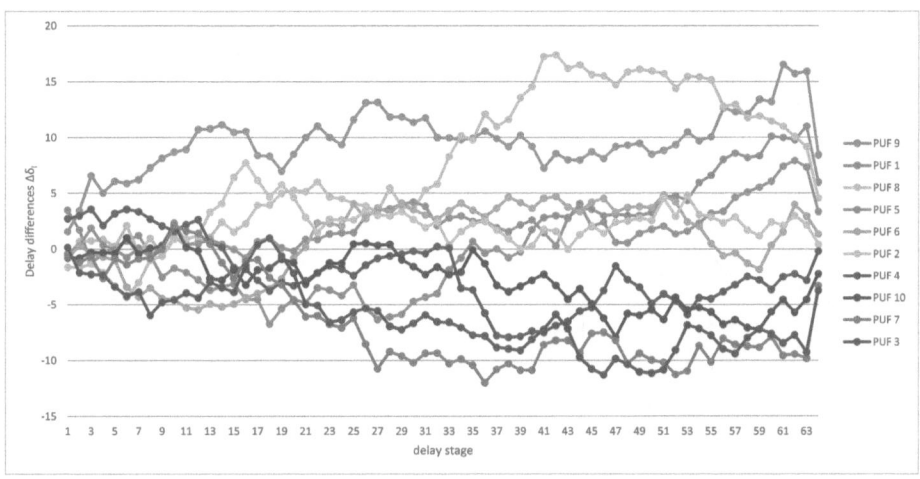

**Fig. 4.** The difference of delay differences with a challenge bit 0 and 1 of the 64 stages of ten randomly placed arbiter PUFs. The time is in dimensionless units because it is derived from a machine learning program. See Eq. (3) for a precise definition of the difference of delay differences.

factor of 29.6 smaller than the differences among chips with a different layout in Fig. 4. This confirms the well known fact that in a multiplexer based arbiter PUF design the delays are dominated by differences in the routing (Morozov et al. [13] found that they dominate by a factor of 25.6 in their FPGA.)

Table 1 shows the fractions of ones for 10 randomly chosen m-challenges on two further chips. An analysis of 1000 m-challenges found that only about 10 % of all m-challenges on chip A also lead to metastable bits on chip B and C. Here a metastable bit is defined as a bit that flips at least once when the challenge is applied 100000 times. This confirms that the responses of m-challenges are strongly influenced by manufacturing variance. Moreover this fraction is much larger than the one for randomly chosen challenges which we found to be 0.72 %[6].

The randomness of the responses of our PUFs was found to depend on the placement strategy. Therefore we needed to test uniformity, uniqueness and reliability of our PUF with the finally chosen placement strategy that is described in Sect. 3.1. Uniformity was determined as the bias[7] of our construction displayed (Fig. 6). The data shown in Fig. 6 have a mean bias of 4.9 %, that is clearly larger than the one expected from statistical fluctuations for our test of 0.3 % but still acceptable for fingerprints that do not have to be perfectly random. Moreover the bias is in a range commonly considered to be acceptable for physical random number generators [6].

The uniqueness of our PUF was quantified as the mean Hamming distance of a "fingerprint" of different chips in the same configuration (Fig. 7). It has a

---

[6] Therefore our PUF construction has $0.0072 \times 2^{64} = 1.3 \times 10^{17}$ m-challenges.

[7] Here we define the bias as $\frac{(\# \text{ of ones}) - (\# \text{ of zeros})}{(\# \text{ of ones}) + (\# \text{ of zeros})}$.

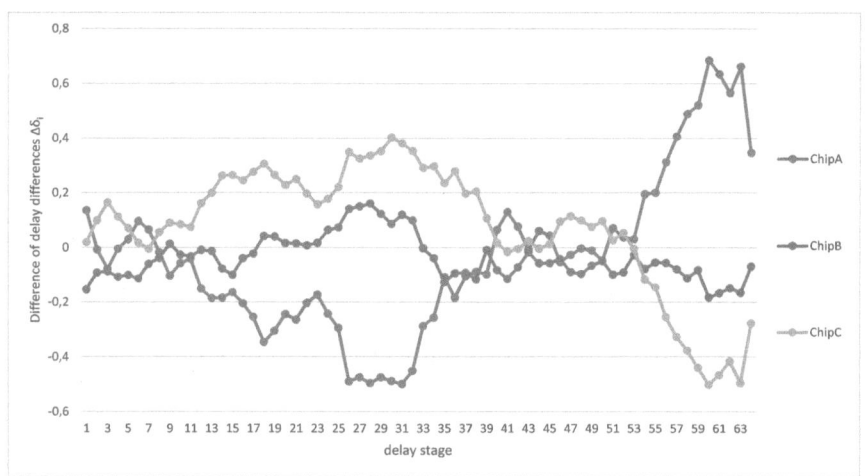

**Fig. 5.** The difference of delay differences of the 64 stages of one randomly placed arbiter PUF in three different chips. The delay difference are plotted relative to the mean of the three values, i.e. only the deviation relative to the mean value is shown.

**Table 1.** The fraction of ones for 10 m-challenges that lead to a metastable response on chip A. Due to manufacturing variance the r-responses mostly do not lead to metastable responses on chip B and C. The first 10 bits of the fingerprint of chip B and C can be read from the table. If the fraction lies between 0 and 100 % the respective bits will be noisy.

| Challenge | Fraction of 1s, Chip A | Fraction of 1s, Chip B | Fraction of 1s, Chip C |
|---|---|---|---|
| 7323654688874139733 | 45,92% | 100% | 0% |
| 11845416167999726454 | 6,66% | 0% | 100% |
| 2814503641960336764 | 53,16% | 100% | 100% |
| 670509234023467077 | 5,24% | 48,61% | 100% |
| 14797980534726803933 | 53,59% | 100% | 100% |
| 16595764706100376029 | 63,21% | 0% | 16,13% |
| 1887583556430087243 | 15,29% | 100% | 0% |
| 1116720592540295842 | 83,56% | 0% | 0% |
| 18126161473406108233 | 68,83% | 0,01% | 0% |
| 11508568743664487972 | 53,34% | 98,39% | 100% |

value of 29.7 which is significantly different from the maximal value of 50, i.e. the relative entropy among two bits from different chips is only 0.88. This is not a problem for our application, as the bits in biometric templates commonly have an entropy smaller than 1. The reduced value can be understood as an effect of our method to choose challenges that yield a metastable response on a reference chip. On the reference chip (see Sect. 3.1) metastability means that routing and manufacturing variation induced delay are exactly balanced. On the chips that are compared, the routing delay will be the same as on the reference chip but the manufacturing induced delay will be different in general. There is a 50 % chance that manufacturing induced delay between the paths will have the same sign as

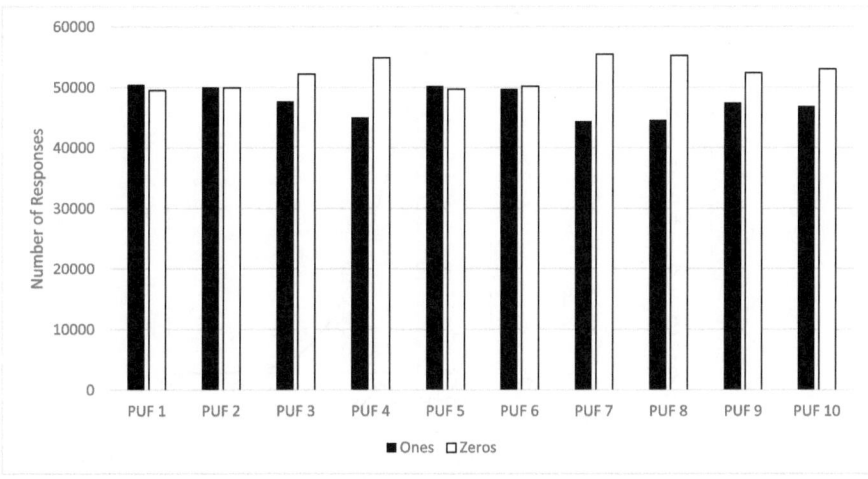

**Fig. 6.** The bias of 10 randomly placed arbiter PUFs displayed for 100000 randomly chosen challenges.

the one of the routing induced delay on the chips to be compared. In this case their response will always be identical. If the delay has an opposite sign on both chips there is a 50 % chance that this will lead to a different response because the distribution of manufacturing and routing induced delays in our selected sample of challenges must be the same by design. This argument predicts a mean Hamming distance of 25 and the value we found is similar. The agreement of the Hamming distances induced by manufacturing variations in delay times in Fig. 7 with a Gaussian distribution is excellent. This suggests that the bits in our "fingerprints" are distributed randomly, because for the mean value of 29.7 a Gaussian is an excellent approximation to the binomial distribution that is expected if the matching probabilities are described by a Bernoullie process.

The reliability was tested by measuring the noise in the "fingerprint" as a function of temperature. We found that the noise is caused exclusively by a metastability of the arbiter that develops when the transit times are nearly exactly balanced so that the both input pulses occur simultaneously. We identified all metastable bits in a sample of 10000 challenges and its fraction of ones $f_1$. The probability P that metastable bit i induces a noise bit, i.e. different responses to consecutive identical challenges is:

$$P_i = 2f_i(1 - f_i) \tag{4}$$

The total noise fraction N determined with j metastable bits is then:

$$N = \frac{\sum_i P_i}{j} \tag{5}$$

In this manner we obtained N = 1.04 % and 1.59 % for two chips. N did not change significantly with temperature in the range 5 °C–60 °C. However we found

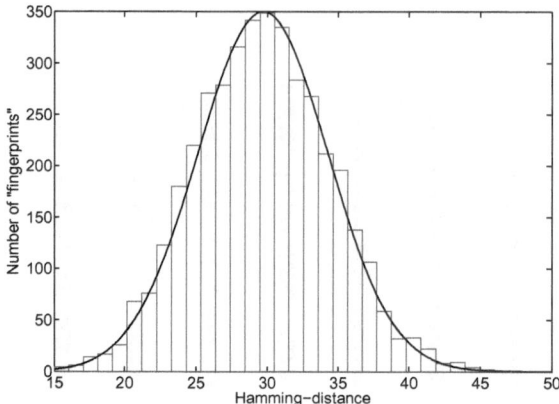

**Fig. 7.** The distribution of 4000 Hamming distances of "fingerprint" of chip B and C. The continuous curve is a Gauss curve with the same mean (29.71) and standard deviation (4.57) as the data points.

that even though its power remained roughly constant the set of metastable bits changed with temperature because some bits became stable and others became metastable. While the mean Hamming distance between consecutively taken responses with random challenges on the same PUF was $0.08 \pm 0.026\,\%$ it rose to $0.35 \pm 0.058\,\%$ when responses taken at $5\,°C$ and $60\,°C$ are compared.

### 4.2   FAR (Interchip Comparison) and FRR (Intrachip Comparison)

Analogously to the common definition in biometrics, the false acceptance rate (FAR) is the probability that the biometric system authenticates a chip incorrectly and the false rejection rate (FRR) is the probability that the system does not authenticate incorrectly. We had seen in the previous Sect. 4.1 that the distribution of matching bits in "fingerprint" taken from two different chips is random and the probability for a non-match has a certain value p ($p = 0.297$ in our case). Under these circumstances we obtain:

$$FAR = \sum_{i=0}^{t} \binom{n}{i} (1-p)^{(n-i)} p^i \qquad (6)$$

where t is the threshold for the number of bits up to which two "fingerprints" that are classified a belonging to the same chip can differ. If we choose $t = 12$ we find that for our construction $FAR = 2.4 \times 10^{-5}$. The FRR is the probability that more than t bit non-matches occur in two "fingerprints" of the same chip. We estimated the FRR by determining the 10000 Hamming distances among "fingerprints" of the same arbiter PUF. Their distribution is plotted in Fig. 8. We then performed a fit of these data to a binomial probability distribution and used this fit to determine the FRR in a manner analogous to Eq. (6) to $FRR = 7.2 \times 10^{-9}$. The underlying

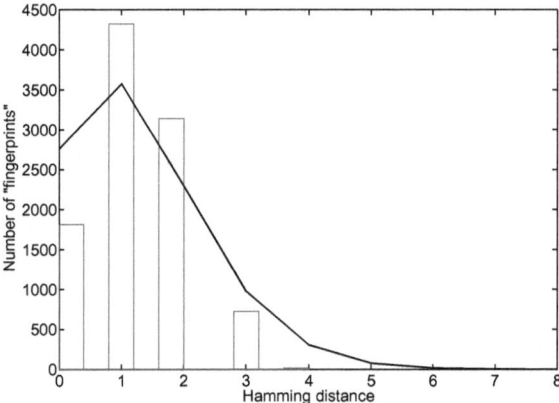

**Fig. 8.** The distribution of 10000 Hamming distances of "fingerprint" of chip B with each other. The continuous curve is a fit to a binomial distribution with the same mean (1,28) as the data points.

extremely conservative assumption of using a binomial distribution to fit these data is that each bit has a mean probability of 1.3 % to have a different value in two consecutive measurements. In reality we found that the noise for the 100 m-challenges we employed to obtain the "fingerprint" comes from six metastable bits with a fraction of ones different from 1 or 0 by more than 0.1 %. It is then much less probable to obtain a Hamming distance larger than 6 than expected by a binomial distribution. As a detailed noise model is beyond the scope of the present paper we contend ourselves with the above conservative upper bound on the FRR.

## 5   Discussion of the Security of Our Design

As a first attempt to break our construction the attacker could try to use the 100 challenge-response pairs that were sent to obtain the "fingerprint" and could be intercepted by her to model the PUF. However we found that it took at least about 2000 challenge-response training pairs for a successful model. It is conceivable that a smaller number might suffice to construct a model, however it seems certain that 100 C-R pairs are not sufficient, because they contain an information content not larger than 100 bits which is insufficient to encode the 64 difference of delay difference values that constitute the model.

Another obvious attack on our construction would be an attempt to model all arbiter PUFs that can be constructed when the PUF is under physical control of the attacker. A conservative estimate of the number of PUFs that can be constructed with our implementation defines PUFs to be different only if they contain different gates, i.e. all PUFs with identical gates that are only put into a different configuration are counted as a single PUF. We then estimate the number of PUFs $N_{PUF}$ as:

$$N_{PUF} = \binom{1428}{128} \approx 4.7 \times 10^{185} \tag{7}$$

Clearly such a number of PUFs cannot even be configured on the FPGA. Even if (theoretically) each reconfiguration could somehow be accelerated to take only a pico-second this would still take $1.6 \times 10^{166}$ years. Therefore the only promising possibility is an attack that faithfully models the timing of the subset of lookup tables selected from the FPGA and the gates used for the routing between them. There are two security mechanisms that make this attack difficult. The first one is largely due to the need for reverse engineering: It will be more difficult to construct a model of a complex dynamical FPGA system than of the simple static arbiter PUF system. It seems likely that as a first step the attacker needs to reverse engineer the FPGA in order to obtain a topological model of the FPGA fabric. This model enables the attacker to identify all components that influence the delays and to predict how these components are combined in the connections between delay elements, the switching matrix for routing and the arbiter. Only equipped with such a construction model she will be able to understand the distribution of the delay times of the stages we determined (but did not understand, yet) in Sect. 4. Without such a model she would need to learn or measure the delays between each delay element and all other delay elements, a number of delays that increases y with the already large number of components. This reverse engineering step is analogous to the one necessary in attacks on authentication secrets stored in conventional memories and protected by sensors or other protection mechanisms. Once the reverse engineering is completed, this security mechanism is broken and further chips can be attacked with relatively little effort. At this point a second, PUF specific, protection mechanism kicks in: Even on a reverse engineered FPGA the attacker needs to find out about the manufacturing variations of the delays of all elements of the PUF that are used in our construction. In our implementation she needs to determine the properties of 1428 lookup tables, i.e. the individual delays of each of them and of all gates that are used in interconnecting them. This makes a complete and linear characterization directly in the hardware (e.g. with techniques developed by Tajik et al. [18]) or with the use of learning programs a time-consuming task on each individual chip that is to be modelled. This security mechanism is easily scaled: if an attacker will succeed to break our security mechanism in an unacceptably short time, one can increase the number of lookup tables out of which the PUFs are constructed. In this manner our PUF construction promises to make cloning impossible based on physical principles rather than lack of knowledge about the protection method and technical skill to break it. Our second protection mechanism requires a level of effort to clone a chip that does not significantly decrease when the protection mechanism is fully understood by the attacker.

# 6   Conclusion

We presented a qualitatively novel concept to increase the security of strong PUFs. Up to now most attempts to make PUFs more secure aimed at making the individual PUF construction more complex, e.g. by performing an XOR between several PUFs. This strategy is limited by the need to keep the final output sufficiently reliable. Our strategy was to keep the individual PUF simple but to force the attacker to model not only the static PUF but a part of a dynamical FPGA system. This concept enabled a qualitative increase the complexity of the system that has to be modelled compared to previous constructions. The only fundamental limit to increasing it further is the available size of the FPGA fabric. Our FPGA-based arbiter PUF design itself is simpler than the ones proposed up to now. The price one has to pay for the gain in security is an additional overhead for the sending of the "2nd challenge" that specifies a reconfiguration of the PUF. However, it is not necessary to introduce this overhead for each authentication. From the 1428 LUTs assigned to our construction in our implementation it is possible to construct 10 arbiter PUFs with one second challenge, so that only every 10th authentication needs the additional overhead.

**Acknowledgements.** We thank Georg Becker, Shahin Tajic, Jean-Pierre Seifert and Marco Winzker for helpful discussions. Georg Becker kindly provided a copy of his machine-learning program to us.

# Appendix

*VHDL Code for our arbiter PUF construction. "above" and "below" stand for the upper and lower signal pathes. [...] stands for the insertion of 62 additional consecutive, identical sub-parts of the code.*

```
-------------------------------------------------------------------------------
----
-- Company: XXX
-- File: Arbiter_PUF.vhd
-- Description:
-- Arbiter Physical Unclonable Function (PUF)
-- Submodul to evaluate response from Arbiter PUF.
-- The input challenge defines the connection of a row of different gates.
-- An Arbiter at the end of this gates evaluates which of the two signals
arrived first
-- and sets the corresponding response.
-- Targeted device: <Family::SmartFusion2> <Die::M2S150> <Package::FG1152>
-- Author: XXX
-- Date: 12.2015
-------------------------------------------------------------------------------
----
library IEEE;
use IEEE.std_logic_1164.all;
use IEEE.numeric_std.all;
```

```
entity Arbiter_PUF is
port (
c : IN std_logic_vector(63 downto 0); -- challenge
enable : IN std_logic; -- enable signal for arbiter puf
dc : IN std_logic; -- don't care input for LUTs
ready : OUT std_logic; -- ready signal
r : OUT std_logic -- response
);
end Arbiter_PUF;

architecture architecture_Arbiter_PUF of Arbiter_PUF is
-- signal, component etc. declarations
attribute syn_keep : boolean;
signal above : std_logic := '0';
signal c0 : std_logic := '0';
signal above0,above1, [...],above64 : std_logic := '0'; --
top arbiter puf signals
signal below : std_logic := '0';
signal below0,below1, [...] ,below64 : std_logic := '0'; --
bottom arbiter puf signals
-- set syn_keep for PUF signals to prevent removing in synthesis optimization
attribute syn_keep of above,above0,above1, [...] ,above64,
below,below0,below1, [...]
,below64,c0 : signal is true;
begin
-- architecture body
above0 <= above when (c0= '0' and dc = '0') else below;
below0 <= below when (c0= '0' and dc = '0') else above;
-- challenge 0
above1 <= above0 when (c(0)= '0' and dc = '0') else below0;
below1 <= below0 when (c(0)= '0' and dc = '0') else above0;
-- challenge 1
above2 <= above1 when (c(1)= '0' and dc = '0') else below1;
below2 <= below1 when (c(1)= '0' and dc = '0') else above1;
[...]
-- challenge 63
above64 <= above63 when (c(63)= '0' and dc = '0') else
below63;
below64 <= below63 when (c(63)= '0' and dc = '0') else
above63;

---- Arbiter to generate response
r <= (below64 and not(above64)) or (below64 and r);
-- ENABLE PROCESS
process--(enable)
begin
wait on enable;
if(enable = '1') then
above <= '1';
below <= '1';
-- wait until response is generated
wait on r;
ready <= '1';
else -- enable = '0'
```

```
above <= '0';
below <= '0';
ready <= '0';
end if;
end process;
end architecture_Arbiter_PUF;
```

# References

1. Becker, G.T.: On the pitfalls of using arbiter PUFs as building blocks. IEEE Trans. Inf. Forensics Secur. **34**, 1295–1307 (2015)
2. Gassend, B., Clarke, D., van Dijk, M., Devadas, S.: Delay-based circuit authentication and applications. In: Proceedings of the 18th Annual ACM Symposium on Applied Computing, pp. 294–301. ACM Digital Library, March 2003
3. Gehrer, S., Sigl, G.: Using the reconfigurability of modern FPGAs for highly efficient PUF-based key generation. J. Circ. Syst. Comput. **25**(01), 1640002 (2016)
4. Katzenbeisser, S., Kocabas, Ü., van der Leest, V., Sadeghi, A., Schrijen, G., Schröder, H., Wachsmann, C.: Recyclable PUFs: logically reconfigurable PUFs. J. Crypt. Eng. **1**, 177 (2011)
5. Lao, Y., Parhi, K.: Novel reconfigurable silicon physical unclonable functions. In: Proceedings of Workshop on Foundations of Dependable and Secure Cyber-Physical Systems (FDSCPS), pp. 30–36 (2011)
6. Killmann, W., Schindler, W.: A proposal for: functionality classes for random number generators (2011). https://www.bsi.bund.de/SharedDocs/Downloads/DE/BSI/Zertifizierung/Interpretationen/AIS_20_Functionality_classes_for_random_number_generators_e.html
7. Machida, T., Yamamoto, D., Iwamoto, M., Sakiyama, K.: A new mode of operation for arbiter PUF to improve uniqueness on FPGA. In: Proceedings of Federated Conference on Computer Science and Information Systems (FedCSIS), pp. 871–878. IEEE Press, New York (2014)
8. Maes, R.: Physically unclonable functions: constructions, properties and applications. Ph.D. thesis, Katholieke Universiteit Leuven (2012)
9. Majzoobi, M., Koushanfar, F., Potkonjak, M.: Techniques for design and implementation of secure reconfigurable PUFs. ACM Trans. Reconfigurable Technol. Syst. **2**, 5 (2009)
10. Majzoobi, M., Koushanfar, F., Devadas, S.: FPGA PUF using programmable delay lines. In: Information Forensics and Security (WIFS), pp. 1–6. IEEE Press, New York (2010)
11. Majzoobi, M., Kharaya, A., Koushanfar, F., Devadas, S.: Automated design, implementation, and evaluation of arbiter-based PUF on FPGA using programmable delay lines (2014). http://eprint.iacr.org/2014/639.pdf
12. Microsemi Corporation SmartFusion2 System-on-Chip FPGAs Product Brief (2013). http://www.actel.com/documents/SmartFusion2_DS.pdf
13. Morozov, S., Maiti, A., Schaumont, P.: An analysis of delay based PUF implementations on FPGA. In: Sirisuk, P., Morgan, F., El-Ghazawi, T., Amano, H. (eds.) ARC 2010. LNCS, vol. 5992, pp. 382–387. Springer, Heidelberg (2010)
14. Pappu, R.: Physical one-way functions. Ph.D. thesis, MIT (2001). Pappu, R., Recht, B., Taylor, J., Gershenfeld, N.: Physical one-way functions. Science **297**, 2026–2030 (2002)

15. Rührmair, U., Sehnke, F., Sölter, J., Dror, G., Devadas, S., Schmidhuber, J.: Modeling attacks on physical unclonable functions. In: ACM Conference on Computer and Communications Security (CCS), pp. 237–249 (2010)
16. Rührmair, U., Sölter, J., Sehnke, F., Xu, X., Mahmoud, A., Stoyanova, V., Dror, G., Schmidhuber, J., Burleson, W., Devadas, S.: PUF modeling attacks on simulated and silicon data. IEEE Trans. Inf. Forensics Secur. **8**, 1876–1891 (2013)
17. Rührmair, U.: Disorder-based security hardware: an overview. In: Chang, C., Potkonjak, M. (eds.) Security System Design and Trustable Computing, pp. 3–37. Springer, Cham (2016)
18. Tajik, S., Dietz, E., Frohmann, S., Dittrich, H., Nedospasov, D., Helfmeier, C., Seifert, J., Boit, C., Hübers, H.: A complete and linear physical characterization methodology for the arbiter PUFFamily (2015). https://eprint.iacr.org/2015/871
19. Tarnovsky, C.: Deconstructing a "secure" processor. In: Black Hat Federal 2010, Washington (2010). https://www.blackhat.com/presentations/bh-dc-10/Tarnovsky_Chris/BlackHat-DC-2010-Tarnovsky-DASP-slides.pdf
20. Tobisch, J., Becker, G.: On the scaling of machine learning attacks on PUFs with application to noise bifurcation. In: Schaumont, P., Mangard, S. (eds.) RFIDsec 2015. LNCS, vol. 9440, pp. 17–31. Springer, Heidelberg (2015). doi:10.1007/978-3-319-24837-0_2
21. Xu, T., Potkonjak, M.: Digital bimodal functions and digital physical unclonable functions: architecture and applications. In: Chang, C., Potkonjak, M. (eds.) Security System Design and Trustable Computing, pp. 83–113. Springer, Cham (2016)
22. Zalikava, S.S., Zhang, L., Klybik, V.P., Ivaniuk, A.A., Chang, C.: Design and implementation of high-quality physical unclonable functions for hardware-oriented cryptography. In: Chang, C., Potkonjak, M. (eds.) Security System Design and Trustable Computing, pp. 39–81. Springer, Cham (2016)
23. Zhang, J., Lin, Y.: Reconfigurable binding against FPGA replay attacks. ACM Trans. Des. Autom. Electron. Syst. **20**, 33 (2015)

# Author Index